101 RIFFS & SOLOS FOR CIGAR BOX GUITAR

ESSENTIAL LESSONS FOR THE 4 STRING
GDGB

WWW.BRENTROBITAILLE.COM

KALYMI PUBLISHING

COPYRIGHT © 2020 BY BRENT ROBITAILLE
ALL RIGHTS RESERVED

UNAUTHORIZED COPYING, ARRANGING, ADAPTING IS AN INFRINGEMENT OF COPYRIGHT.

OTHER BOOKS BY BRENT ROBITAILLE

The Complete Cigar Box Guitar Chord Book
Cigar Box Guitar - Jazz & Blues Unlimited Book One & Two
Cigar Box Guitar Blues Overload
101 Riffs for Cigar Box Guitar
3 - 4 String Cigar Box Guitar Tablature Reference Books
Celtic Collection for Cigar Box Guitar
The Ultimate Collection – How to Play Cigar Box Guitar Vol. 1 & 2
Cigar Box Guitar - The Technique Book
The Pop Rock Looper Pedal Book
The Blues Guitar Looper Pedal Book
Standard Guitar Tuning - Celtic Collection
Open D Guitar Tuning - Celtic Collection
Open G Guitar Tuning - Celtic Collection
Improve Your Guitar Chord Playing
Slide Guitar Collection
Celtic Collection Fiddle - Tab & Notes
Holiday Collection for Fiddle - Tab & Notes
Traditional Collection Fiddle - Tab & Notes
Fiddle Tab - Celtic Collection
Celtic Collection for Mandolin
Celtic Collection for Ukulele
Holiday Collection for Cigar Box Guitar

Recordings - Ebooks - Sheet Music
Available at:

www.brentrobitaille.com

KALYMI PUBLISHING

PUBLISHED BY KALYMI PUBLISHING
©2020 Kalymi Publishing

Although the author and publisher have made every effort to ensure that the information in this book is in public domain at press time, the author and publisher do not assume and hereby disclaim any liability to any party. Any copying of this material whole or in part with the express

101

RIFFS AND SOLOS

for FOUR STRING CIGAR BOX GUITAR

CONTENTS - 101 Riffs & Solos for 4-String Cigar Box Guitar

Introduction and Slide Tips 6
How to Read Tablature 8
How to Read Rhythms 9
How to Play Slide 12

RIFFS & TECHNIQUES

Riffs: 1 - 4 – Hammer Ons & Pull Offs 16
Riffs: 5 - 8 – Easy Slide Riffs 17
Riffs: 9 - 12 – Triplet Rhythms 18
Riffs: 13 - 16 – G Blues Scale 19
Riffs: 17 - 20 – D Blues Scale 20
Riffs: 21 - 24 – C Blues Scale 21
Riffs: 25 - 28 – Muting Technique 22
Riffs: 29 - 32 – Barre with Slide 23
Riffs: 33 - 36 – Extended Slides 24
Riffs: 37 - 40 – Vibrato 25
Riffs: 41 - 44 – Palm Muting 26
Riffs: 45 - 48 – Fingerstyle Riffs 28
Riffs: 49 - 52 – Double Stops & Slide Chords 30
Riffs: 53 - 56 – Strumming and Muting 32
Riffs: 57 - 60 – Undetermined Slides 34
Riffs: 61 - 64 – Slide and Fingerstyle 36
Riffs: 65 – 68 – Boogie Bass Patterns 38
Riffs: 69 - 72 – Blues Shuffle Patterns 40
Riffs: 73 - 76 – Tapping and Harmonics 42
Riffs: 77 - 80 – Playing in Different Keys 44
Riffs: 81 - 84 – Playing in Different Time Signatures 46
Riffs: 85 - 88 – Intros, Turnarounds and Endings 48

SOLOS

Riffs: 89 – 91 – Soloing over Major Chords 50

Riffs: 92 – 94 – Soloing over Minor Chords 52

Riff: 95 – Pop Solo #1 53

Riff: 96 – Pop Solo #2 54

Riff: 97 – Dominant 7th Solo 55

Riff: 98 – Country Solo 56

Riff: 99 – Rock Solo 58

Riff: 100 – Blues Solo #1 60

Riff: 101 – Blues Solo #2 62

CHORD TONES - SCALES - NOTE CHARTS

Chord Tones - Major, Minor & Dominant 7th – All Keys 64

Scales – Major, Minor & Blues – All Keys 80

Cigar Box Guitar Fingerboard and Note Charts 104

Cigar Box Guitar Notation Guide 107

Other Books available from Kalymi Publishing 110

Introduction

"101 Riffs and Solos" is arranged for the four-string fretted or fretless cigar box guitar tuned to GDGB. An excellent resource for beginners and a good review of useful techniques for players of all levels and styles, including blues, rock, country, popular and more. The riffs cover all the main slide techniques with tips and playing instructions for each of the 101 riffs and solos. For beginners or those in need of a refresh, read the pages on *how to read tablature, how to read rhythms*, and *how to play slide*. Download the 101 free audio mp3's from my website to help learn the riffs and solos. To further your knowledge, check out the section on scales and chord tones. You will also find a few pages of the fingerboard charts, and the notation/tablature guide at the back of the book. Please visit my website at www.brentrobitaille.com for more information.

Slides

Finding the right slide is a challenge of its own! For many year's slide players would have to conform to commercial slides that are often too big or too narrow. Fortunately, there are now many more slide manufacturers that cater to the different finger sizes and materials (glass, metal, ceramic, bone). Take the time to experiment with the different tones the materials produce and to get the right fit for your finger. Of course, the slide you choose will depend on which finger your wear the slide. Most players put the slide on the 3rd or 4th finger, which allows the use of the other fingers to play simultaneously with the slide. There are no rules, so try the slide on different fingers and do what feels natural to you. See *how to play slide* pages that show the main techniques of slide playing.

Tuning

Playing in tune is the first technique to learn with slide playing. The note is in tune when the slide is placed directly on top and in line with the fret. Sometimes, the magic of the slide is to play intentionally "out of tune," producing that slide vibe necessary to the overall feel and sound. To help with your tuning, try to memorize the riffs and solos in whole or part when more significant hand movements are required. Memorizing helps keep your eye on the fingerboard and the slide in line with the fret. It is also good to practice without looking at your fingers to develop your sense of touch and developing your ear to keep the notes in tune. Another tip is to use a clip-on tuner to see how accurate you are when moving from note to note. A slide is notated with a diagonal line, and the grace note tells you where to slide from. The grace note is a quick note played before the main note and written as a small note or number.

Muting

The "mute" technique is essential and will refine your slide playing to the next level. Knowing how to stop the strings ringing is sometimes as important as playing the notes. The gap between the notes is indicated with a rest or "x." The sound of the slide gliding between notes is the main reason you play slide, but often a combination of sliding and muting adds greater variety to your playing. Many of the riffs and solos in this book require a variety of sliding and muting techniques but develop your own approach to master this essential technique.

Vibrato

Vibrato is another important technique to learn for an authentic slide feel. Vibrato means to move the slide back and forth of the fret and divided into two main techniques: speed and width. The speed is how fast the slide moves and the width of how far or wide the slide moves back and forth from the fret. Vibrato is frequently used on long sustained notes but also effective pretty much anytime. Experiment with the speed and width of your vibrato to create your own "style" of playing.

Pressure

Another vital aspect of slide playing is how hard to press the slide down against the string(s), referred to as "string pressure." The action (the distance of strings to the neck) on your guitar determines how hard you will need to press on the string. Lower actions are tricky as the slide will knock against the frets making an unwanted buzzing clank that often produces dropped and muted notes. Try adjusting your bridge for a higher action to make your instrument more conducive to slide playing. For the most part, try and keep good, even pressure on the strings.

Please visit my websites for more cigar box guitar books, videos and audio tracks at:

https://www.brentrobitaille.com/101-riffs-and-solos

or

www.brentrobitaille.com

Good luck and happy riffin'

HOW TO READ TABLATURE (TAB)

To read tablature, you need to know four things:

1) What string is the note on? - Strings are thin (1st) to thick (4th).
2) What fret is the note on? - Fret numbers are left to right.
3) Which finger do I use? - Keep all fingers in position (1-2-3-4) where possible when playing single notes, and most comfortable fingerings for chords.
4) How long to let the note ring? - Based on the song's rhythm but generally keep fingers on fretboard as long as possible to let notes ring throughout.

Fingerboard Number Chart

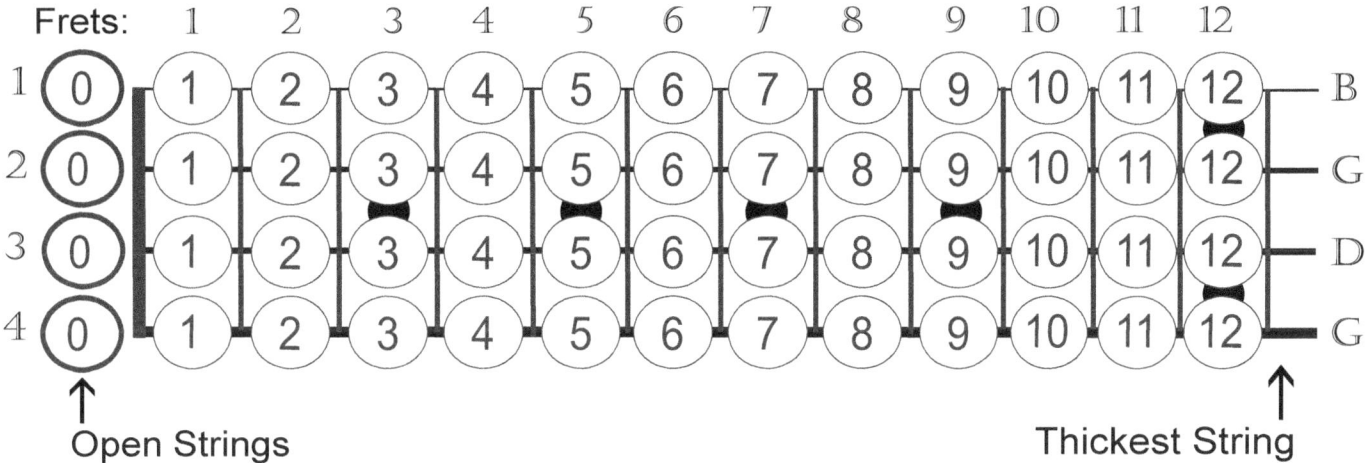

Examples:

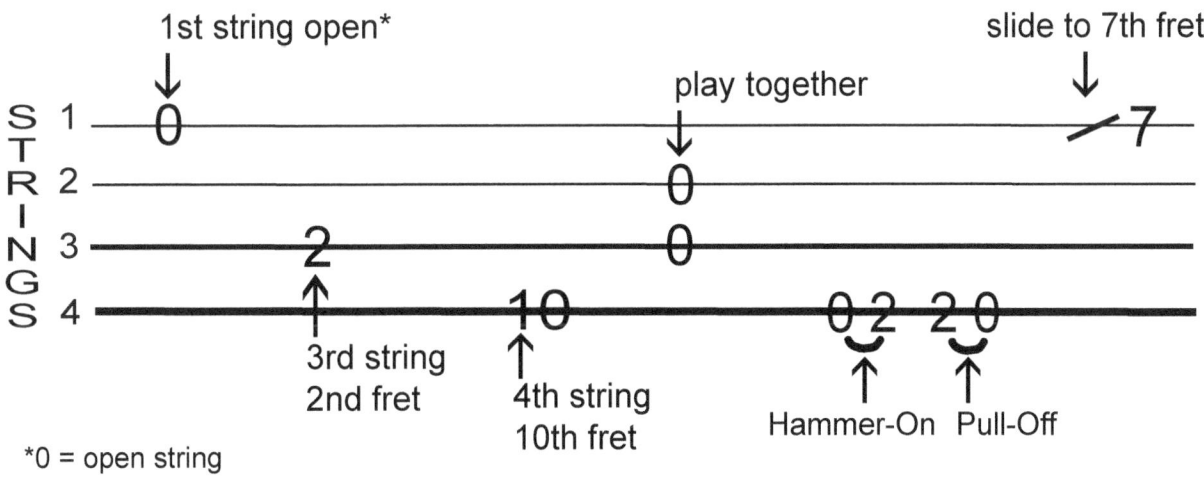

*0 = open string

How to Read Rhythms

① Tap foot (x) with second hand on clock or set metronome to 60 beats per minute. Count 1 - 2 - 3 - 4 and repeat.

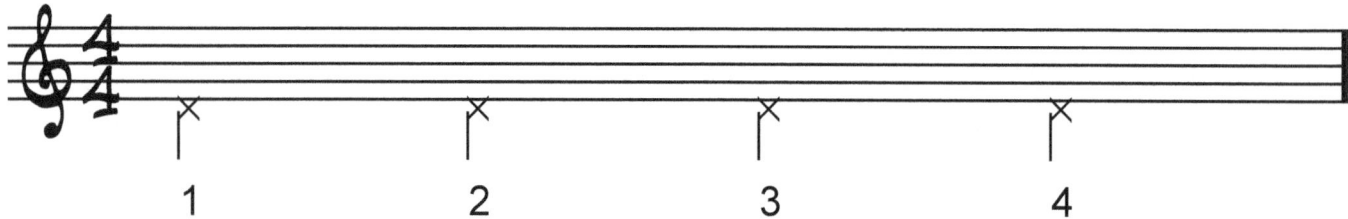

② Whole note: o   Play note on 1st tap or "beat" and let ring for a count of 4.

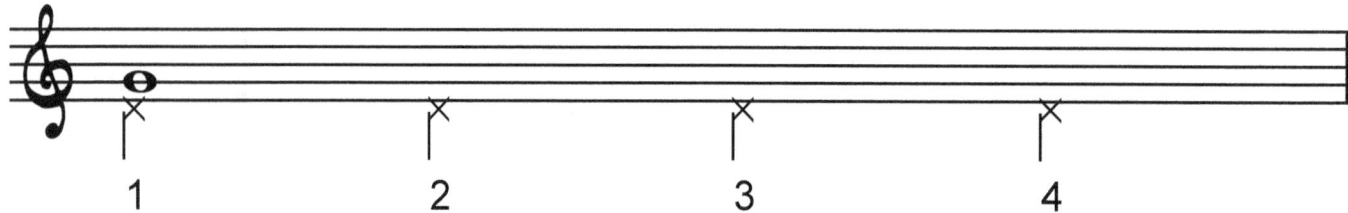

③ Half note: ♩   Play note on 1 and 3. Let ring for 2 taps (beats) each.

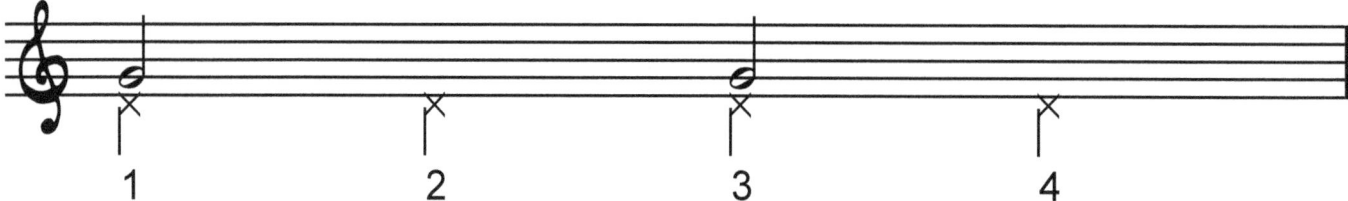

④ Quarter note: ♩   Play note on every beat and count to 4.

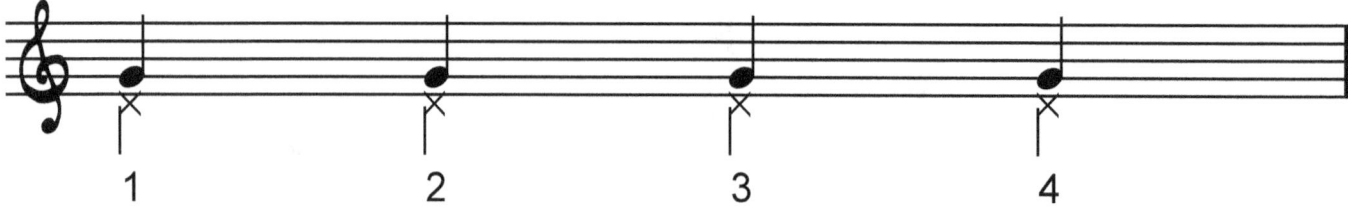

Eighth note: ♪ Play two even notes for every tap. Say "&" between numbers. Use down and up picking. This is called alternate picking.

(5)
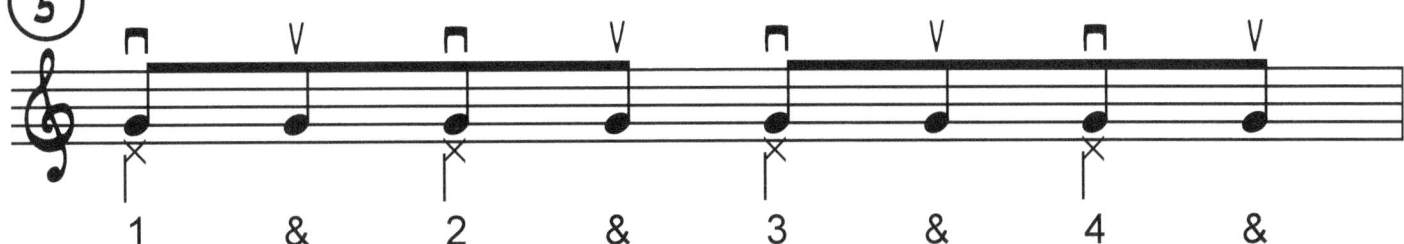

Eighth note Triplets. Play three even notes for every tap. Count "1 & a 2 & a" etc..

(6)
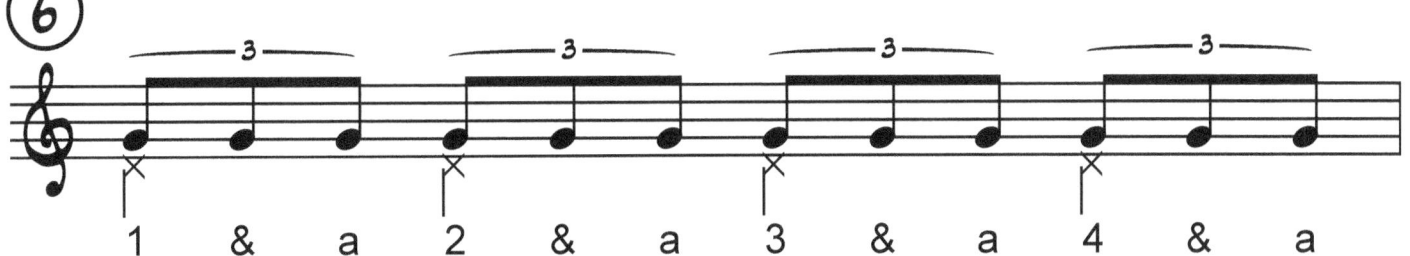

Shuffle rhythm. Divide each beat into 3 equal notes like triplets but play on the 1st (1) and 3rd note (a). Count: "1 a 2 a." Long - short rhythm.

(7)
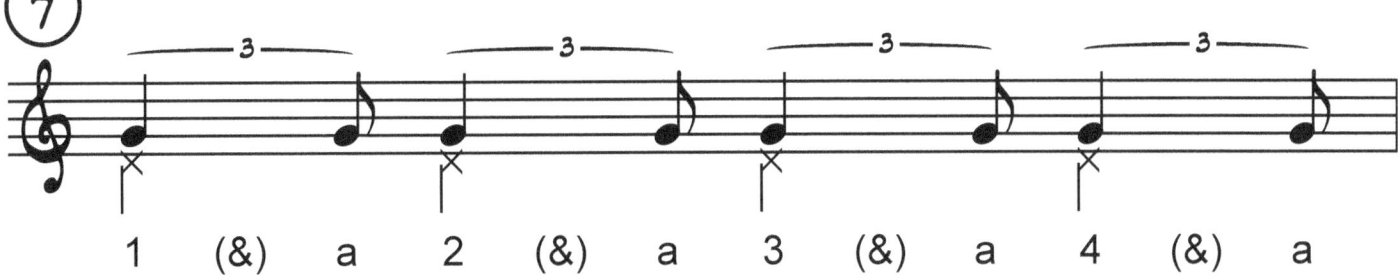

Sixteenth notes. Play four even notes for every tap. Count "1 e & a 2 e & a" etc.. With pick: use down/up picking. With fingers: alternate index and middle fingers.

(8)

⑨ Eighth and sixteenth notes. Play on "1 & a." Say: boom chick-a.

⑩ Eighth and sixteenth notes. Play on "1 e & ". Say: chick-a boom.

⑪ Tied notes (⌒) join two notes together. Only play first note and let ring for duration of second note. In this example, don't play on the 3rd beat.

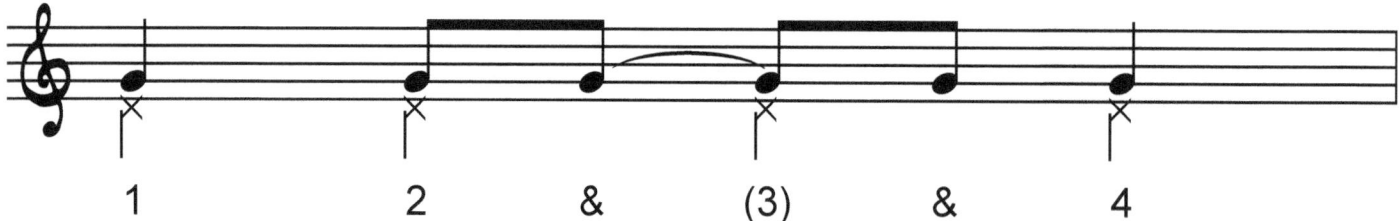

⑫ Dotted note. The dotted note rings longer when a dot is placed beside it. In this example, the note rings longer by an extra eighth note (1 + 1/2).

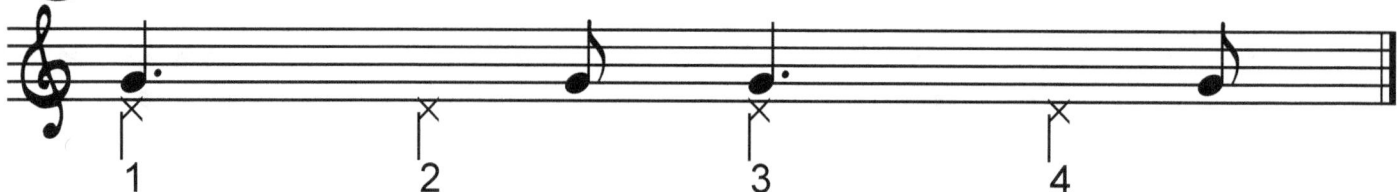

How to Play Slide

1. Keep the slide directly over the center of the fret to play in tune. Don't press down too hard on the string. The string should glide over the frets.

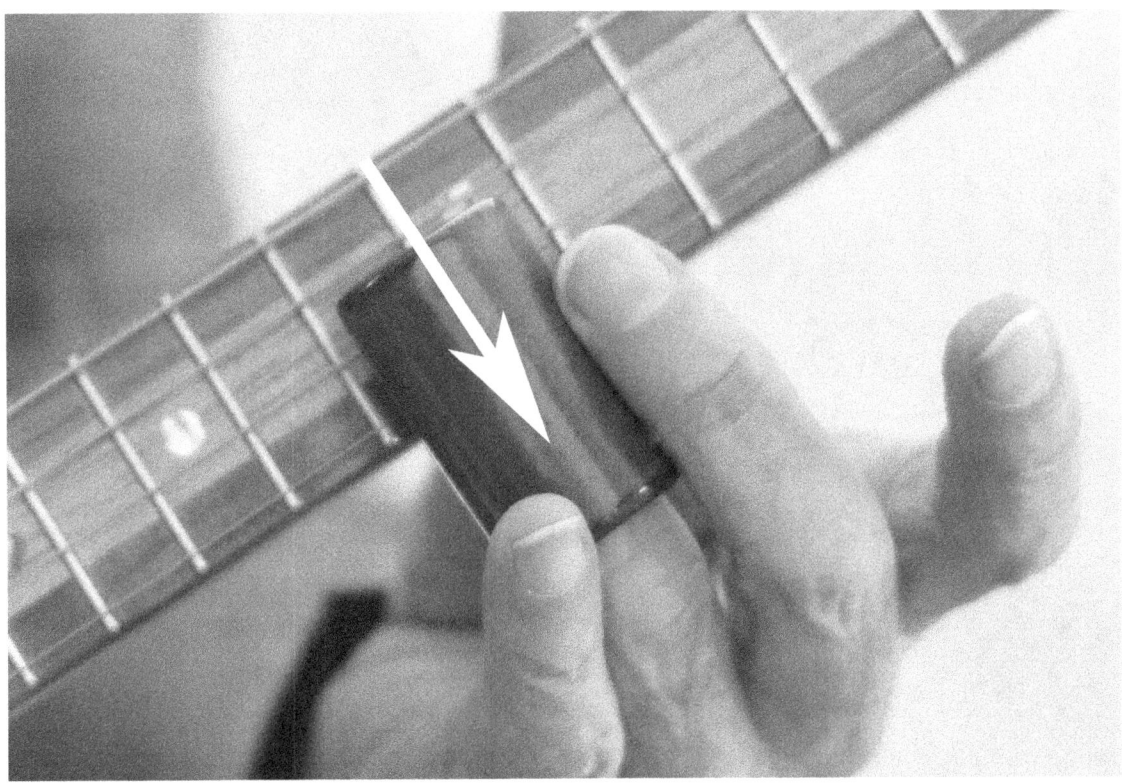

2. Tilt the slide to play a single note or to let other strings ring.

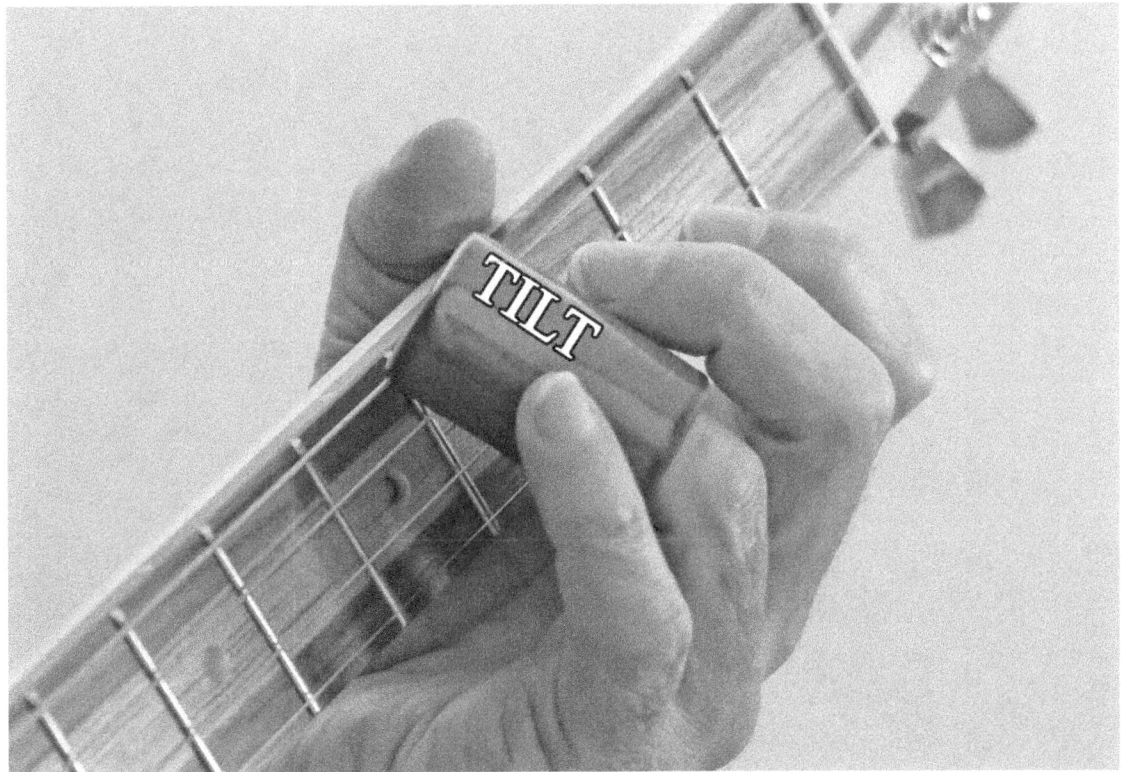

3. Hold the slide down and play a note behind the slide.

4. Hold the slide down and play a note in front of the slide.

5. Mute the string(s) by placing the right-hand fingers or pick on the strings.

6. Mute the strings by placing the left-hand finger(s) on the string.

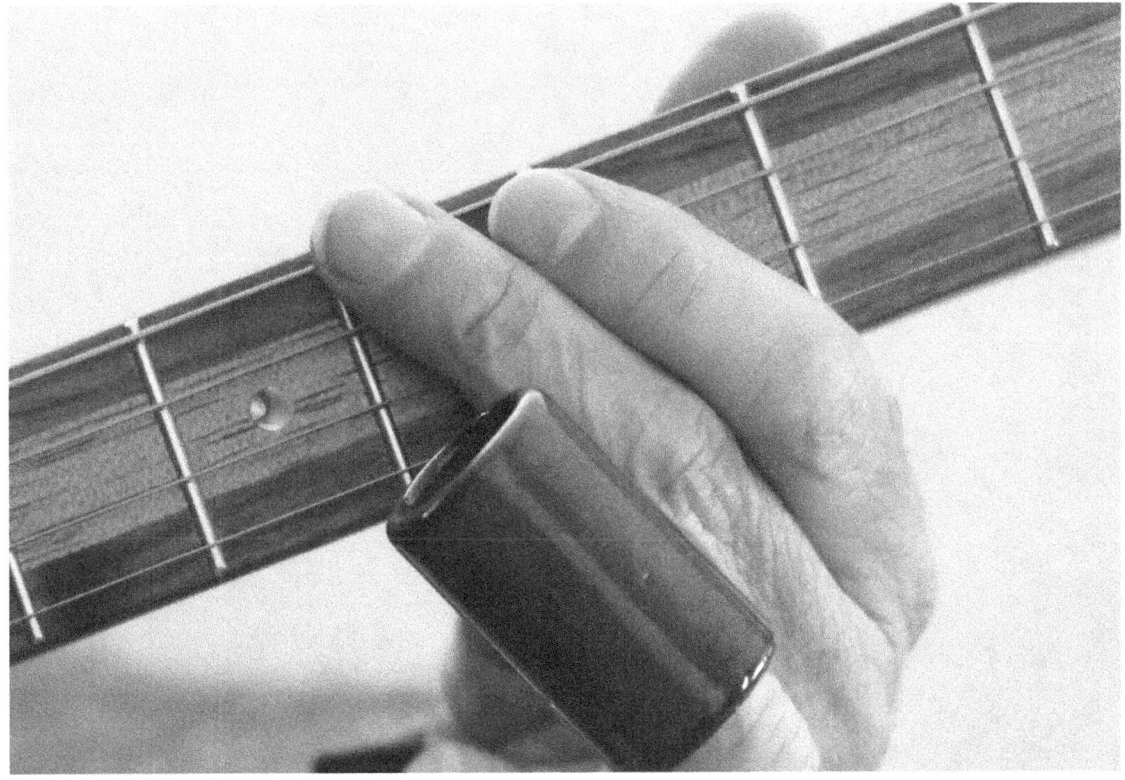

Vibrato

7. Move the slide back and forth of the fret and use the thumb as a pivot.

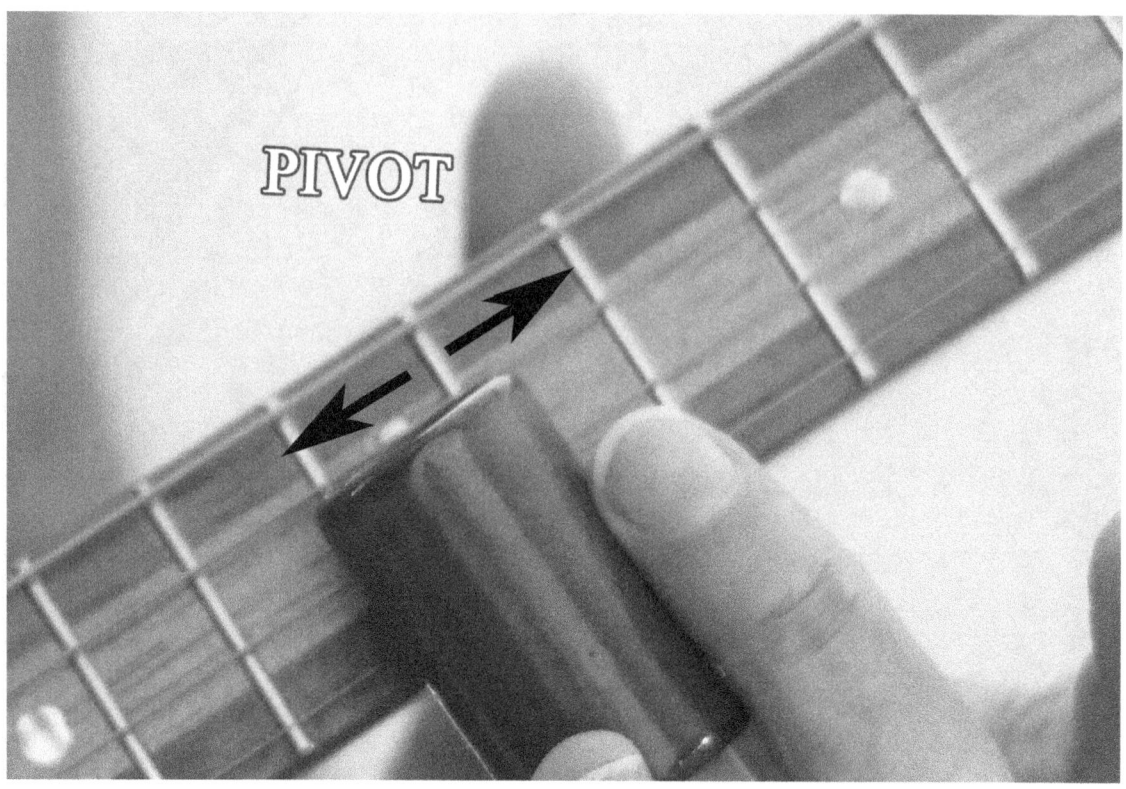

8. Keep a loose wrist. Focus on the wrist, not the slide.

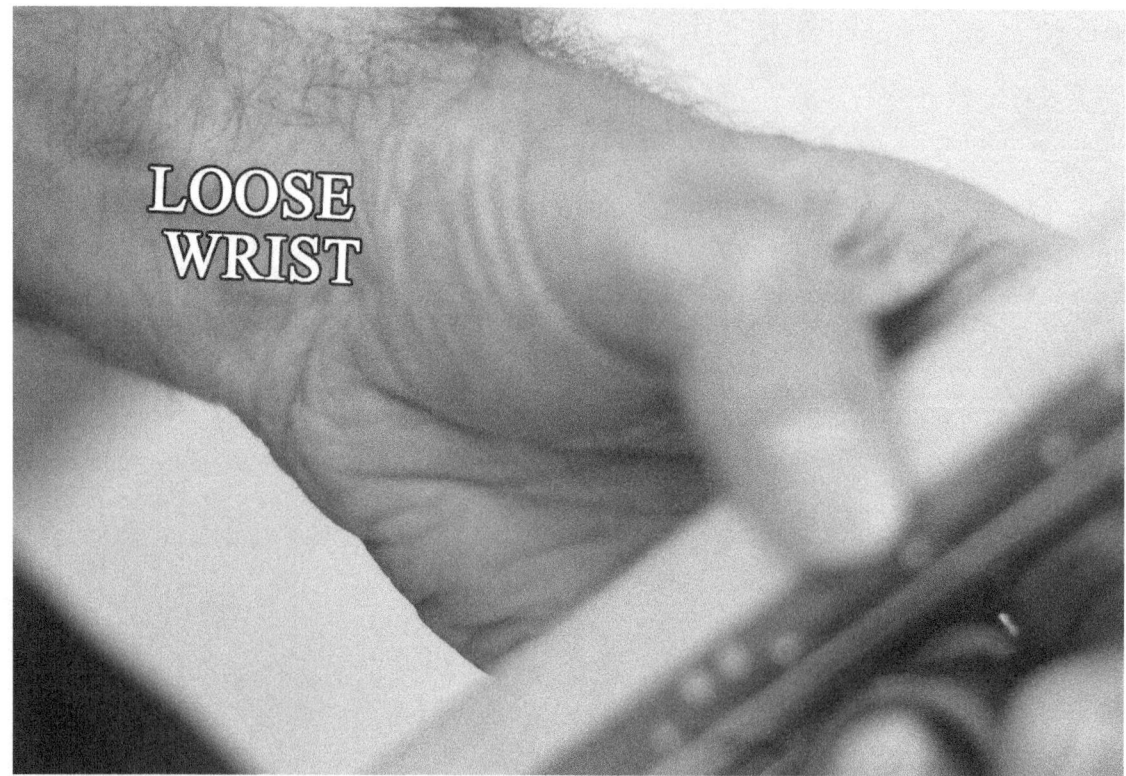

RIFFS: 1 - 4
HAMMER ONS & PULL OFFS

1

Let's start by taking the slide (or finger) on and off the 1st string 3rd fret. Line up your slide in line with the fret to play in tune.

2

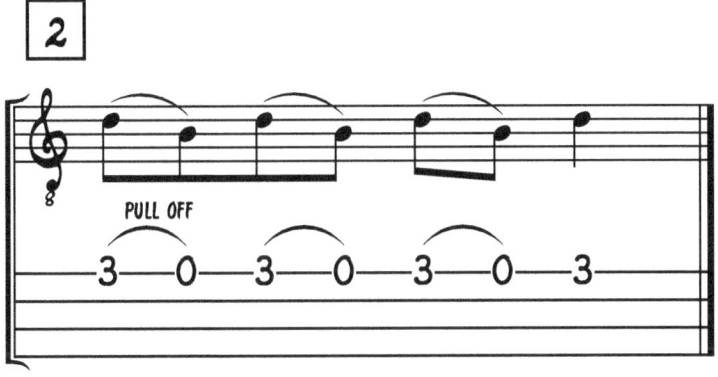

A curved line over two different notes on the same string is called a "pull off." The pull off goes from a higher to lower note. Place slide on the 1st string 3rd fret. Play the 3rd fret note then pull off slide from the string without playing the open string again.

3

The curved line also represents a "hammer on." A hammer on is when you go from a lower to a higher note. In this example, play the 1st string open then hammer on the slide or finger to the 3rd fret without playing the 3rd fret note again.

4

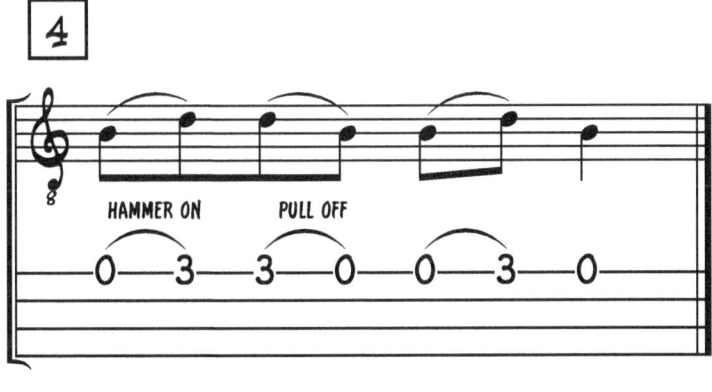

Ok, now let's try to combine the hammer on & pull off in riff 4. Start with the hammer on to the 3rd fret then do a pull off to the open string. Keep an even rhythm and the slide in line with the 3rd fret.

RIFFS: 5 - 8
EASY SLIDE RIFFS

A smaller note or number (♪) is called a "grace note" - this shows which fret you start the slide. A diagonal line represents a slide - When leaning to the right, move the slide to a higher note and when leaning to the left, move the slide to a lower note. In this riff, slide quickly up from the 2nd to 3rd fret.

In riff 6, slide down quickly from the 3rd to 2nd fret then play the open 1st string. Repeat on all strings for extra practice.

Start this riff on the 3rd string open, slide up from the 2nd to 3rd fret, and play the open string. Then slide down from the 3rd to 2nd fret before playing the open 2nd string.

Riff 8 is similar to riff 7 but with a slide down on the 3rd string, then slide up from the 2nd to 3rd fret on the 2nd string.

RIFFS: 9 - 12
TRIPLET RHYTHMS

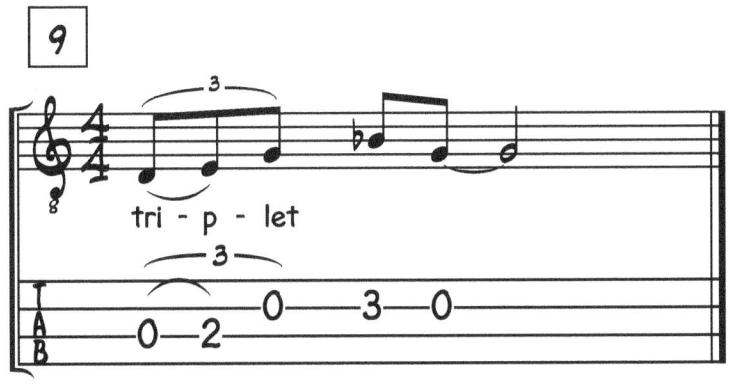

Riff 9 introduces the eighth note "triplet" rhythm. An eighth note triplet is when you play three eighth notes in the space of one quarter note. You can say "tri-p-let" to divide the beat into three. Start with a triplet then switch to the eighth notes to play this riff.

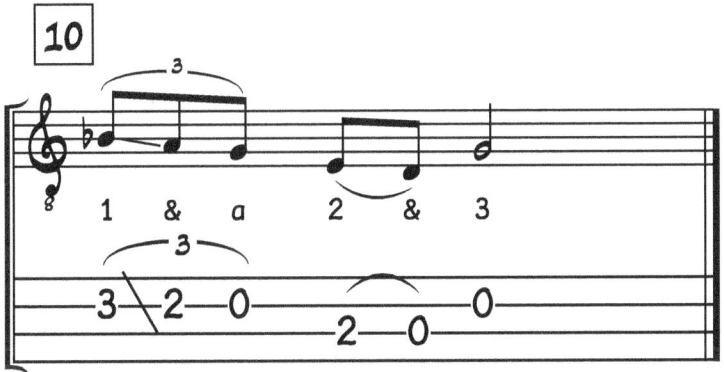

Another way to count out the triplets is to say 1 & a - 2 & a, etc. This riff combines the triplet with a slide and a pull off—practice tapping or hearing the rhythm in your head before you play.

Riff 11 has two groups of triplets with slides. Practice playing the triplet notes while you tap your foot on the beat. In other words, tap your foot on the 1 - 2 while you count 1 & a 2 & a. Try to get an even subdivision of three notes per beat.

Riff 12 is similar to the last riff but with three triplets. Say "1 & a 2 & a 3 & a" tapping your foot or counting in your head on the 1 -2 -3. Tilt the slide on the 3rd and 4th string to hear the 2nd string ring clearly.

RIFFS: 13 - 16
G BLUES SCALE

13

Here is the one-octave G blues scale. Slide from the 3rd to 5th fret then play the 6th fret on the 4th string. Hammer on the open 3rd string to 3rd fret, then play the 2nd string open. You can use a shuffle "or" straight eighth note rhythm (see "How to Read Rhythm").

14

Here' the same G blues scale descending. Pull off from the 3rd fret to open 2nd string then slide down from 6th to 5th fret on 4th string. Finish with a pull off on the 3rd fret 4th string to open.

15

Here's the G blues scale again but moving up the neck. Slide from the 3rd to 5th fret, then 2nd to 3rd fret and 6th to 8th fret on 1st string. Listen carefully to your tuning.

16

And here's the G blues scale moving down the neck. Slide from the 6th to 3rd, then 2nd to 1st fret on the 1st string. Finish with a pull off on the 2nd string. Keep an even shuffle or straight rhythm.

RIFFS: 17 - 20
D BLUES SCALE

17

Here's the one-octave D blues scale ascending. Play open 3rd string and hammer on to 3rd fret, then play open 2nd and slide from 1st to 2nd fret, and finish with 1st to 3rd fret slide on 1st string.

18

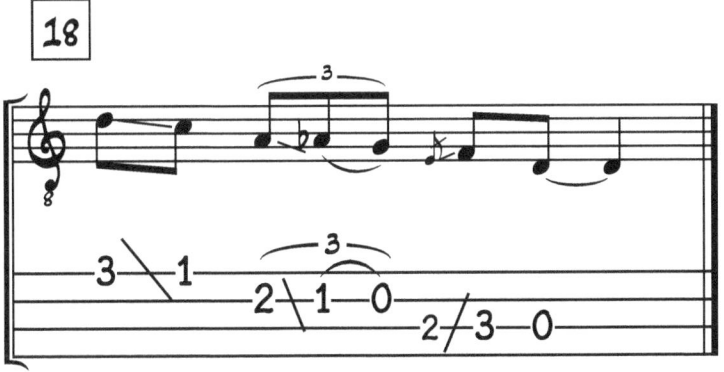

Now the D blues scale descending. Slide down from 3rd to 1st fret, then slide down from 2nd to 1st fret, then pull off to open 2nd string with a triplet rhythm. Finish with a quick slide up from 2nd to 3rd fret then play the open string.

19

The D blues scale moving up the neck. Slide from the 3rd to 5th and 6th to 7th fret on 3rd string then finish with a slide from 5th to 7th fret on the 2nd string.

20

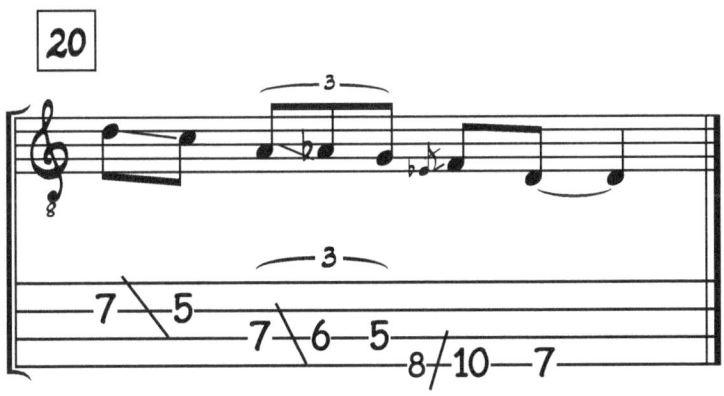

The D blues scale moving down the neck. Slide down from 7th to 5th fret, then 7th - 6th - 5th on 3rd string with a triplet rhythm. Finish with a quick slide up from 8th to 10th fret ending on 7th fret on 4th string.

RIFFS: 21 - 24
C BLUES SCALE

The C blues scale ascending. Slide from 1st to 3rd fret on 3rd string then 3rd to 5th fret on 2nd string. Practice with straight and shuffle rhythm. Notice fingering in the staff line above.

The C blues scale descending. Slide down from 5th to 3rd fret on 2nd string, then a triplet slide: 5th - 4th - 3rd on the 3rd string. Finish with a quick slide down from the 8th to 5th fret on 4th string.

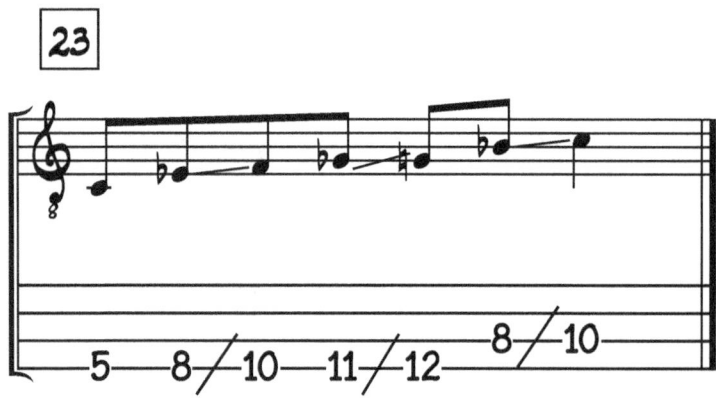

The C blues scale ascending the neck. Slide from 8th to 10th then 11th to 12th fret on the 4th string. Finish with a slide up from 8th to 10th fret on the 3rd string. Keep your slide aligned with the fret for the best tuning.

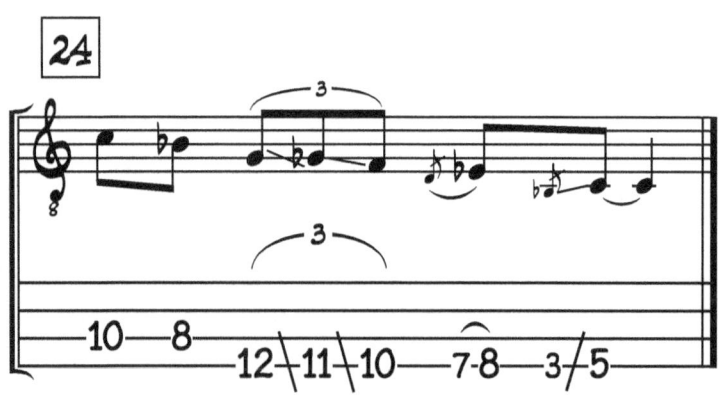

The C blues scale descending. Play the 10th then 8th fret followed by a triplet slide 12th -11th -10th on the 4th string. Hammer on the first and second finger on the 7th to 8th fret, then finish with a quick slide up from the 3rd to 5th fret on 4th string.

RIFFS: 25 - 28
MUTING TECHNIQUE

An essential technique to master the slide is called "muting." Muting means to stop the string from ringing, particularly when you are moving the slide from fret to fret. Here are a few ways to mute the sting: If you are playing with fingers, then place the finger on the string after you play a note. If you are using a pick, put the pick and finger(s) against the string to mute. Try to eliminate the sound of the slide, so you only hear the notes in riff 25.

Here's a great slide practice with the G blues scale on the 2nd string. Mute the 2nd string after each note without the sound of the slide. Watch the tuning and repeat going up and down the string.

This riff requites a quick jump from the 2nd to 5th fret. Mute the 2nd string after playing 2nd fret note while quickly moving slide to 5th fret with no slide noise then slide from 8th to 9th fret. Keep an even rhythm throughout.

Play the first six notes of "The Star-Spangled Banner" without any slide noise. There are no rests indicated, so apply the muting technique after each note.

RIFFS: 29 - 32
BARRE WITH SLIDE

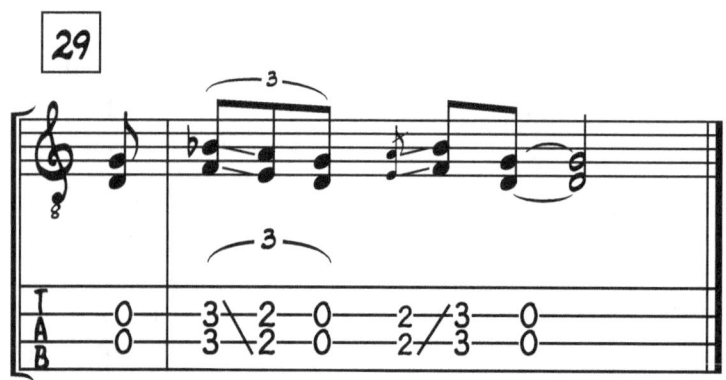

Place the slide over the 2nd and 3rd string and form a "barre." Slide down on both strings from the 3rd to 2nd fret, then play both open strings together with a triplet rhythm. Finish with a quick slide up from the 2nd to 3rd fret then open strings again.

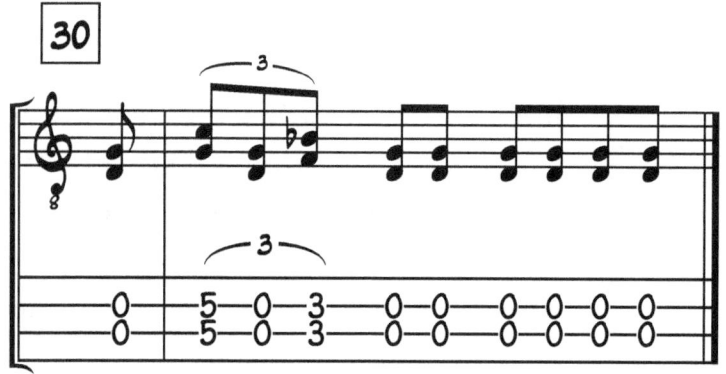

Make a barre with the slide on both 2nd and 3rd strings and play the triplet rhythm on the 5 - 0 - 3 frets. Play the open strings together with a shuffle blues rhythm.

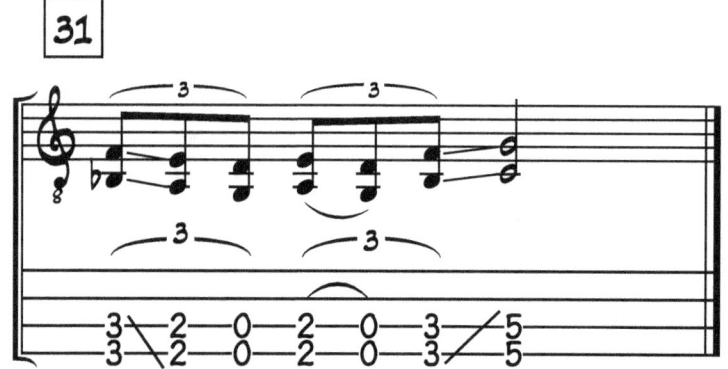

Make a barre on 3rd and 4th strings and play the triplet rhythms. Pull off slide from 2nd to open on the second triplet rhythm. Finish with slide up from the 3rd to 5th fret.

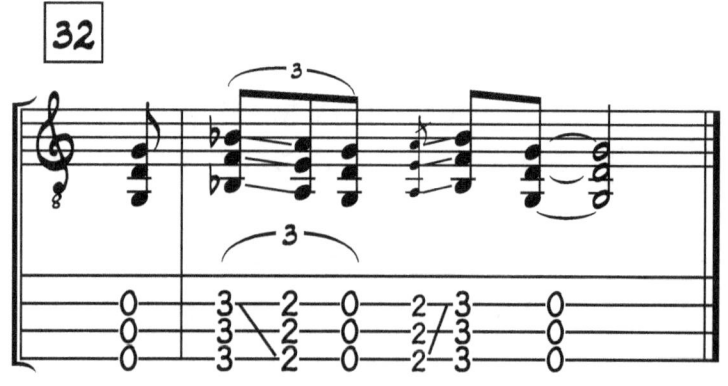

Place slide on three strings and slide from 3rd to 2nd fret then play open strings with the triplet rhythm. Finish with a quick slide up from 2nd to 3rd fret then play the open strings.

RIFFS: 33 - 36
EXTENDED SLIDES

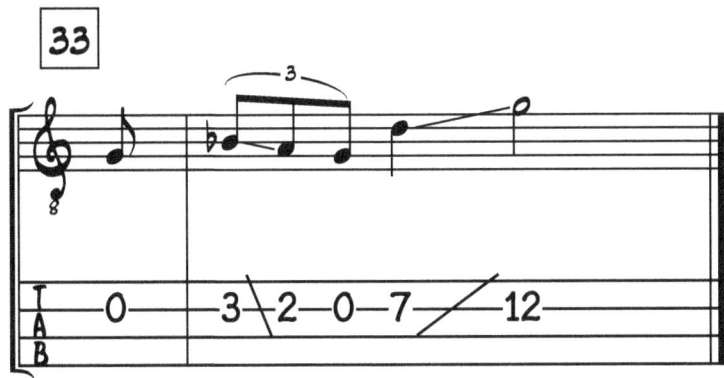

Here are some riffs using a long slide up and down the neck. In riff 33, play triplet rhythm sliding from the 3rd to 2nd fret then play open 2nd string. Quickly move the slide to the 7th fret then do a long slow slide from the 7th to 12th fret. Pay attention to your tuning.

This riff is similar to riff 33 but playing two notes together (barre). Slide from 3rd to 2nd fret on both strings then play open strings with a triplet rhythm. Do a long slide up the neck on the 2nd and 3rd strings from 5th to 10th fret.

This riff might look easy, but it's pretty tricky to do a double slide without muting. The challenge is to play the three notes (7th - 6th - 5th fret) without taking the slide off the string and clearly hear the three notes. As always, keep an ear for accurate tuning.

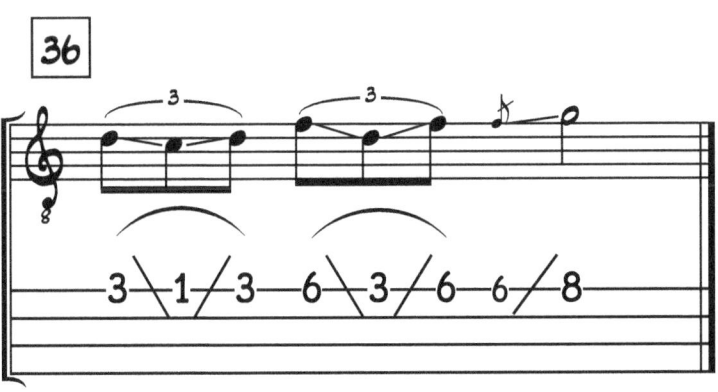

Here's an even trickier riff with these double slide triplets. Slide from the 3rd - 1st - 3rd fret without taking the slide off 1st string, "then" mute the 1st string and move quickly up to the 6th fret. Repeat this technique at the 6th - 3rd - 6th fret and finish with a slide up to the 8th fret.

RIFFS: 37 - 40
VIBRATO

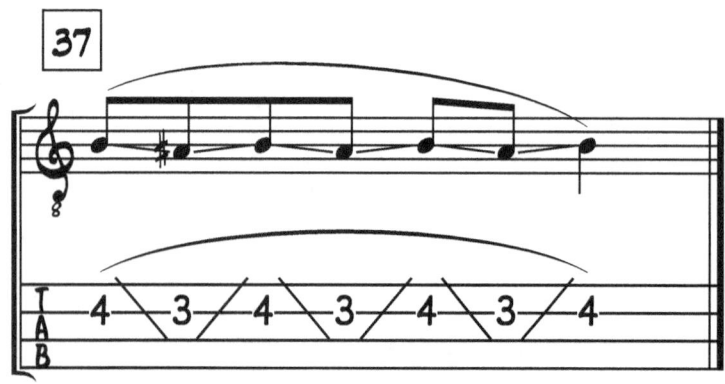

Add expression to your slide playing with vibrato. Start with a fret to fret vibrato in riff 37 by moving the slide back and forth between the 4th and 3rd fret on 2nd string. Keep your wrist loose!

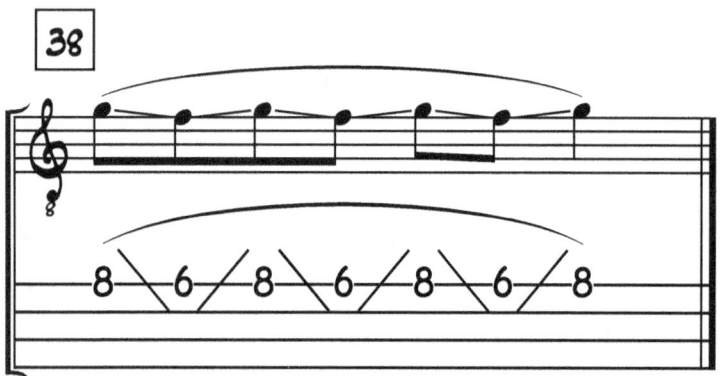

Here's a wide two fret vibrato. Move slide back and forth between 8th and 6th fret on 1st string. Keep an even rhythm with attention to pitch.

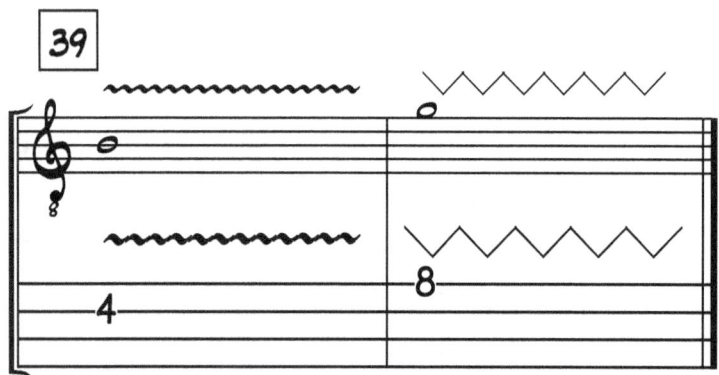

Usually, vibrato is written with a squiggly line above the note or tab. In measure 1, quickly move your wrist back and forth of the 4th fret but keep the slide tighter to the 4th fret and narrow -this is a fast vibrato. In measure 2, move your slide in a slightly wider arc - this is a wide vibrato.

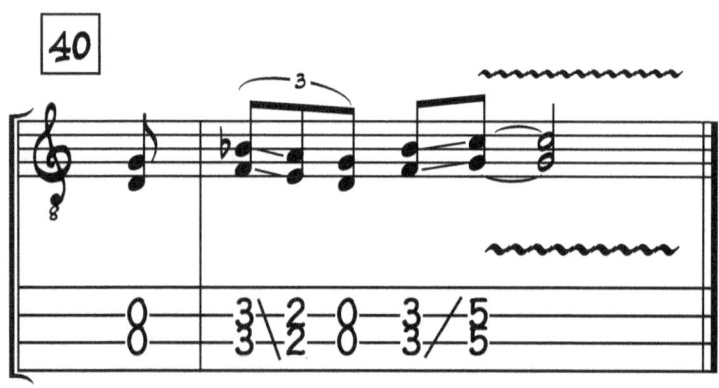

Riff 40 is an example of a barre vibrato playing on two (or more) strings. Experiment with different vibrato speeds and vibrato widths to make it your own and listen to other slide players!

RIFFS: 41 - 44
PALM MUTING

Palm-muting is indicated above with P.M and dashed line. Place your picking hand directly on the strings close to the bridge. Keep your hand on the strings while you pick to produce a muted sound. There is a "sweet spot" position that will make the strings ring less yet produce a muted "pizzicato" sound. Experiment with different hand placements to find the many sound variations this technique provides.

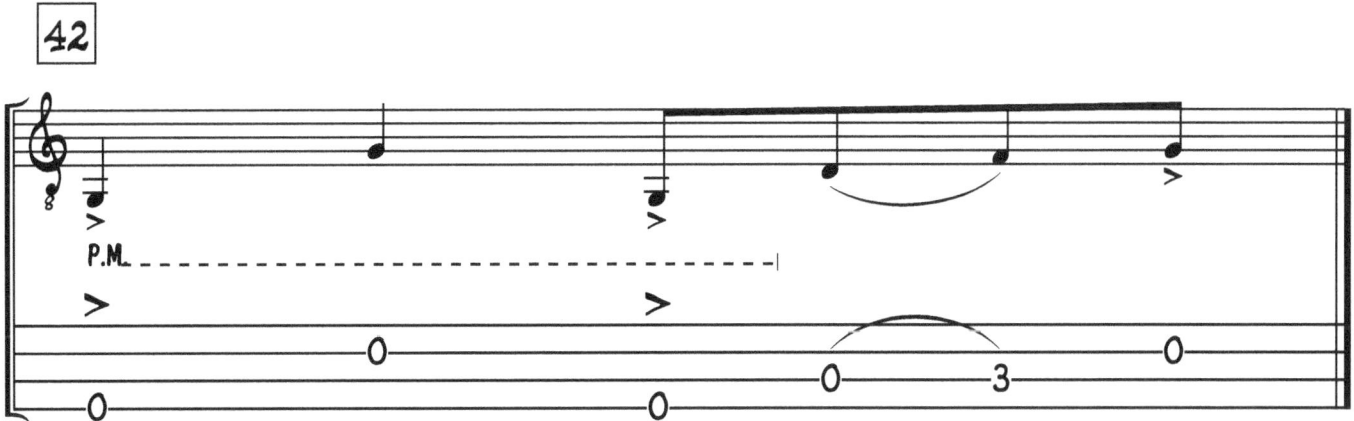

Palm-muting with an accent and hammer on. Like riff 41, place your palm on the strings near the bridge. Play the open 4th string with an accent. Take your palm off the strings where the dashed line ends and play the open to 3rd fret hammer on. Practice with a shuffle blues rhythm.

Palm muting on one string only. Palm mute the 4th string while fingerpicking with the index and middle fingers on the 2nd and 3rd string. This riff can also be played with a pick. In that case, use a down stroke on the muted 4th string and an up stroke on the 2nd and 3rd strings. End with a triplet slide down from the 3rd to 2nd fret.

Palm muting chords. Place your palm on the strings and make a barre with the slide. Keep slide in line with frets to play chords in tune. Slide between chords where desired. For example, you could slide down from the 9th to the 5th fret. Keep an even tension on the strings as you move your barre up and down the neck.

RIFFS: 45 - 48
FINGERSTYLE RIFFS

Here are some riffs with fingerpicking or sometimes referred to as fingerstyle. Alternate between the thumb on the 4th string and the index (1st) finger on the 3rd string. This riff can be played with a straight or shuffle rhythm. Tilt the slide in line with the 3rd and 5th frets while playing 3rd string open.

Fingerstyle with a slide. Alternate between the thumb and index finger while playing this riff. Tilt the slide on the 4th string sliding quickly from the 3rd to 4th fret, then 4th to 5th fret while maintaining a steady rhythm.

Alternate between the thumb on the 4th string and middle finger (or index) on the 2nd string. Keep a steady rhythm while alternating fingers. In measure one, a quick slide from the 2nd to 3rd fret, then play open 2nd string and move the slide to 5th fret keeping in line with fret.

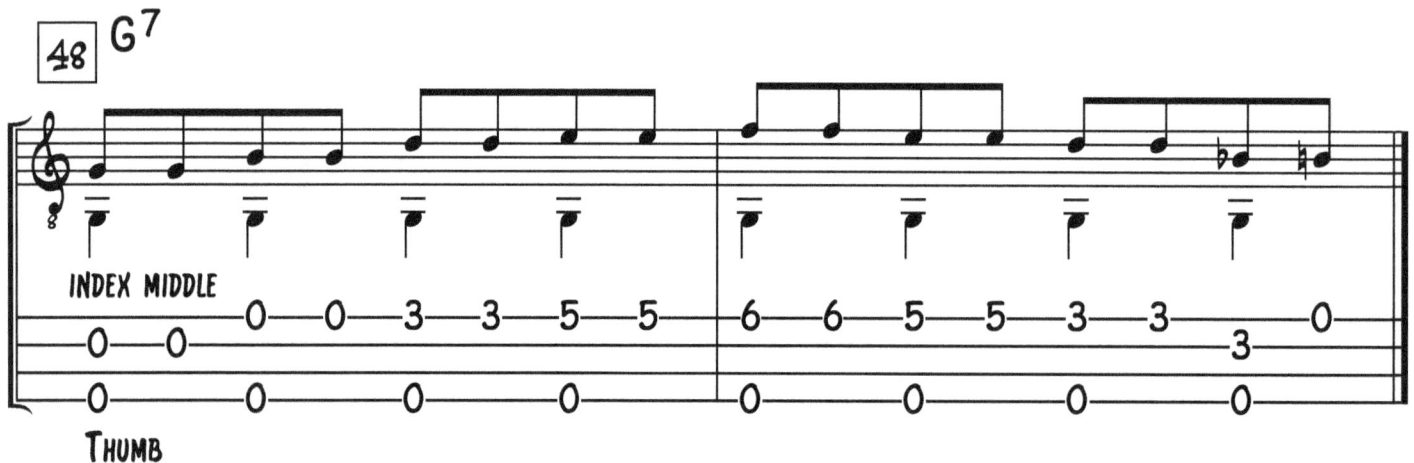

Riff 48 is an example of a boogie blues pattern. Alternate between the index and middle finger on the 2nd and 1st strings while keeping the thumb steady on the 4th string. Practice slowly with a focus on alternating the fingers. Gradually pick up the speed going between the straight and shuffle rhythm.

RIFFS: 49 - 52
DOUBLE STOPS & SLIDE CHORDS

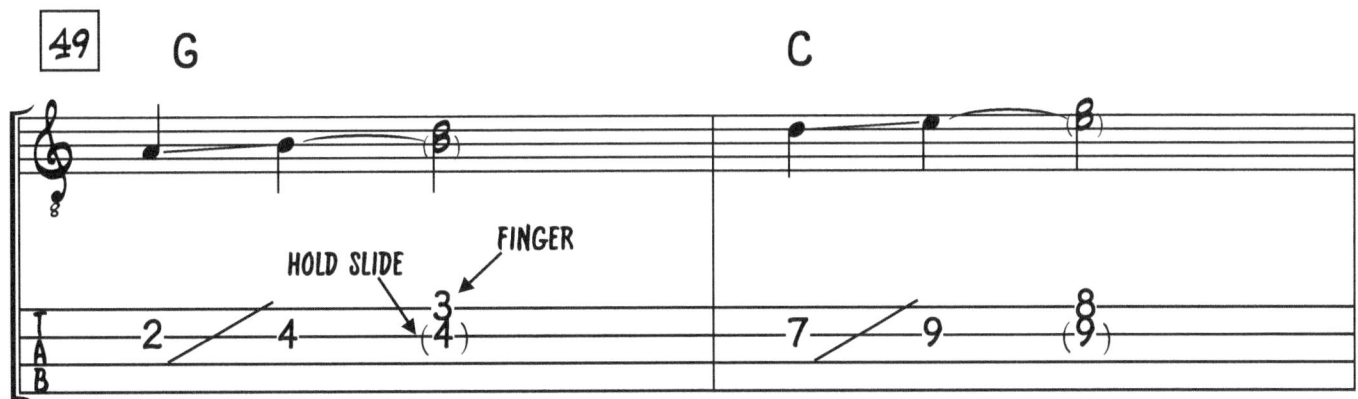

Playing notes behind the slide. Slide up from the 2nd to 4th fret. Keep the slide on the 4th fret while placing a finger behind the slide on the 3rd fret. Don't replay the (4) in brackets; this is a tied note. Keep the slide off the 1st string so you can hear both strings ring together. Repeat the same technique when playing at the 8th and 9th frets over the C chord.

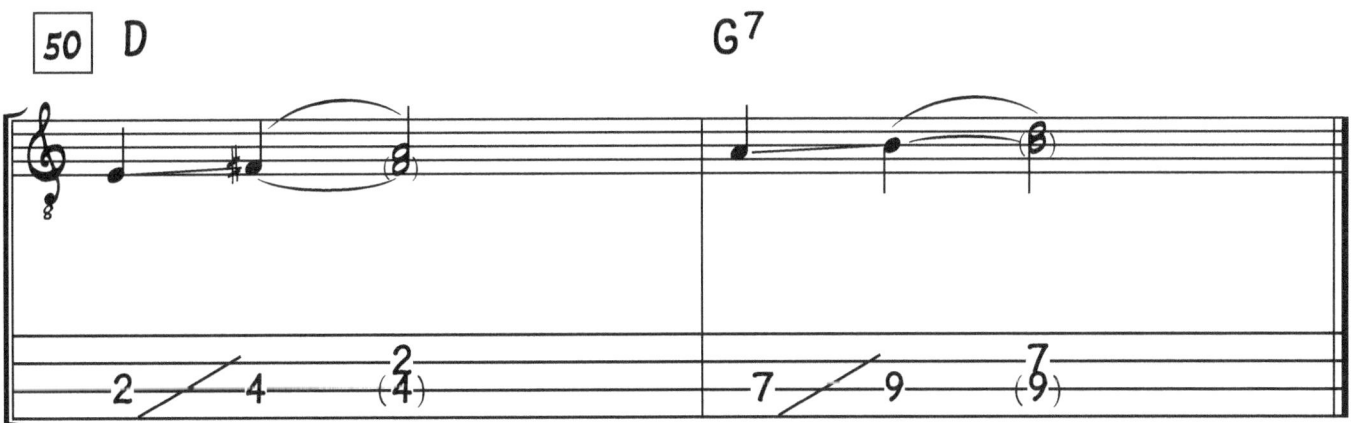

Similar to riff 49 but with a two fret stretch. Hold the slide down and place index finger two frets behind the slide. Slide from the 2nd to 4th fret keeping the slide on the 4th fret then put your index finger behind slide at 2nd fret. Repeat this technique at the 7th and 9th fret. This produces a minor 3rd interval.

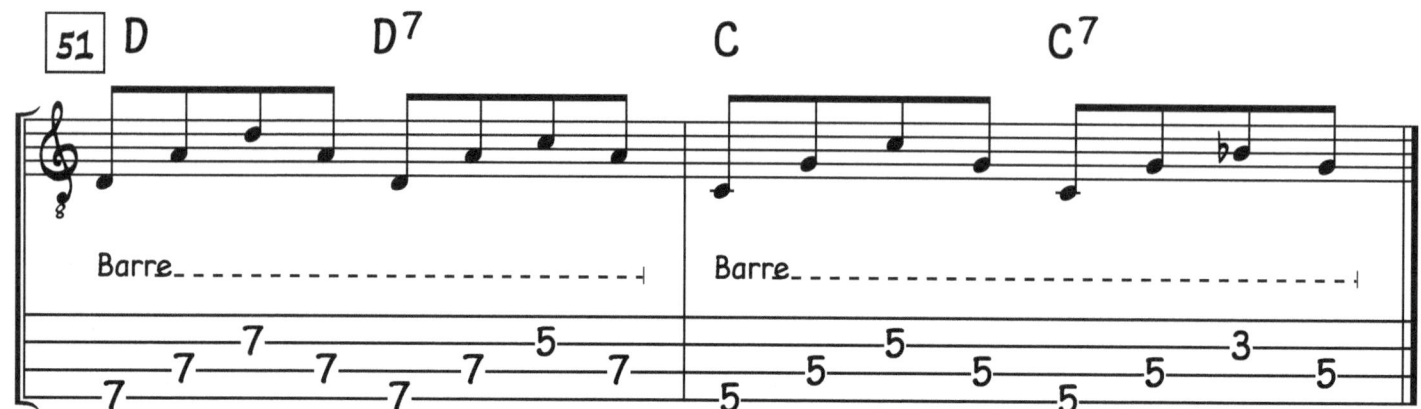

Slide barre chords. Place the slide on the 7th fret and hold while you pick the D chord up and down the strings. Keep holding slide at the fret while you push your index finger down behind slide at the 5th fret - this now produces a D7 chord. Repeat the same technique at the 5th fret to play the C and C7 chords.

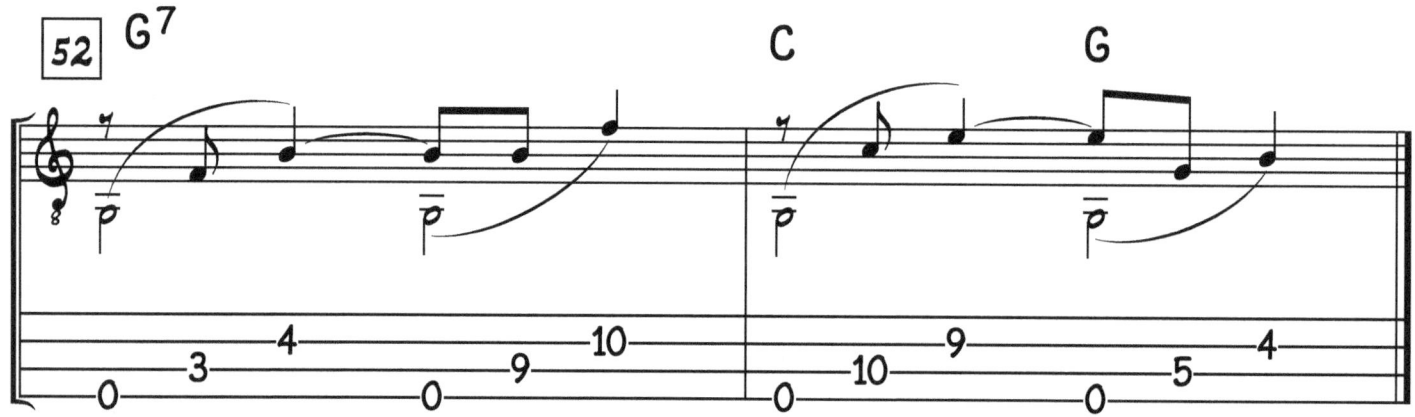

In riff 52, you can practice playing chords with an open string, finger and slide. This riff is a little harder getting the slide in the right position but doable with some practice. Play the G on the 4th string open and let it ring while placing the 1st finger on the 3rd fret 3rd string and the slide in front of the finger on the 4th fret 2nd string. Let all three notes ring together. Repeat up the neck at the 9th and 10th fret. In measure two, reverse this technique and play the finger behind the slide on the 3rd string while placing your index finger on the 2nd string. Listen carefully for tuning and practice slowly.

RIFFS: 53 - 56
STRUMMING & MUTING

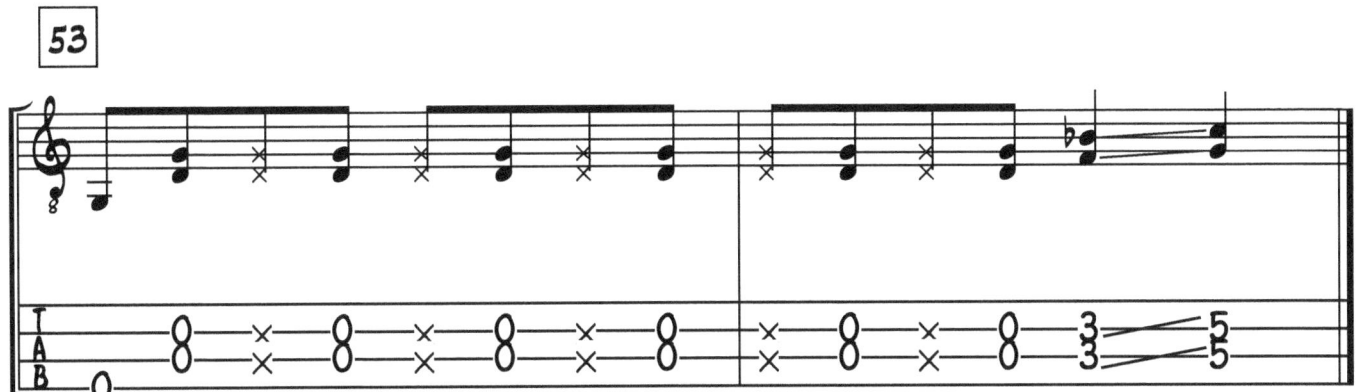

Muting (x) open strings. This technique requires you to mute the strings by placing your right-hand fingers or palm on the strings. Play the 4th string open then play 2nd and 3rd open strings together. Quickly put the index and middle finger (or palm) back on the strings to stop the open strings from ringing. If you are using a pick, then mute the strings with the pick and middle finger. Try to make a rhythmic clicking sound at the "x" by striking the strings harder with the right hand.

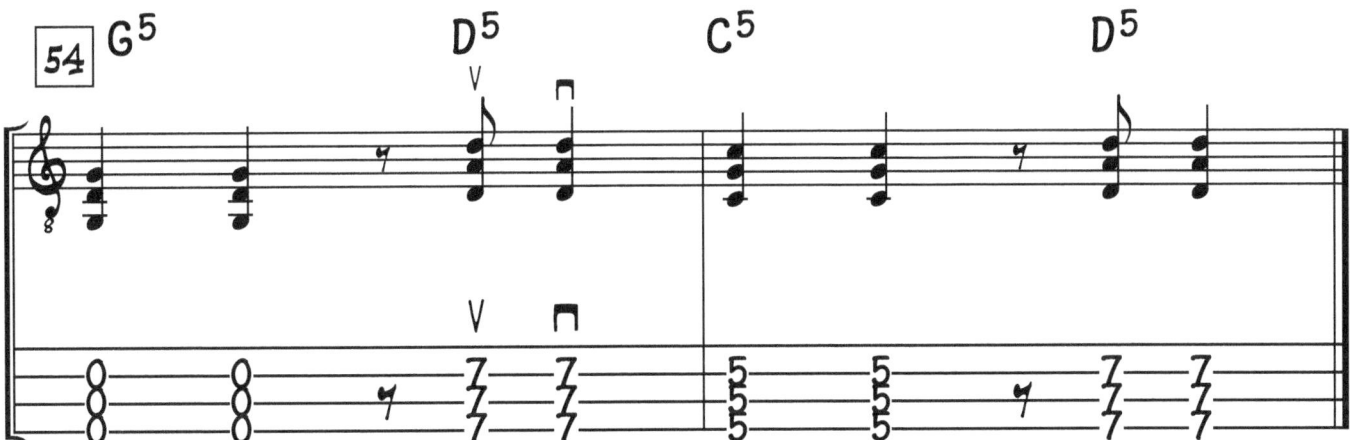

Similar to riff 53, mute the strings with the palm or fingers of your strumming hand at the rest (𝄿). If you are using a pick, do an upstroke at the first 7th fret (D5) chord followed by a downstroke. Keep the slide in a straight line with fret to play chords in tune and get a nice even groove.

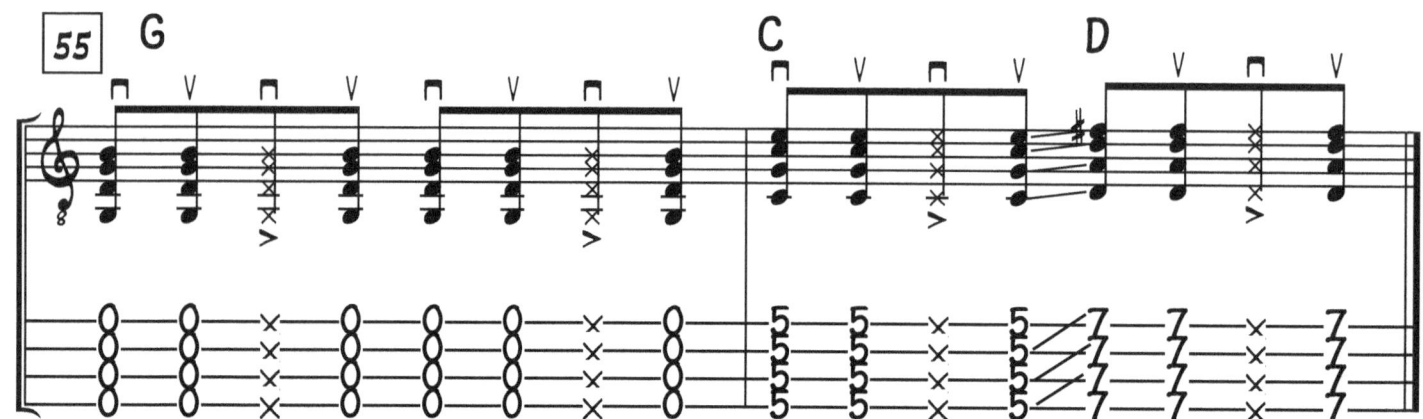

Strum down (⊓) and up (∨), then mute all the strings with your strumming hand at the x's. This type of muting is sometimes called a "pick slap" and frequently occurs on the 2nd and 4th beat of the measure similar to a snare drum effect Emphasize with an accent on the 2nd and 4th beat and get a loud clicking sound.

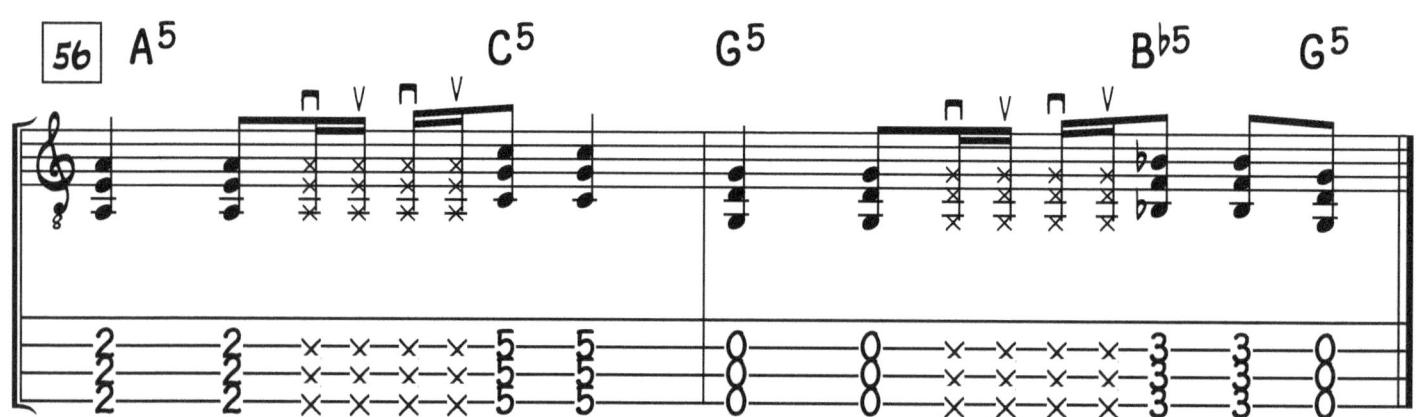

The muting in riff 55 requires a quick sixteenth note: down/up-down/up strum. The big difference: the muting is done with the left hand (fretting hand). Take the slide off the strings at the mute (x) and place a left-hand finger(s) lightly on the strings and strum the muted sixteenth-note pattern. Make sure to mute all the strings with your left hand - so no notes are ringing. Practice this riff until you get a nice muted sound with the left hand and produce a rhythmic clicking sound.

RIFFS: 57 - 60
UNDETERMINED SLIDE

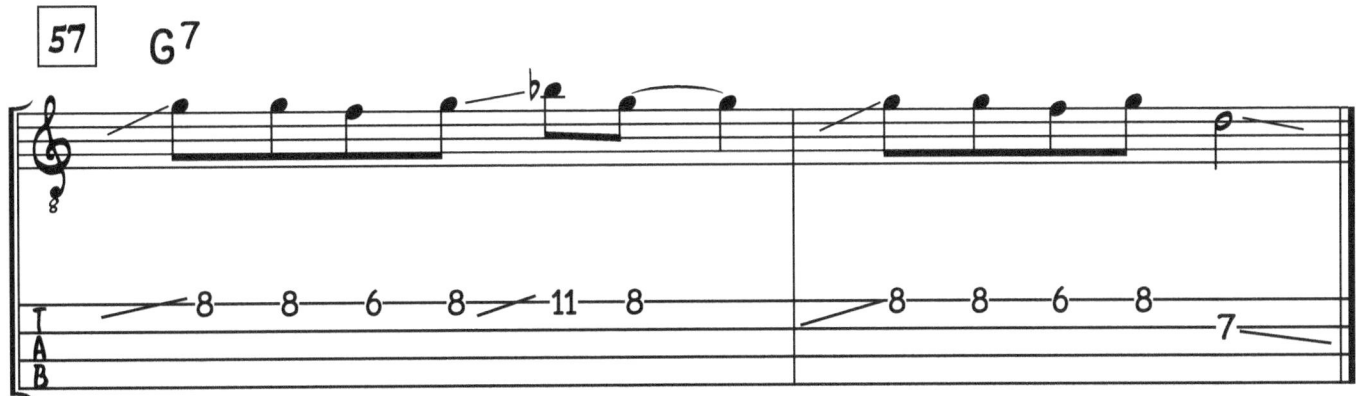

An undetermined slide means you can slide up or down to your target note at a fret you choose. In other words, the slide does not have a specific note to slide from, so you can slide from any note(s). In measure one slide up to 8th fret from a fret of your choice. Though it is undetermined, often you slide from one or two frets lower but at the discretion of the player. Take the same approach on the slide down at the end of measure two. Often the slide down is to a chord tone meaning another note in the chord.

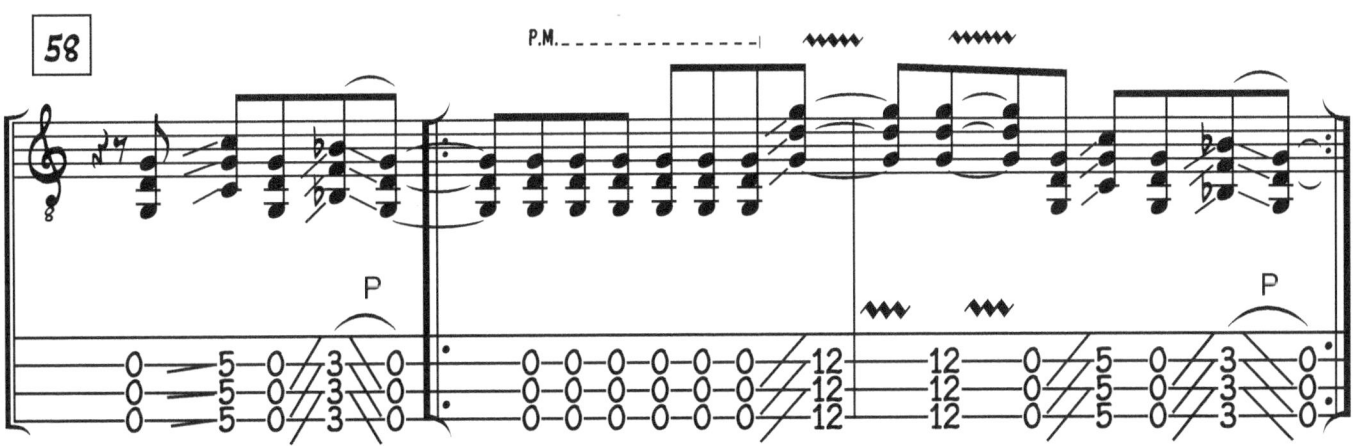

Undetermined slide making a barre with the slide. Slide up to the 5th fret and play the open strings, then slide up to 3rd fret then back down to open strings. A pull off is frequently used when sliding to open strings. Slide up at 12th fret from a fret of your choice, adding vibrato at the 12th fret. This type of slide playing is usually more aggressive. Keep a steady rhythm and turn up your amp loud!

Riff 59 can be played with a pick or fingerstyle. Play the open string picking pattern, then mute all strings at the rest (𝄾), place the slide at the 5th fret and slide down the neck to an undetermined fret of your choice-you can stop the slide at a fret or slide down to open strings. To finish, slide up from the 3rd fret.

Riff 60 has a combination of undetermined and determined slides with single and double notes. To begin, slide up to 8th fret then pluck 8th fret again. Play a triplet rhythm from 8th to 6th fret then play the open 2nd string. Slide up to 3rd fret from any string below on both 2nd and 3rd strings. Repeat in measure two but end with a determined slide up from the 3rd to 5th fret.

RIFFS: 61 - 64
SLIDE AND FINGERSTYLE

Fingerstyle and slide riffs. Use your thumb on the 4th string, index on 3rd string and middle finger on 2nd string. Start with a hammer on (H) using the index finger of your picking hand. Tilt the slide and play the 2nd string open using your r.h. middle finger and continue with your thumb on the 4th string, index on 3rd and middle finger on the 2nd string. The riff should sound like one continuous flow of notes. When played smoothly, this is called "legato."

This riff is a little challenging, so take it slow, trying to keep a steady rhythm and proper tuning with slide. Begin with a quick slide up from the 3rd to 5th fret tilting the slide on the 3rd string. Hold the 5th fret note down and play the 1st string open. Keep the thumb steady on the open 4th string. The next part will take some practice. Slide up on the 2nd string from the 2nd to 4th fret, hold the 4 with the slide and bring the index or middle finger of right hand behind the slide. You should hear all the strings ringing. Continue with the same technique at the 5th to 7th, holding the 7th and playing the 6th behind the slide. All while keeping the thumb steady. Good luck!

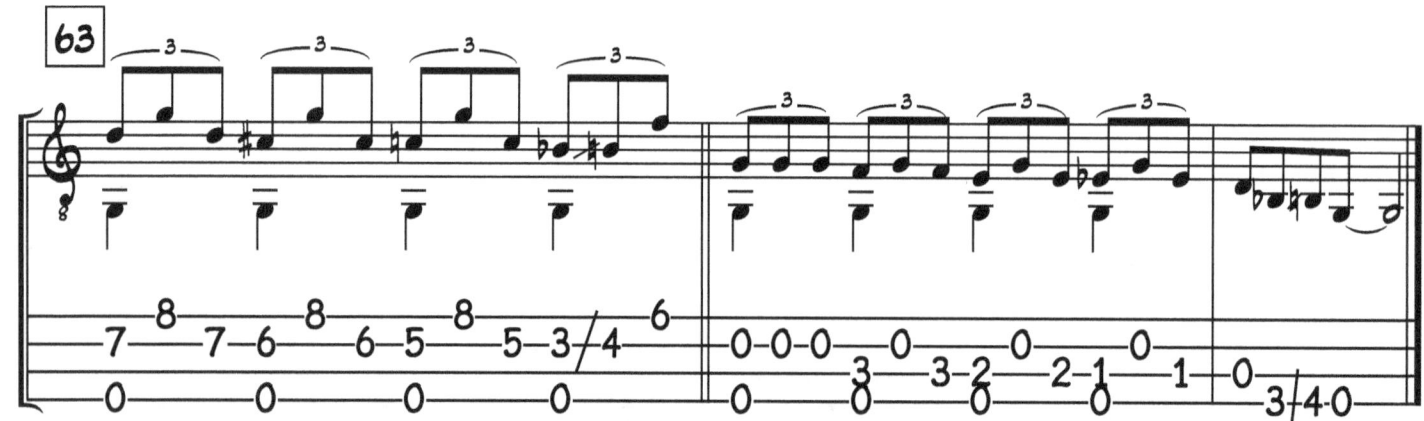

Riff 63 is more of a fingerstyle riff without the slide but can also be played by putting the slide on the 4th pinky finger. Use the following fingering on the picking hand: thumb on 4th, index on 3rd, middle on 2nd and ring on 1st string. If you are playing with a slide, place the slide in front of the fingers on the 1st string. Keep the slide in line on the 8th fret while you stretch the fingers back. Play with even triplets and a steady quarter note rhythm with the thumb. This riff is a typical blues ending.

Keep the thumb on the 4th string, and middle and index or middle and ring finger on the 1st and 2nd string. The rhythm is triplet, eighth notes, then triplet. Use the techniques you have learned thus far: tilt slide, playing behind the slide, and use the proper right-hand fingering.

RIFFS: 65 - 68
BOOGIE BASS PATTERNS

65

Here is a familiar boogie bass blues pattern. This riff can be played with either a straight or shuffle rhythm and with or without a pick. Use alternate up and down picking if you are using a pick and your thumb or thumb finger combination if you are playing fingerstyle. Keep the rhythm steady and experiment with different tempos. Notice the triplet at the end of the riff.

66

Here is a cool little rockabily riff to work on. Tilt the slide moving up neck and down the neck. Alternate between thumb and middle or index finger of your picking hand. There are several options for fingering on 2nd string: index only, middle only, or alternating between index and middle. Keep the slide on 4th string without muting between notes. Play fast!

This riff is based on a common blues/rock riff. Use the thumb on the open 4th string, the middle finger on the open 2nd string and the index finger on the 3rd string. In measure one, try to minimize slide noise and let notes ring clearly by tilting the slide on the 3rd string. In measure two, repeat the same pattern adding a slide from the 2nd to 3rd fret. Throw on the distortion!

Here is another bluesy riff with a "call and answer." Measure one calls out and measure two answers. Alternate between the thumb and middle or index finger. Tilt the slide to play the notes on the 4th string and let the 2nd string ring out. Experiment with muting techniques and straight or shuffle rhythms. Make it slow and dirty!

RIFFS: 69 - 72
BLUES SHUFFLE PATTERNS

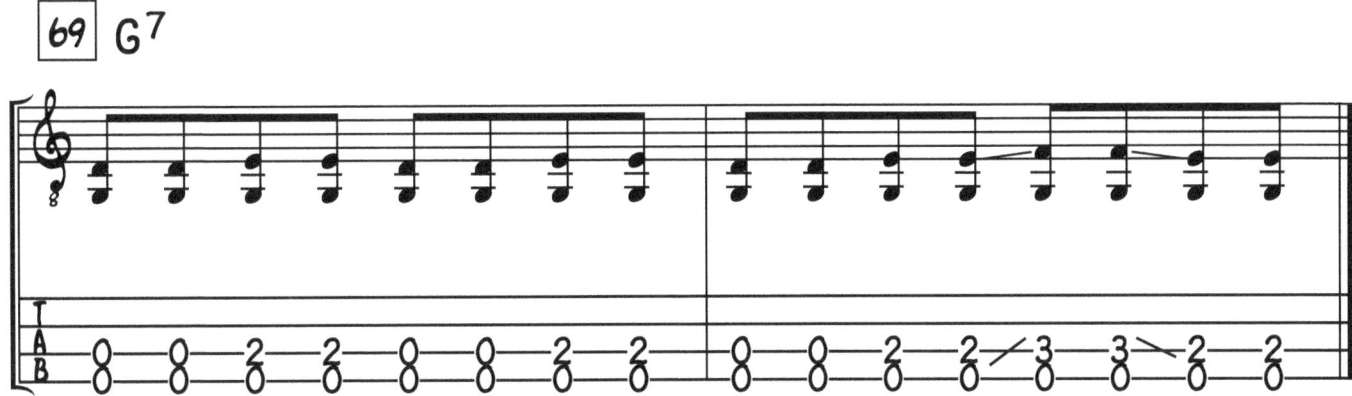

Here are the nuts and bolts of blues accompaniment. Riff 69 is probably the most common pattern associated with blues. Play the open 4th and 3rd string together with your pick or thumb. This riff can be played with or without the slide. If you play with the slide, try not to touch the 4th string to avoid any slide rattle. Experiment with the straight or shuffle groove.

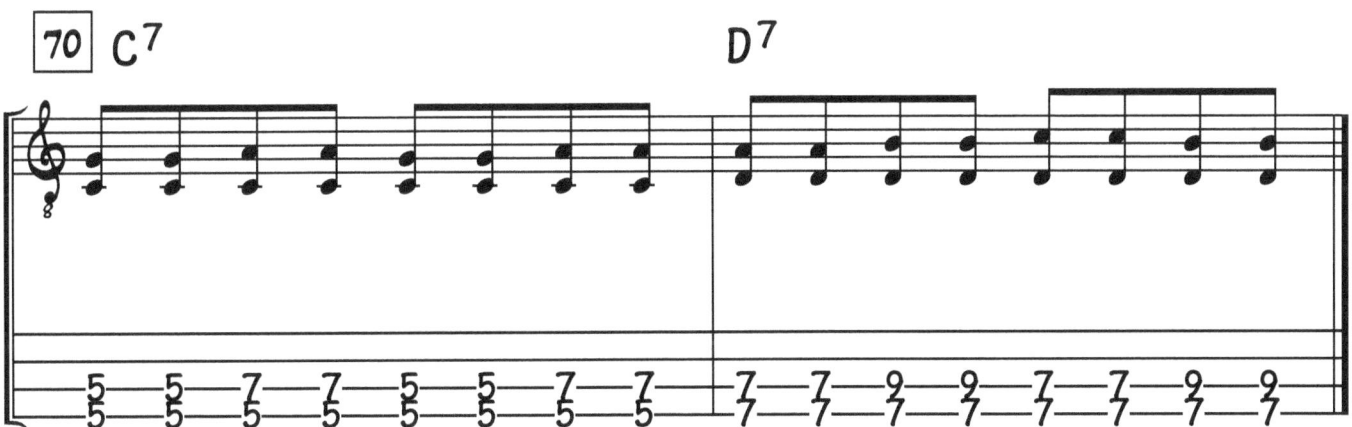

Riff 70 works with riff 69 when playing a 12 bar blues in the key of G. Make a barre with the 1st finger at 5th fret and play the 4th and 3rd string together. Keep the 1st finger barre down while taking the 3rd (or 4th) finger on and off the 7th fret of the C7 chord. Repeat at the 7th fret to play over the D7 chord. This pattern can be played with or without the slide. For a challenge, experiment with different left-hand fingers while holding the barre down.

Here's another variation on a blues shuffle pattern. Keep a steady rhythm with the thumb on the 4th string. Take the slide on and off the 3rd string while alternating the fingering in picking hand: index- middle, or with a pick using downstrokes only. When you are ready, try making up your own shuffle variations using the blues scales provided in the scales section.

The riff 72 rhythm switches between triplets and eighth notes. Play with a shuffle rhythm alternating between the thumb and fingers. Let the open strings ring while moving slide. Tilt the slide where necessary. Practice with a metronome or drum machine if you have one. If not, tap your foot evenly, trying to distinguish between triplets and eighth notes.

RIFFS: 73 - 76
LEFT HAND TAPPING & HARMONICS

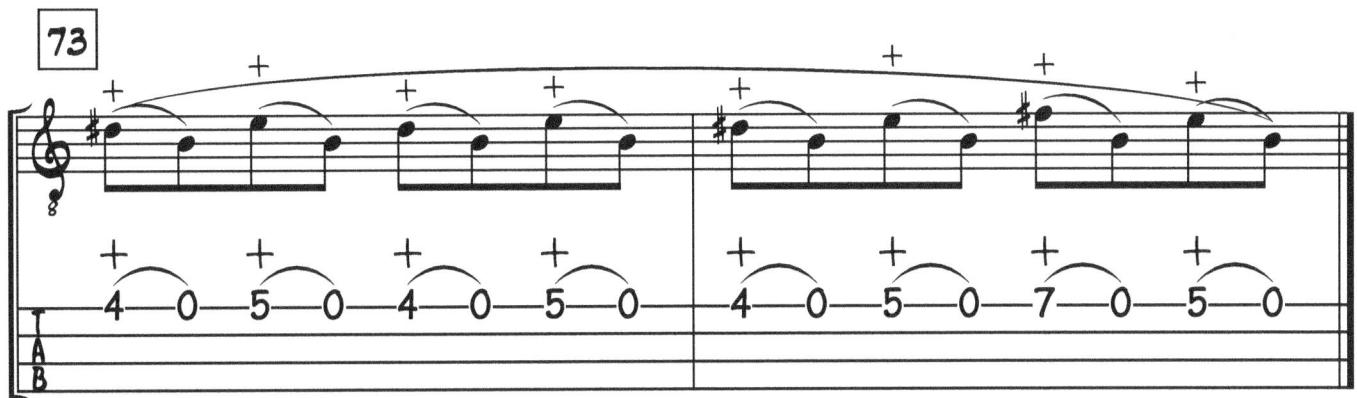

Here are a few classic rock techniques to practice. First, pluck the note on the 4th fret 1st string, then pull off your finger or slide without plucking again. Go to the 5th fret, but this time tap (+) your finger on the string "without plucking." In other words, once your pluck or pick the first note of this riff, you don't pick again. This riff can be played with or without the slide. If you are using the slide, start slow and gradually pick up the tempo paying attention, as usual, to your tuning.

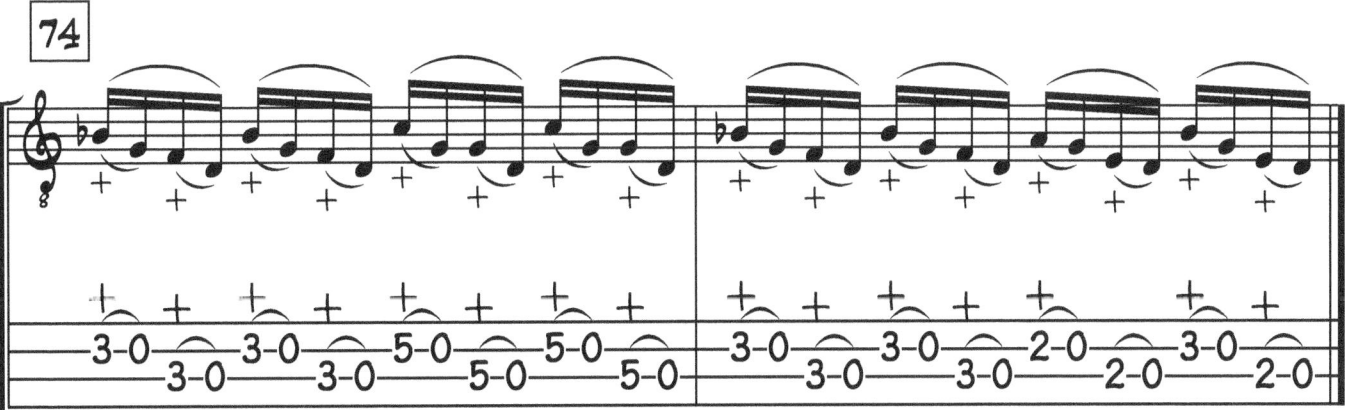

This rock tapping riff is similar to riff 73, but switching between the 2nd and 3rd strings. Gently tap slide on and off, paying attention to tuning and keeping an even rhythm. This technique works best with fingers or with a short or small slide. Tilt the slide and angle your wrist to avoid stopping the open strings after the tap.

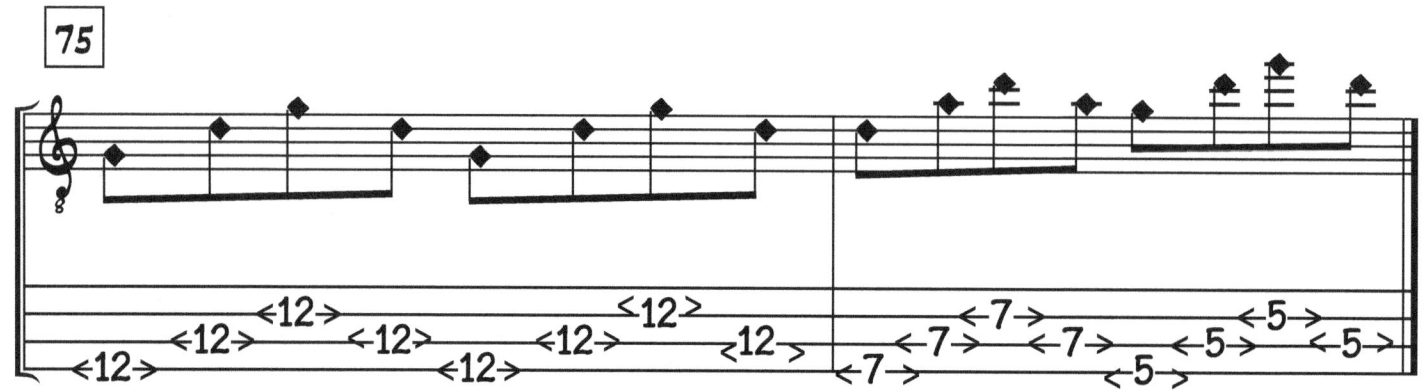

Riff 75 introduces a technique called "harmonics." To play harmonics, place your finger directly over the fret touching the string but not pushing down onto the neck. When you pluck the string, you should hear a note that is higher in pitch, almost sounding like a little bell. Harmonics are indicated with a diamond shape-note on the notation line and with brackets (<>) on the tablature line. Make a barre with your finger at the 12th fret and gently hold down while you play the harmonics. Repeat this at the 7th and 5th fret. Try plucking the string closer to the bridge for a brighter tone.

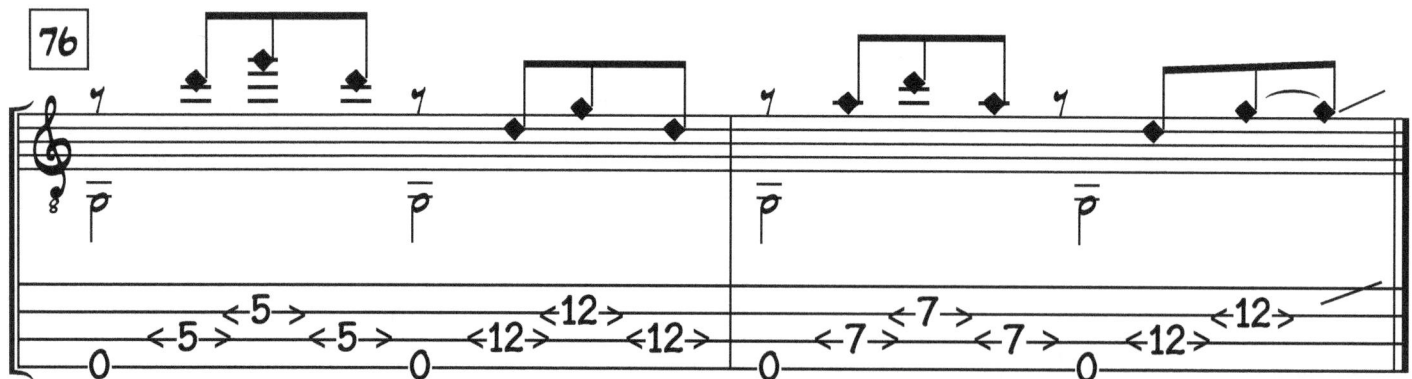

Riff 76 also has harmonics though combined with open strings. To start, play the open G 4th string then lightly touch your finger over the 5th fret on the 2nd and 3rd string, letting all the notes ring out. Repeat the same approach at the 12th and 7th fret. On the last note, play a harmonic on the 12th fret, then gently slide your finger, or slide, up the fingerboard. This slide up produces a "glissando" or "portamento" effect. It is essential to get the pressure just right and keep the finger on the string as you slide up the neck.

RIFFS: 77 - 80
PLAYING RIFFS IN DIFFERENT KEYS

The most accessible key to play in on the cigar box guitar in standard G-D-G tuning is the key of G. Not all tunes are in G, so it is necessary to transpose into other keys. The following four riffs are repeated in different keys and cover many of the slide techniques you learned so far. Notice the triplet rhythms and quick grace note slides (remember that grace notes don't take any extra time in the measure). Listen to the audio tracks for help with the correct rhythm. As usual, use tilt slides to avoid hitting other strings.

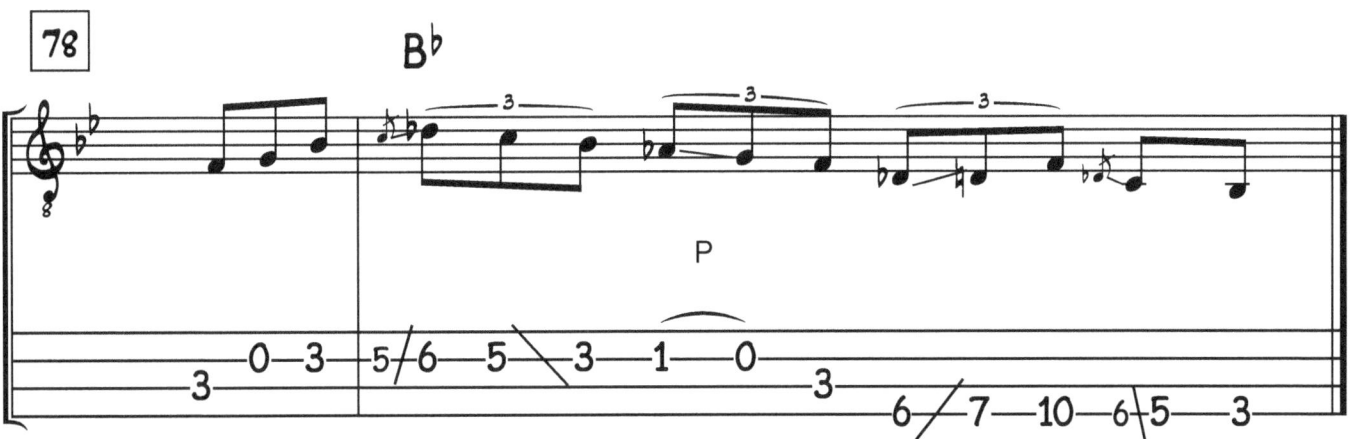

Riff 78 is the same as riff 77 but in the key of "Bb." The key of Bb has two flats: Bb and Eb. The key of Bb is a standard blues key, especially when playing with any horn players. It's a good idea to practice the Bb scales from the scale section to become familiar with the fingering in this key.

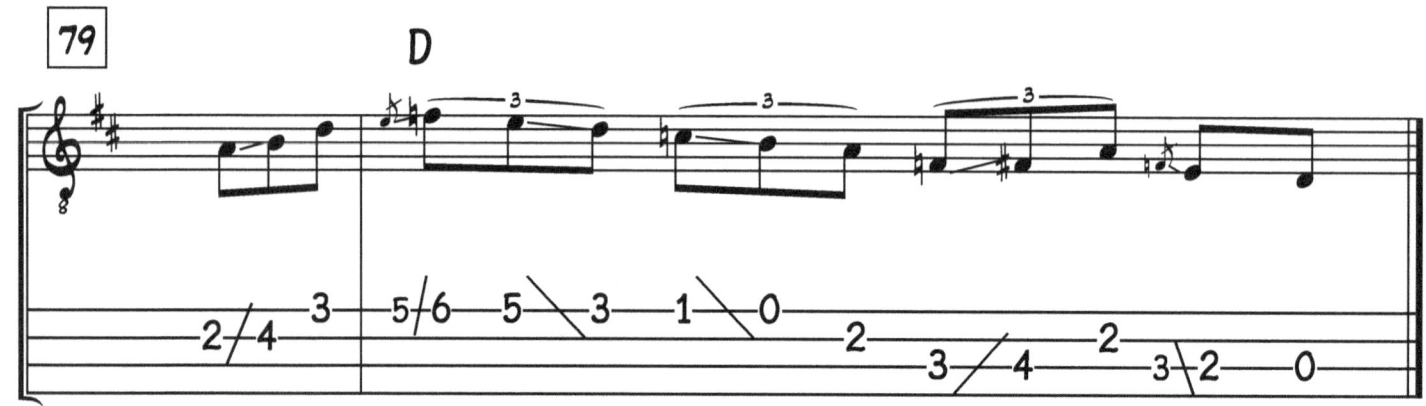

Riff 79 is in the key of "D." The key of D has two sharps: F# and C#. This key is also popular on the cigar box guitar. In this version of the riff, start with a slide up from the 2nd to 4th fret and play the 1st string 3rd fret behind the slide, as explained in earlier lessons. The notes in the key of D are: D E F# G A B C# D.

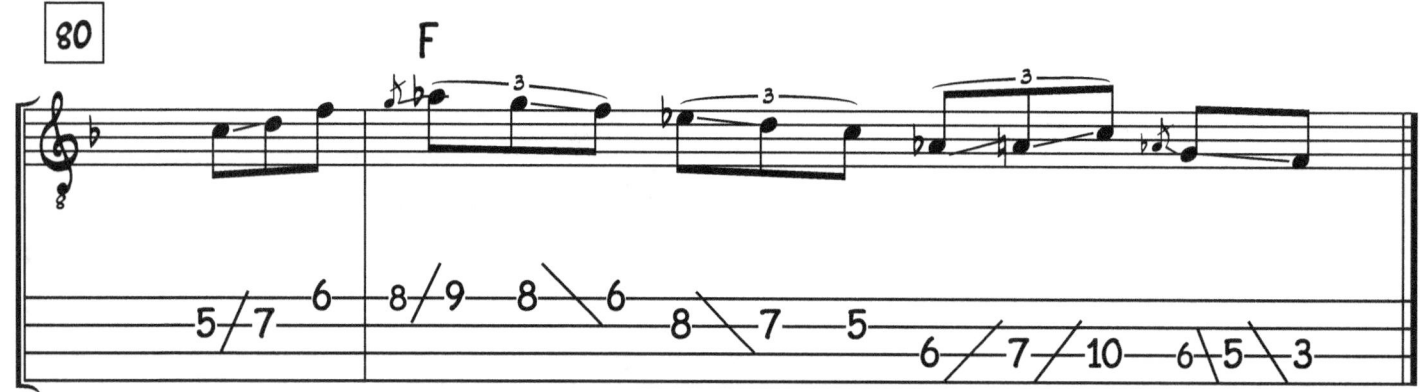

The last riff in this series is in the key of "F." The key of F has one flat: Bb. This version of the riff is transposed into a higher position on the neck. Playing up the neck requires more care as the frets are closer together, making the tuning is more sensitive. Pay attention to the amount of slide pressure applied on the 1st and 2nd string to get a clean full tone.

RIFFS: 81 - 84
PLAYING IN DIFFERENT TIME SIGNATURES

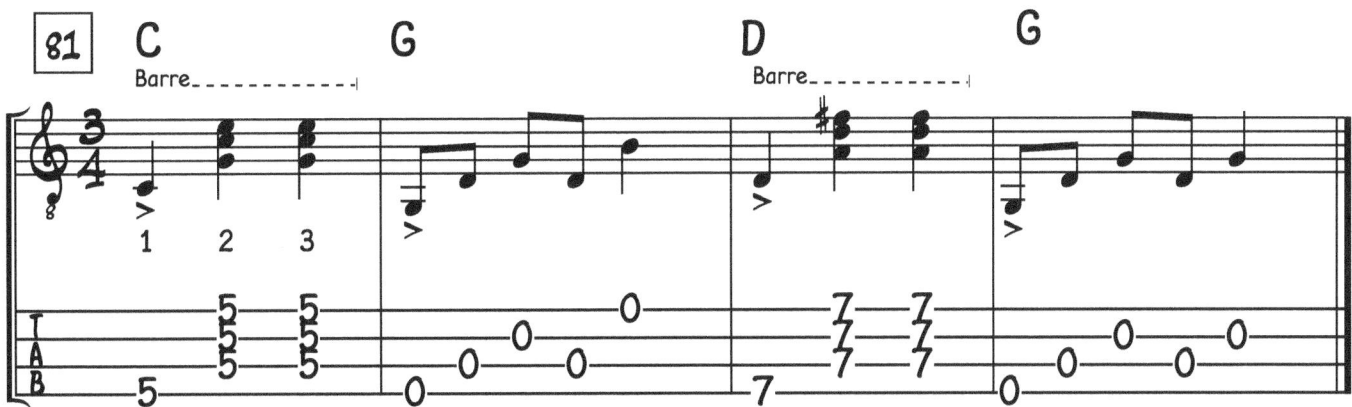

The next series of riffs will use different time signatures other than 4/4. Riff 81 is in 3/4 time - meaning three beats per measure. 3/4 is common in waltzes and some ballads. Begin this riff by making a barre with the slide or finger on the 5th fret. Put an accent on the 1st beat of each measure and count to three. This riff can be played with a pick or fingers on the right hand.

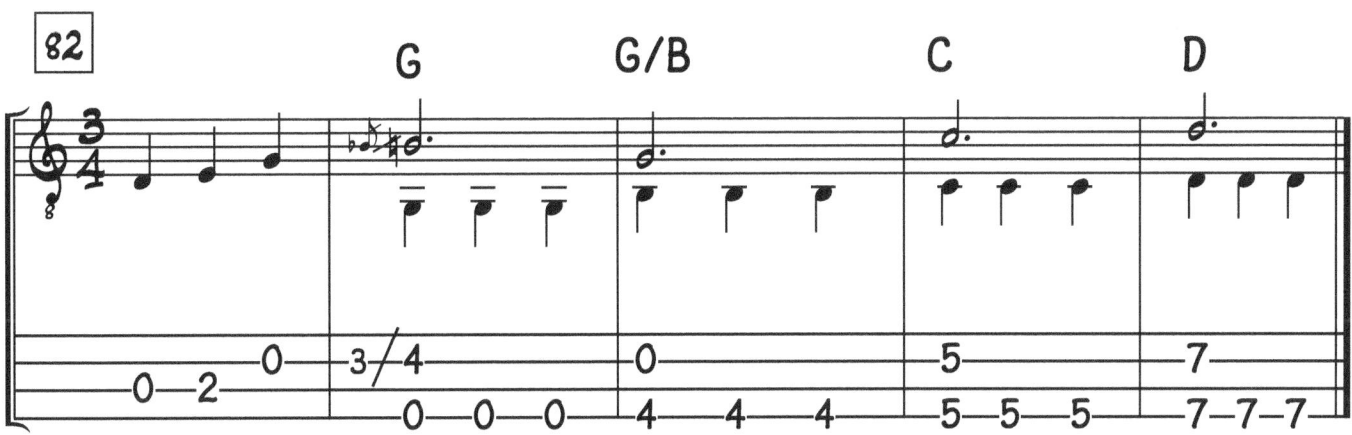

Riff 82 is also in 3/4 time. Keep an even three-beat rhythm with your thumb on the 4th string accenting the first beat in each measure. If you are using a slide, the third measure provides an added challenge to move the slide from the 2nd to 4th string on the G/B chord. Practice slowly until the entire riff can be played smoothly.

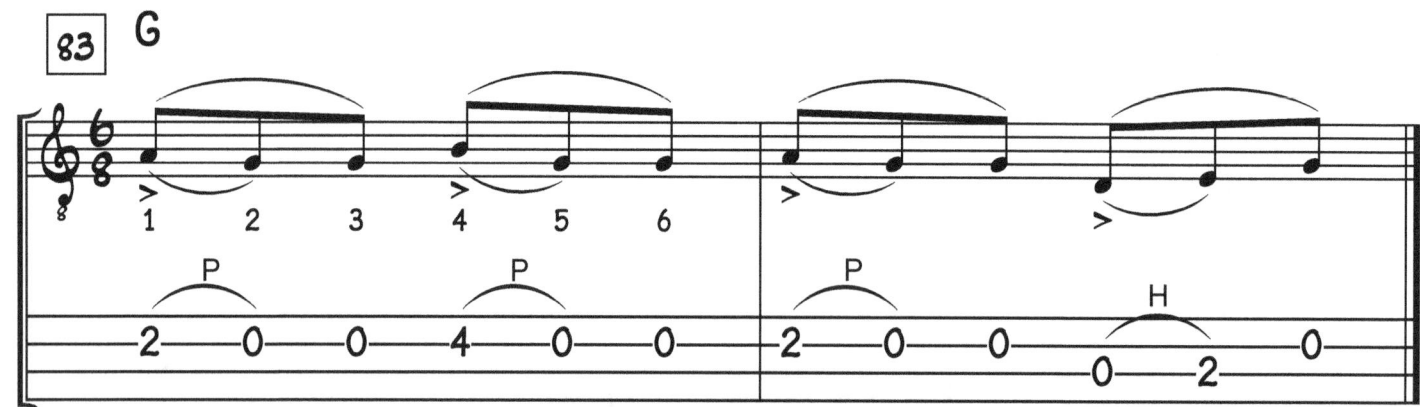

Riff 83 is in 6/8 time. 6/8 means there are six beats per measure, usually counted in two groups of three (1-2-3 / 4-5-6). This time signature is typically heard in jigs, polkas, marches and some rock music. This riff uses a combination of pull offs and hammer ons. Use the tilt slide technique, accent the first and 4th beat of each measure, and count to six.

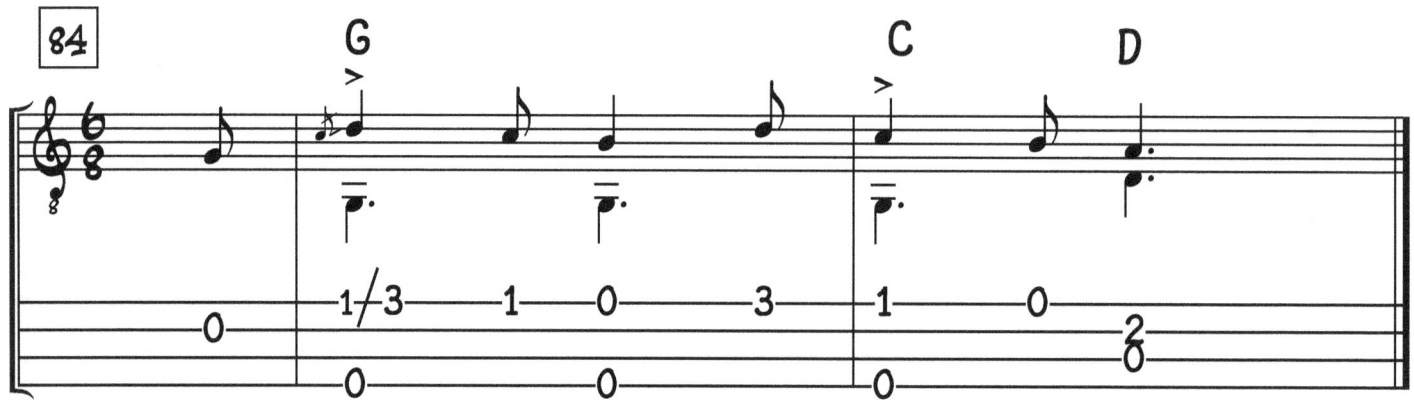

Here's another riff in 6/8 time that can be played with fingers or slide. Try to create a clean melody on the 1st and 2nd strings while keeping the thumb steady on the 1st and 4th beats.

RIFFS: 85 - 88
INTROS, TURNAROUNDS & ENDINGS

Riff 85 is an excellent example of a standard blues intro or turnaround. A turnaround occurs at the end of the tune, harmonically setting up a return to the beginning. You can insert this 12 bar G blues turnaround in measure 11 of a 12 bar blues form. To play this riff alternate between the thumb and fingers or go down and up with a pick. Tilt your slide at the 12th fret and gradually move down the neck. End the riff with a barre slide up the neck from the 5th - 6th to 7th fret.

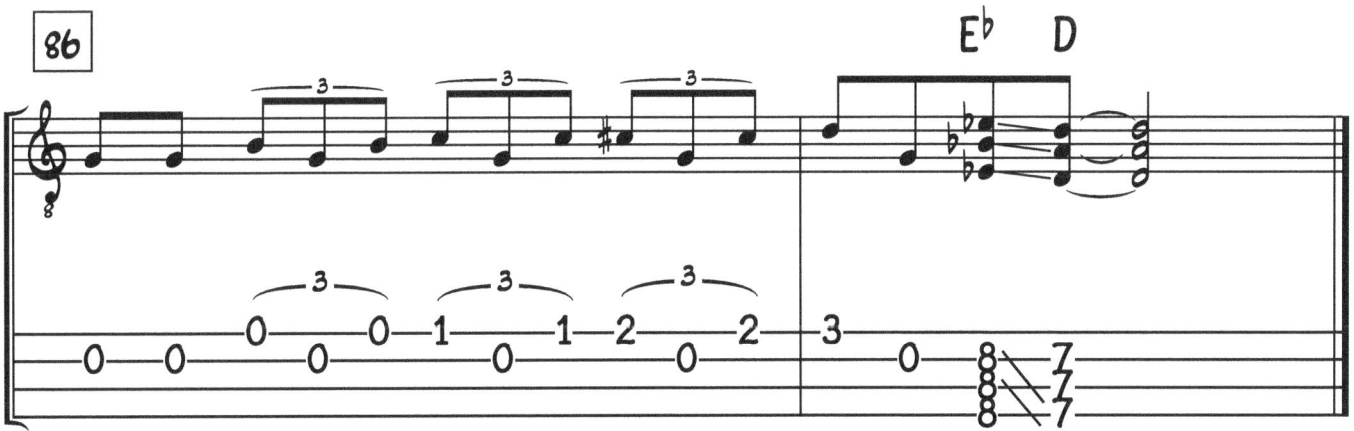

Here's another good example of a blues intro or turnaround. Begin with two eighth notes on the open 2nd string then play three consecutive triplets alternating between the 1st and 2nd strings before playing the 3 - 0 in measure two. Use your fingers or pick and finish with a barre slide on the Eb to D chord. Pay close attention when switching between the eighth notes and triplets, and keep a steady shuffle groove.

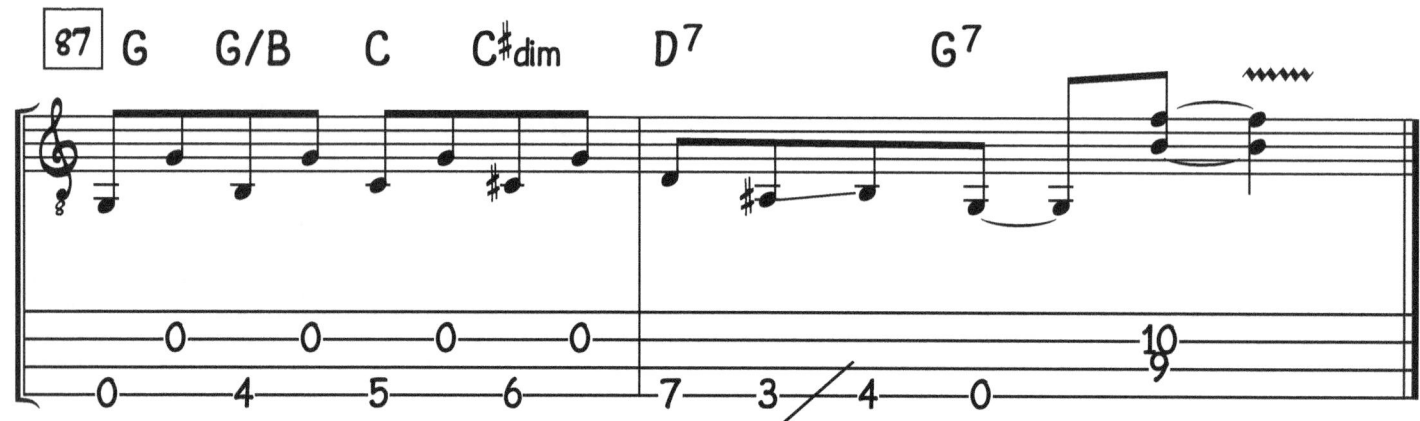

Riff 87 can work as a blues ending when inserted at measure 11 of a standard 12 bar blues. Alternate between the thumb and fingers or use alternate picking. Tilt the slide on the 4th string, working your way up the neck.

Here's another example of a blues ending. Let the open 4th string ring while you move your slide down the neck from the 8th fret. Play behind the slide on the last two notes of measure one (4 - 3). Finish with a slide up on strings 1 and 2 from the 9th to 10th fret. The last chord has an F and A with the G; this is a G9 chord.

RIFFS: 89 - 91
SOLOING OVER MAJOR CHORDS

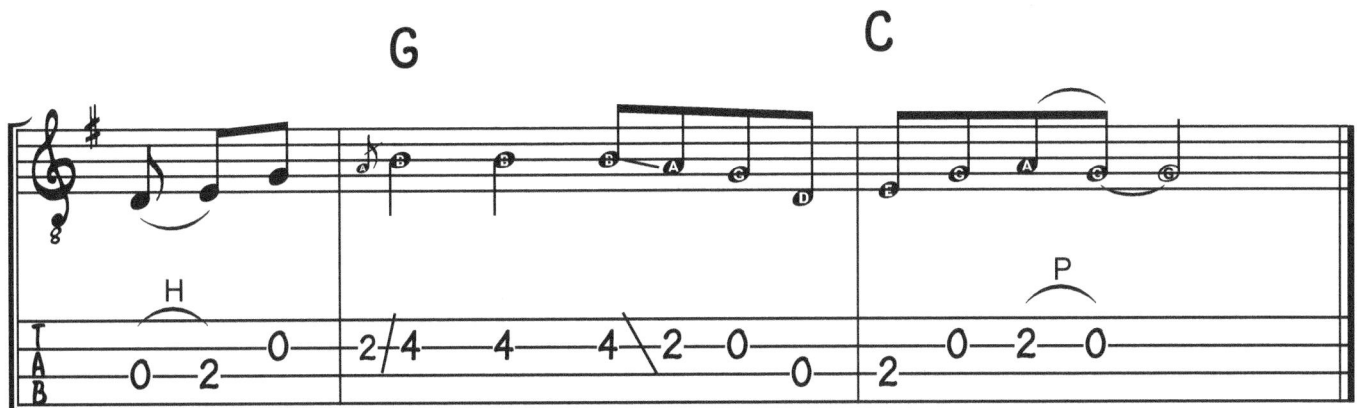

Here are a few tips for soloing over major chords. The notes in a G chord are (G-B-D). These notes are called "chord tones." When you play a chord tone, there is a sense of stability, meaning it sounds right over the G chord accompaniment. Add some interest to your solo by using both chord tones and non-chord tones. The non-chord tones are notes not in the chord but from the G scale or chromatic notes. In measure 3, the chord tones are C-E-G.

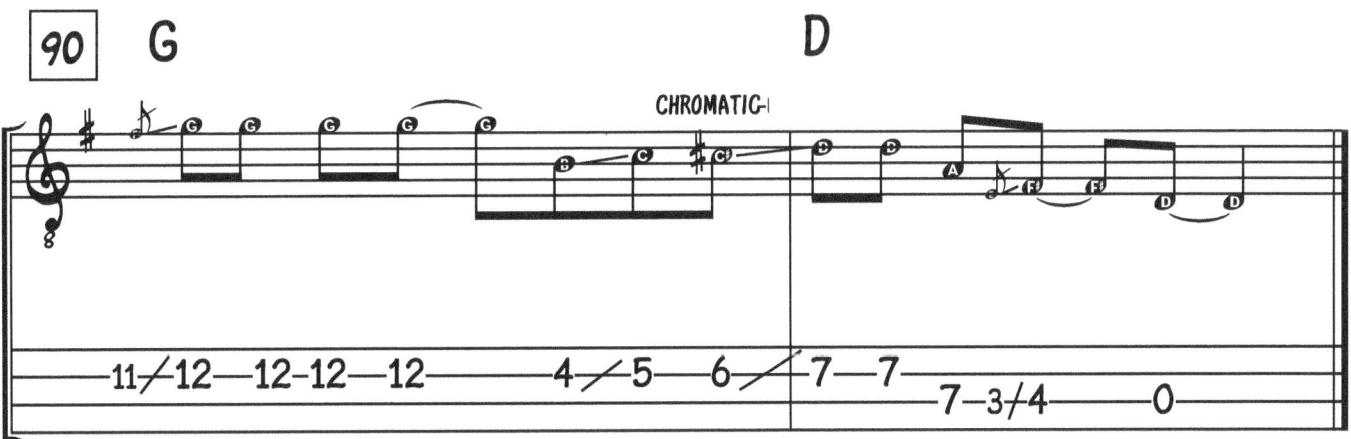

Riff 90 is an example of a riff going from the I chord (G-B-D) to the V chord (D-F#-A). Try to play a combination of chord and non-chord tones in your solos to add tension and release. Notice the use of a chromatic note (C#) at the end of measure one. A chromatic note is a note that is not from the key scale. Chromatic notes are often used on a weaker beat or for a shorter time.

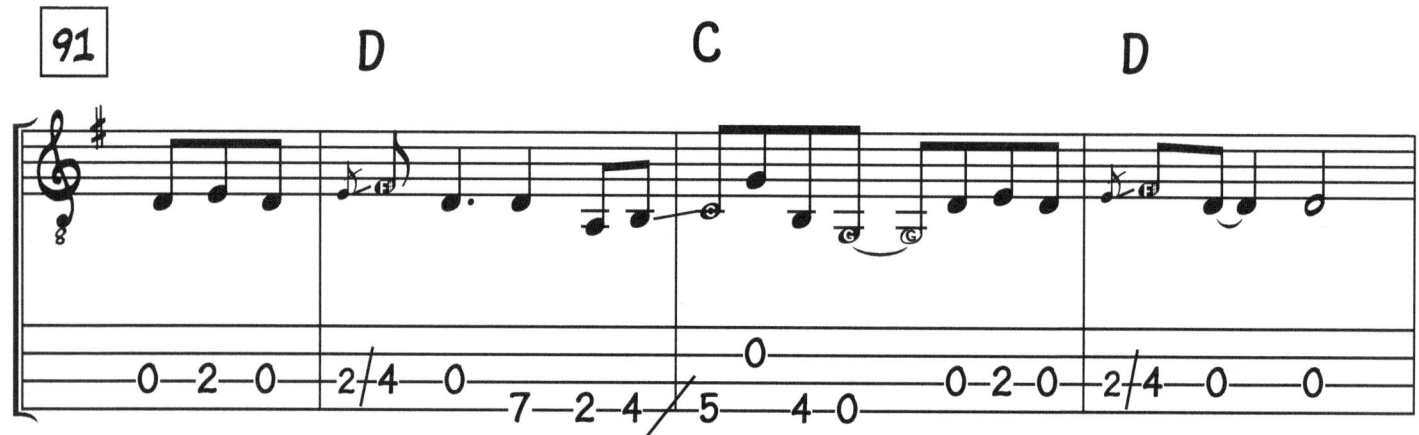

Soloing over D and C chords in the key of G. Land on a chord tone on the strong beat of the measure - in this case, slide into the F# on beat one. In measure three, slide into the C chord tone, and in measure four slide into the F#.

RIFFS: 92 - 94
SOLOING OVER MINOR CHORDS

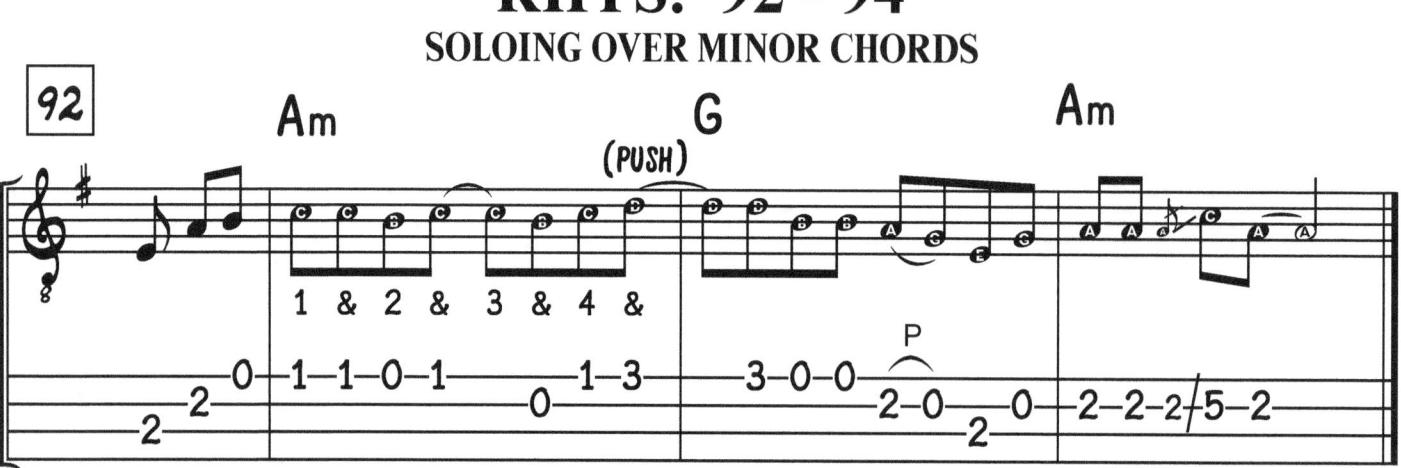

Apply the same approach with the minor chords as done in the major chords. The chord tones in an Am chord are A - C - E and G - B - D in the G chord. This riff also has a rhythmic "push," which means a rhythmic anticipation comes before the note typically lands. The push is at the end of measure two on the 1st string 3rd fret (D). The D note comes earlier than anticipated before the change to the G chord. Experiment with pushes while keeping an even tempo and counting or tapping your foot.

RIFFS: 93 - 94
SOLOING OVER MINOR CHORDS

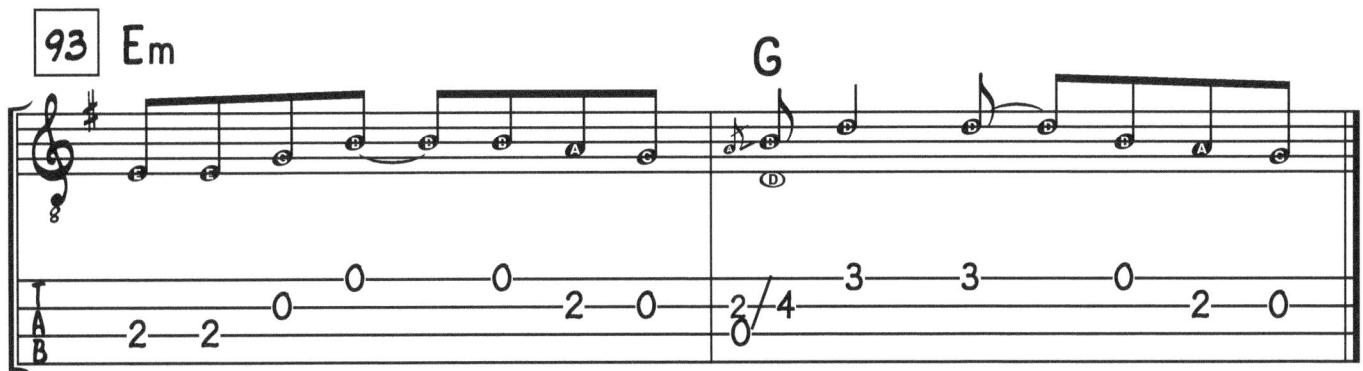

Riff 93 begins by outlining the Em notes (E-G-B) starting on the E - 3rd string 2nd fret, the G - open 2nd string, then the B - 1st string open. The second chord is G (G - B - D). Measure two starts by playing two notes together - play the 3rd and 2nd string together. Let the open 3rd string drone as you play the other notes.

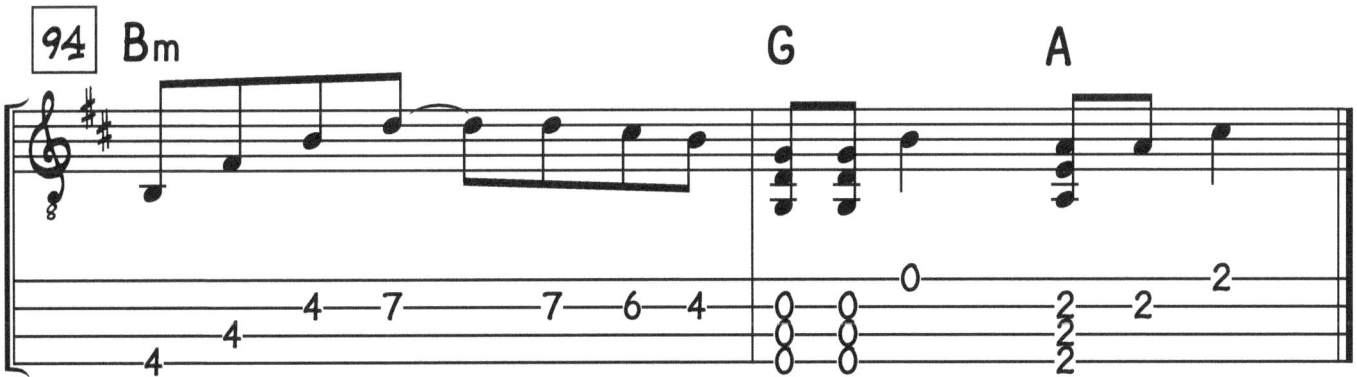

The chord tones for Bm are B - D - F#. Make a barre with the slide to play the Bm notes on the 4th fret. Move the slide quickly on the 2nd string up to the 7th fret (D). Play the G chord in measure two then move up to the A chord on the 2nd fret. This riff/solo uses a combination of single notes and chords, which adds variety.

RIFF: 95
POP SOLO

   This solo is based on a popular chord progression: G, D, Em and C. Riff 95 has several examples of playing non-chord tones, meaning notes, not in the accompanying chord (*). In measure two, the first note over the G chord is an "A," but the A is not in the G Chord (G-B-D) - this is an example of using a note not in the chord but from the G major scale. Using non-chord tones creates what's called a "tension."

   As explained in an earlier riff, using a combination of chord and non-chord tones plus chromatic notes help add interest to your solos. The non-chord tones placed on a strong beat, like beat 1 or 3, create more tension and usually resolve to a chord tone. In measure three, the open G is a non-chord tone that resolves up to the chord tone A. This solo is in the key of G major and uses notes from the G major scale. Try to create original solos with this chord progression using the G major scales found in the scale section of this book.

RIFF: 96
POP SOLO #2

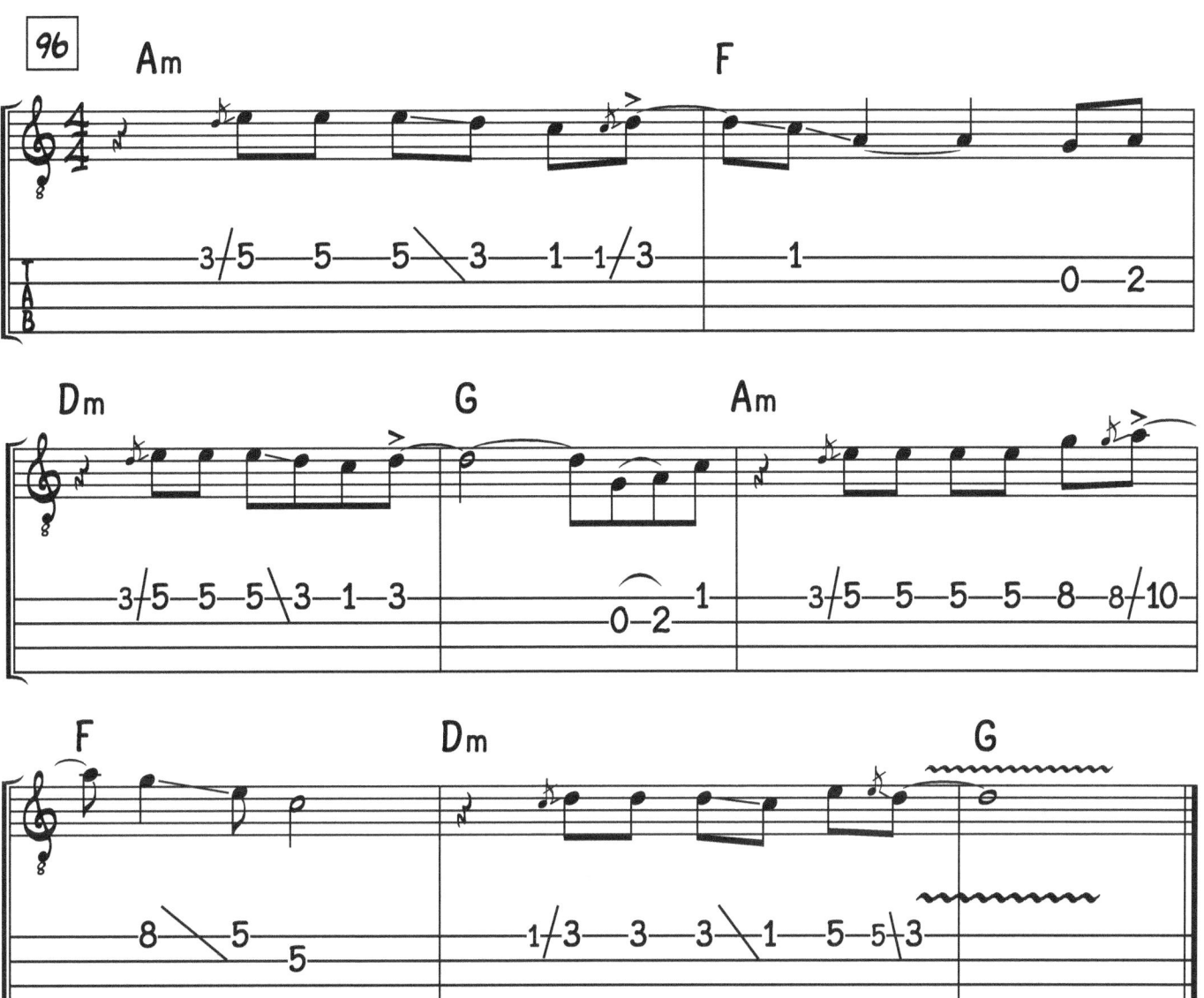

Here's another solo using a popular chord progression in a minor key: Am F Dm G. Notice, in measures 1, 3, 5 and 7, a similar rhythmic and melodic riff is repeated to create a "motif." A motif is a short repeating musical idea and can also be called a motive, riff, lick, figure or cell. Many musicians use the motifs to create and extend solos by repeating the same or similar idea throughout the solo. This repetition gives the solo a sense of unity or continuity and engages the listener.

This solo also has several examples of pushed notes on the last note of the 1st, 3rd, 5th and 7th measures. To play this riff, use a combination of sliding and muting techniques learnt thus far and add vibrato where appropriate.

RIFF: 97
DOMINANT 7TH SOLO

A relatively easy way to create a solo is to outline the notes in the accompanying chords, as shown in **Riff 97**. The chord progression in this solo uses a series of dominant 7th chords, and there are four chord tones in each dominant 7th chord, meaning there are four notes to form a dominant 7th chord: the 1st, 3rd, 5th and b7th. So in the first G7 chord, the notes are: G (1) - B (3) - D (5) - F (b7).

It's a good idea to learn the chord tones or "arpeggios" for each chord in the song you solo over. Study the chords in your songs and write in the chord tones above and practice playing them in several positions on the neck. Of course, experiment with a combination of chord tones, non-chord tones, and chromatic notes. Here are the chord tones from the chords in this example:

G7 - G B D F / B7 - B D# F# A / E7 - E G# B D / A7 - A C# E G / D7 - D F# A C

For more practice, play the chord tones by going through the circle of 5ths. The circle of 5ths arranges the chords/notes five notes apart from each other. For example, play the chord tones in C, then move to G and D and so on. Here are the notes of the circle of 5ths starting on C:

C - G - D - A - E - B - F# - C# - Ab - Eb - Bb - F

RIFF: 98
COUNTRY SOLO

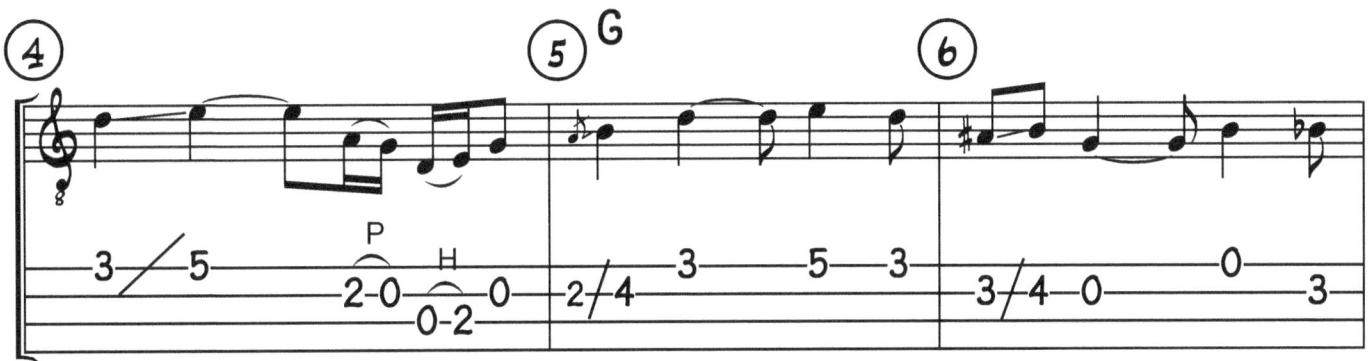
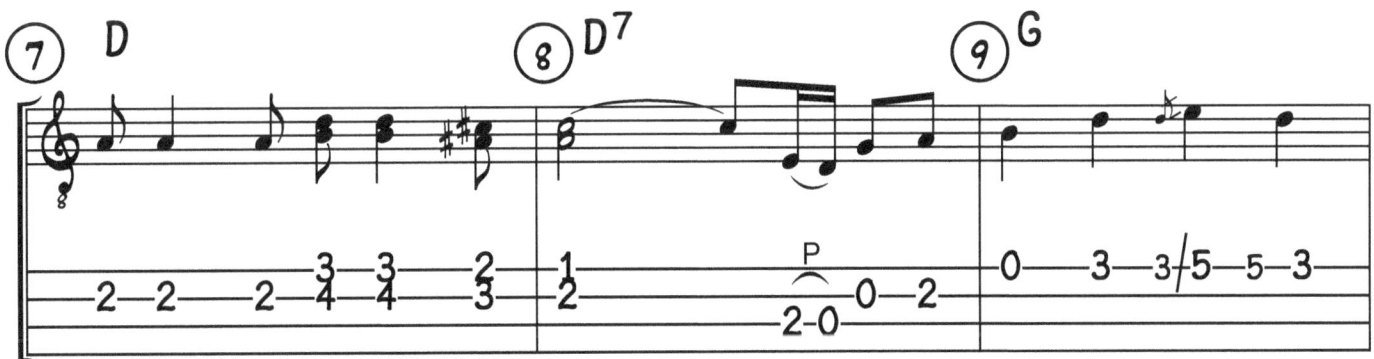
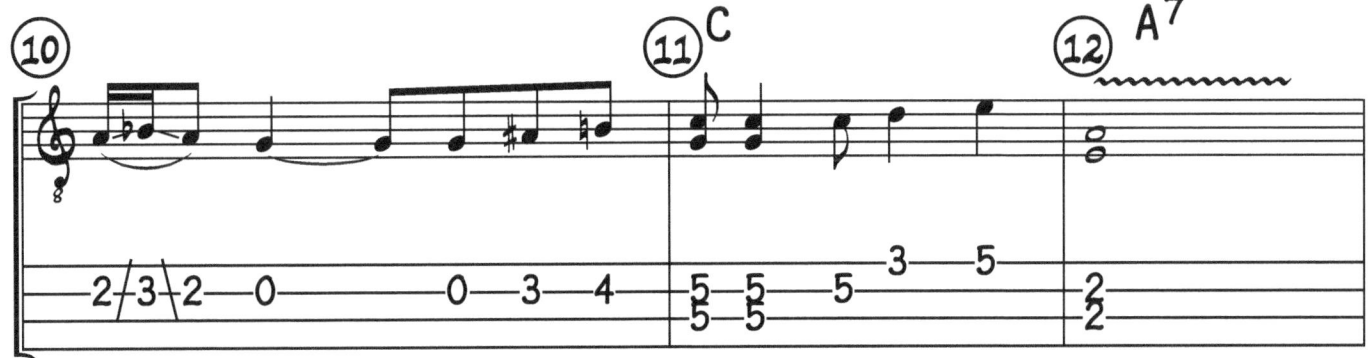

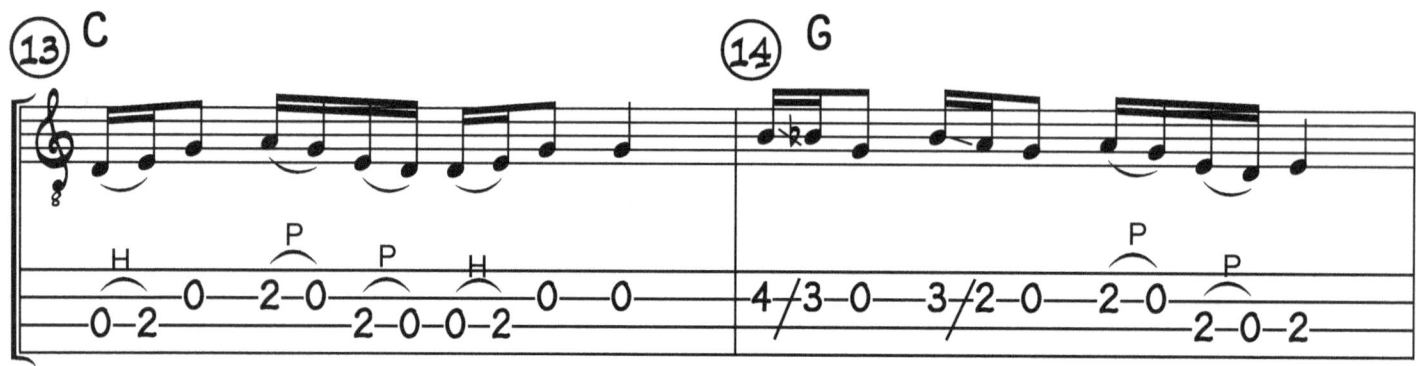

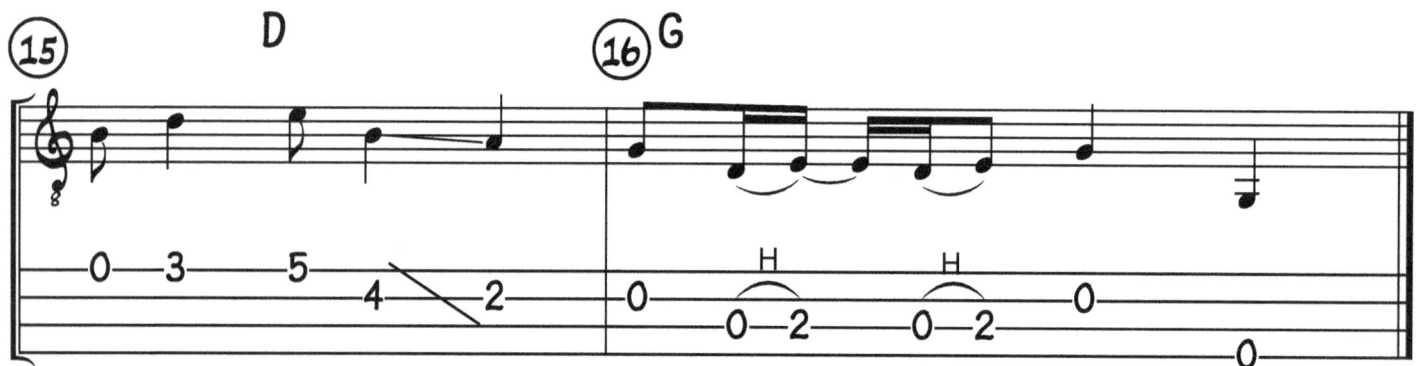

Here's an example of a 16 bar bluegrass/country solo. This solo covers many of the techniques covered in this book. Here are the instructions for the more challenging sections:

Measure 4: At the end of measure four, there is a pull off - hammer on combination. Isolate this little riff and practice slowly using the tilt slide technique.

Measure 7-8: Here is an example of descending thirds. Tilt your slide and place it on the 2nd string 4th fret, put your first finger behind the slide on the 1st string 3rd fret and play the two notes together (double stop). Hold the slide and finger in the same position and move down to the 3-2, then 1-2 frets. This part is a little tricky, so practice slowly keeping the tuning in mind and the spacing between the slide and fingers even.

Measure 13: Ok, this part of the solo will take some practice for sure. Measure 13 is more accessible if you play the combination hammer ons and pull offs with your index finger, that is, provided you wear your slide on the 3rd or 4th finger. Playing with your fingers and slide is a great technique to develop and opens up many possibilities for complicated passages such as this one.

Measure 14: Slide down from the 4th to 3rd and 3rd to 2nd fret, then with your index finger, play the pull offs from the 2nd to open strings. So, use your slide at the first part of measure 14, then your index finger at the end on beats three and four.

RIFF: 99
ROCK SOLO

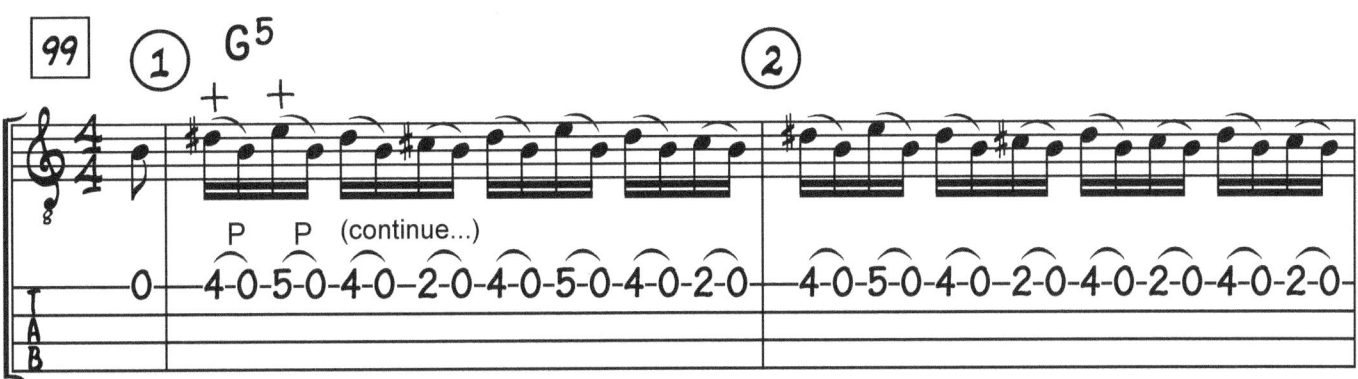

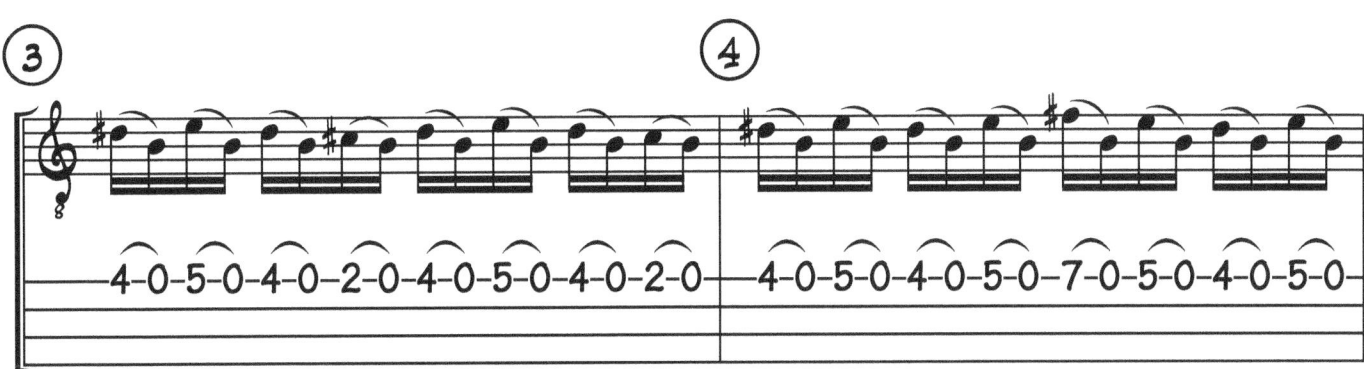

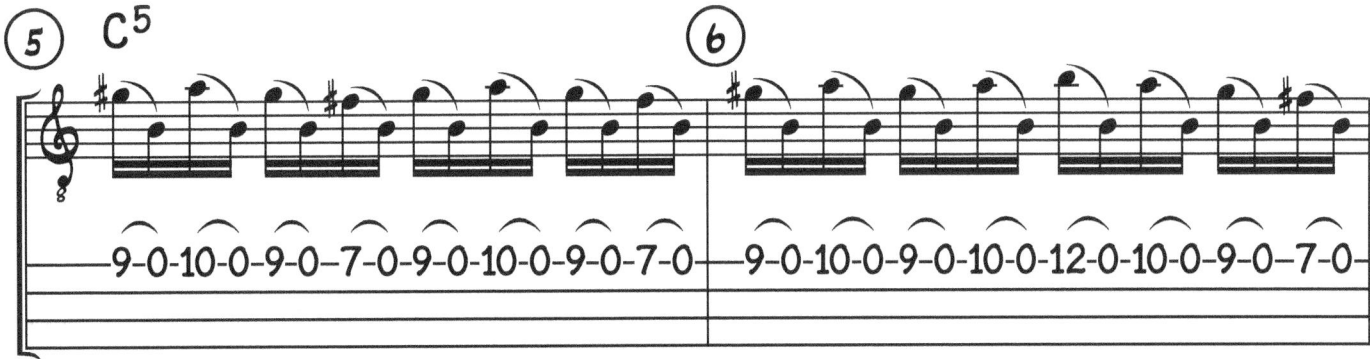

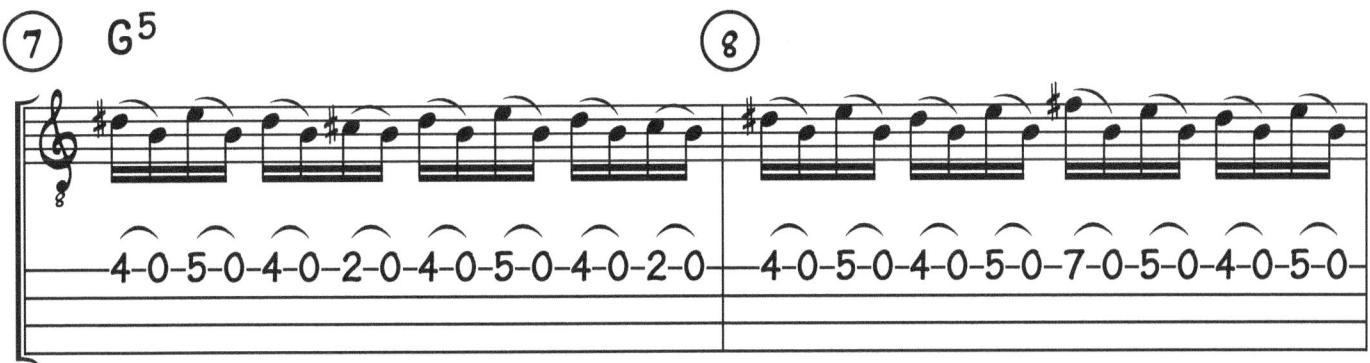

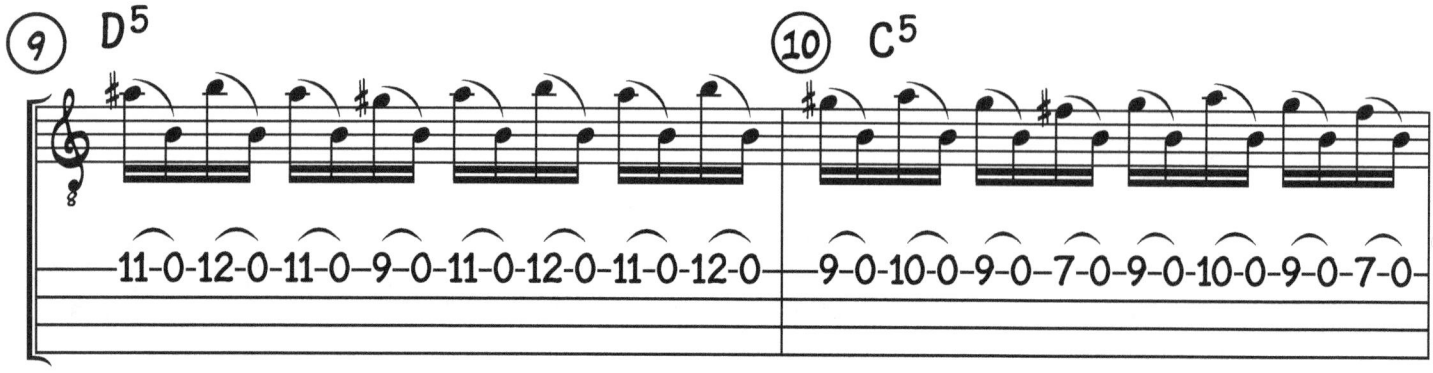

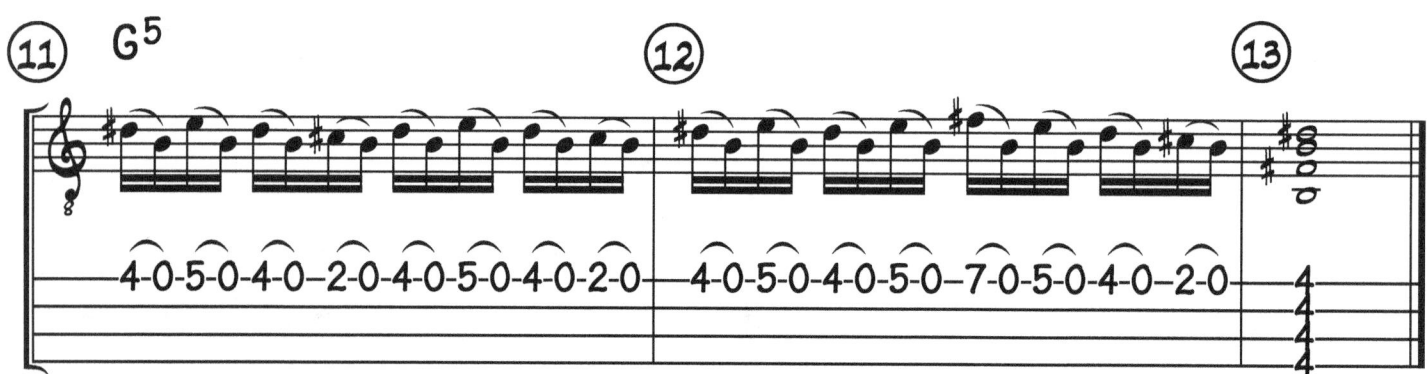

Here's a classic 12 bar rock riff/solo that is a typical rock guitar technique and fun to play. Riff 99 is based on a repeating pull off to open string figure that can be performed using the slide, fingers, or combination thereof. There are a few methods to approach this riff/solo: 1) plucking each fretted note, then pull off to the open string or, 2) Use a combination of tapping hammer ons and pull offs without plucking any strings. Here's a breakdown of the two methods:

Method 1) Place finger or slide on the 1st string 4th fret. Pick the note then pull off quickly to the open string note. Do not pick the open string. Move your finger or slide to the 5th fret, play the 5th fret and again pull off to the open string. Continue this method for the rest of the tune.

Method 2) Tap (+) your finger or slide on the 4th fret to produce note then pull off to open string without picking. The big difference between the two methods is you don't pick the string in method two; you only tap the string with your left-hand finger without picking with your right hand.

Both methods can be applied and exchanged at will. As usual, try to keep your slide in line with the frets for accurate tuning and keep a steady beat throughout.

RIFF: 100
12 BAR BLUES SOLO #1

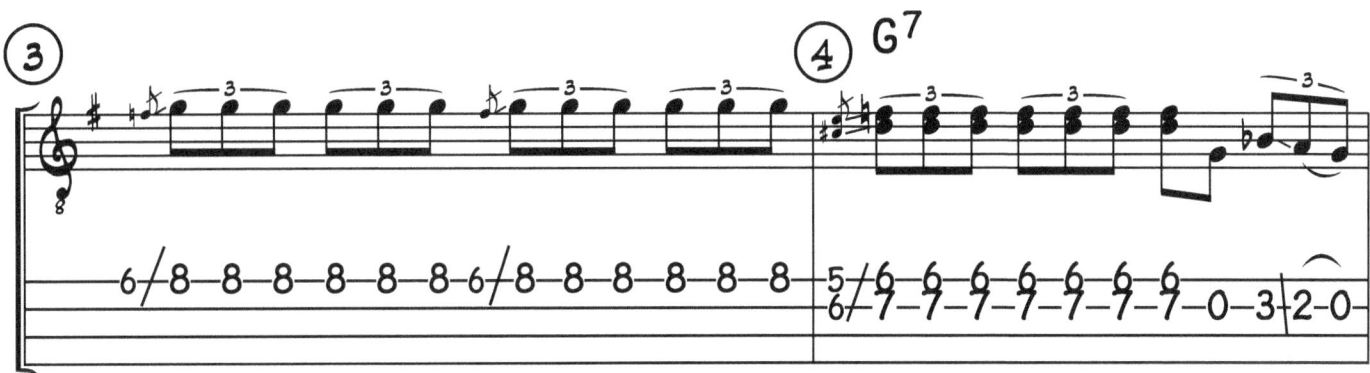
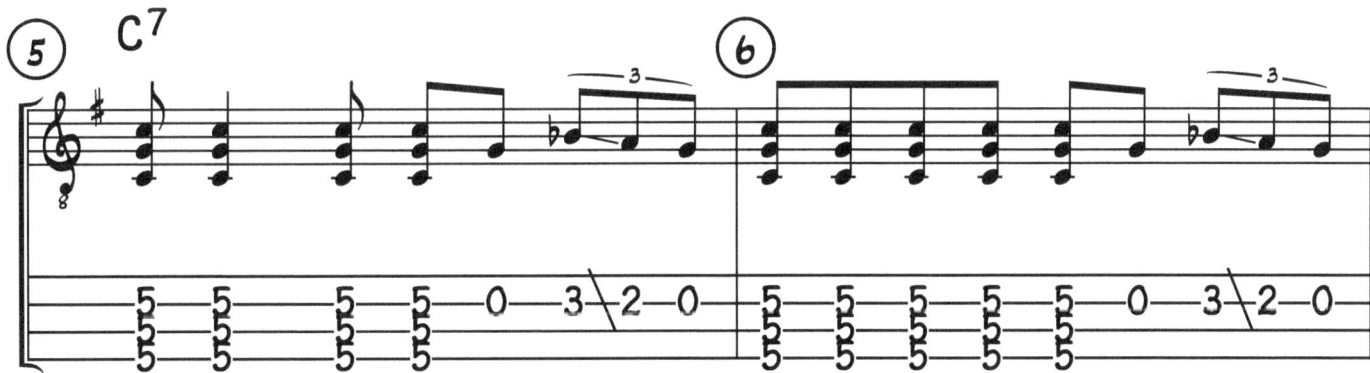
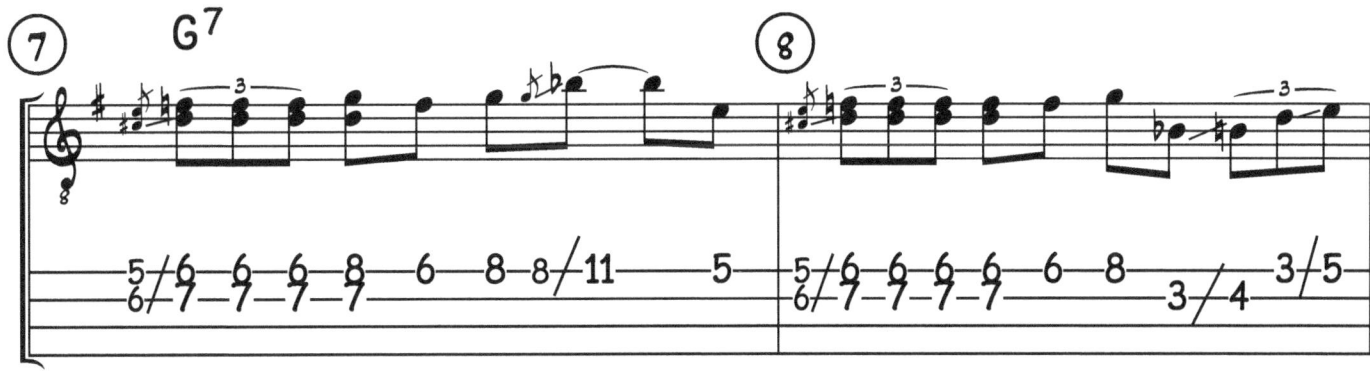

RIFF 100

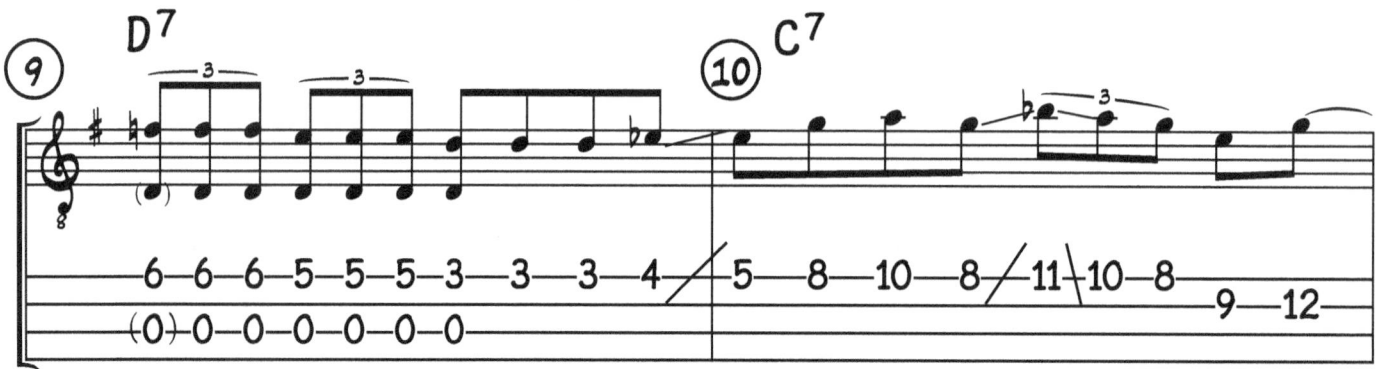

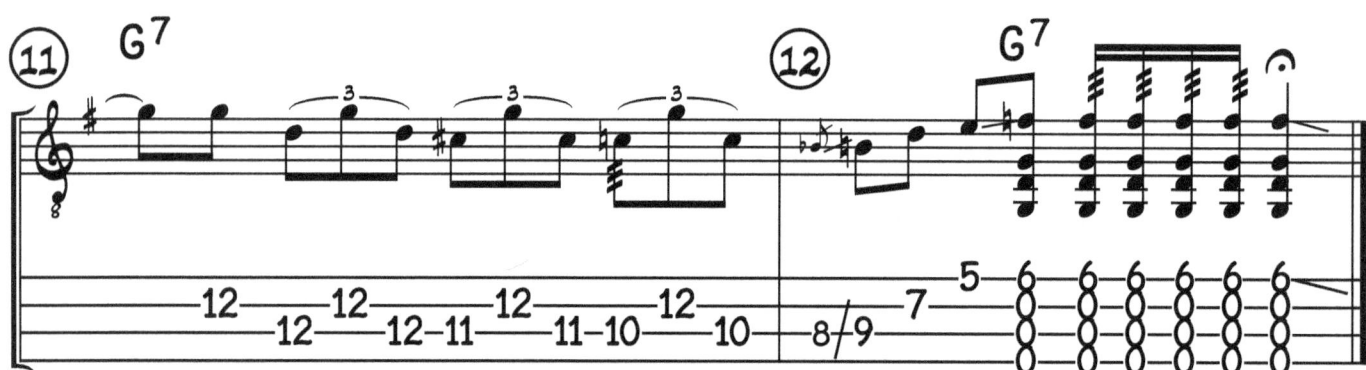

Here's a traditional 12 bar blues solo in the key of G. This solo covers many of the techniques learnt so far plus a few new ones. Here are instructions for the more challenging sections:

Measure 4: Start with a double slide to the 6th and 7th fret from one fret below and play both the 1st and 2nd string together. Make sure to play the first two beats of measure four as triplets, followed by eighth notes, then back to triplets.

Measure 7-8: Just like the double notes in measure four - tilt the slide on the 7th fret and place the finger behind the slide on fret 6.

Measure 9: Here's a new technique to try playing on two separate strings. This technique is best-played fingerstyle but can also be played with a hybrid pick style, that is, if you are using a pick. 1) Fingerstyle: use your thumb on the 3rd string and, at the same time, use the slide on the 6th fret on the first string. Play both strings together with the triplet rhythm, 2) Hybrid picking: hold the pick like usual between the thumb and index finger and play the 3rd string open, at the same time, use your middle finger to pluck the 1st string.

Measure 10: Combination of eight notes and triplets. Use the muting technique as preferred to minimize slide noise.

Measure 11: This typical blues ending in measure 11 is a little challenging if you are using the slide. Keep the slide in line at the 12th fret and stretch your 1st finger back to the 11th then 10th fret as you play behind the slide.

Measure 12: On the last G7 chord, play the note on the 6th fret and the open strings and strum the chord with a quick down and up strumming (𝄌 = tremelo).

RIFF: 101
BLUES SOLO #2

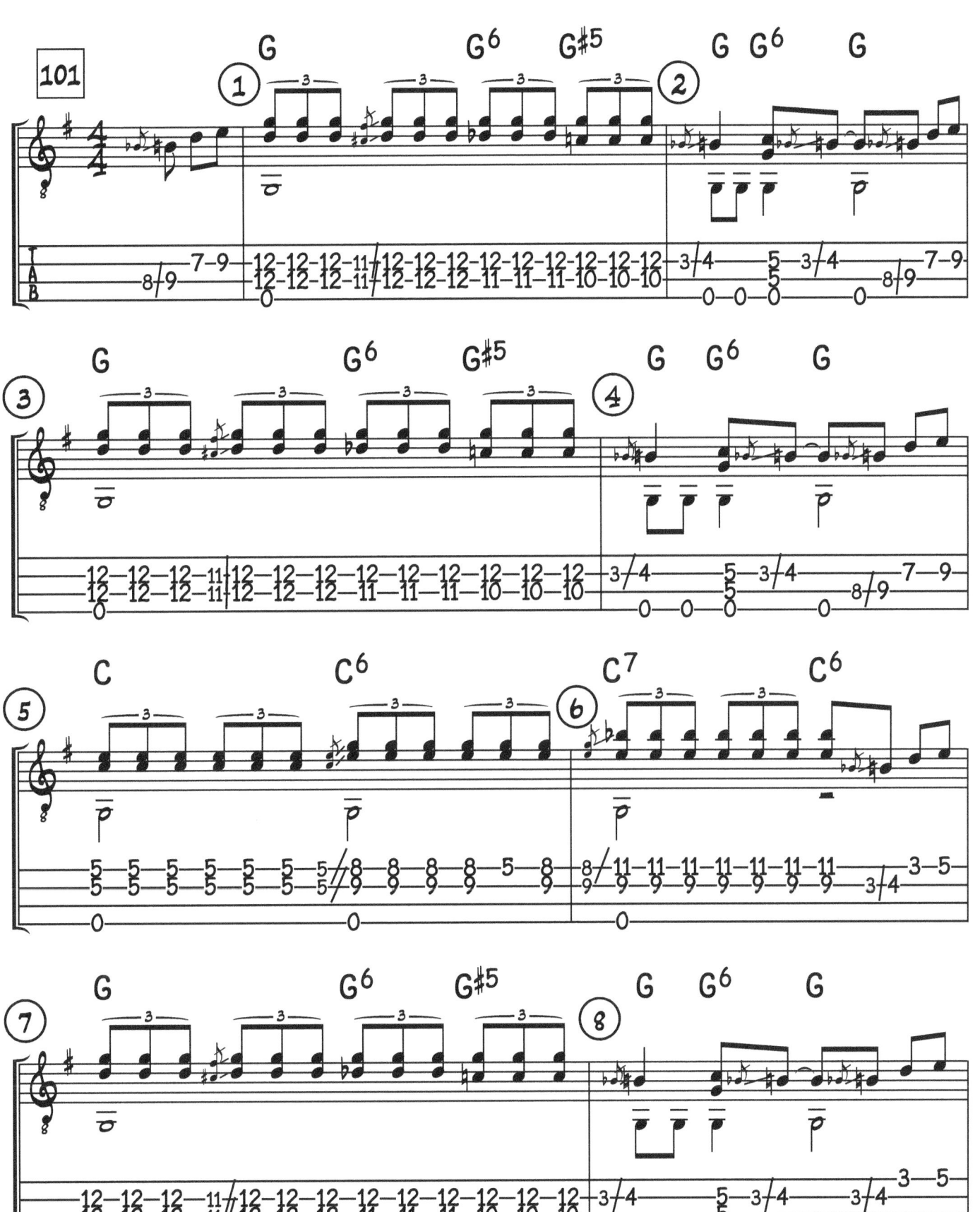

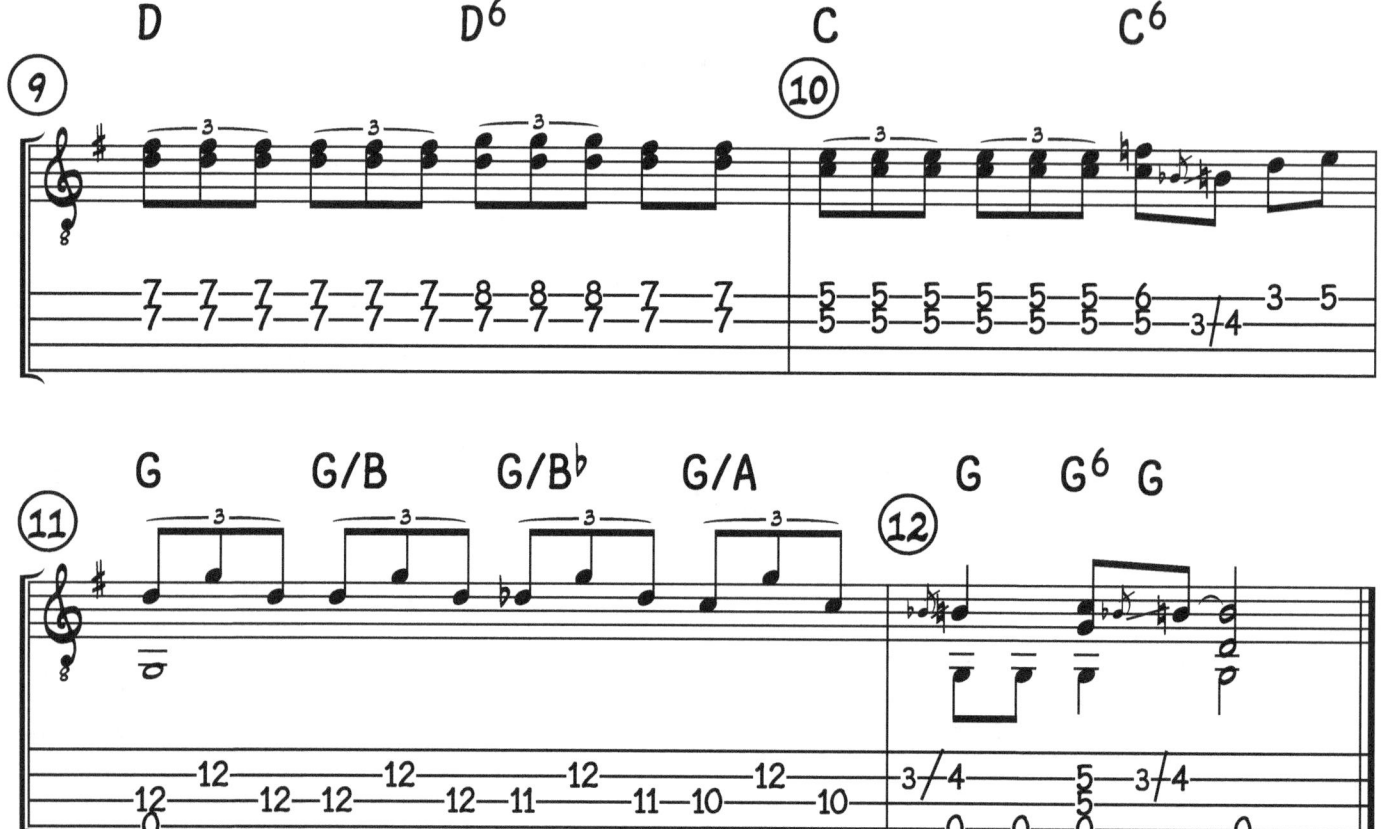

Blues solo #2 is a fingerstyle solo that uses a combination of tilt slides, barres, playing behind the slide, and double stops. Here are instructions for the more challenging sections:

Measure 1: This first little riff repeats several times throughout the solo. Try to keep the slide in a straight line at the 12th fret as your index finger plays the 11th, then 10th fret. Notice the triplet rhythm and the thumb on the open G string (4th).

Measure 2: Slide from the 3rd to 4th fret playing the open G 4th string at the same time. A common mistake is to play the 3rd fret first then play the 4th fret and open string together, but the correct way is to play the 3rd fret and the open 4th string together. On the second beat (0-5-5), play the open 4th and make a barre up to the 3rd string to play both 5's. Avoid the slide touching the 4th string to prevent string rattle.

Measure 5-6: Play the half-barre at the 5th fret and move up with the slide on the 9th fret and the index finger on the 8th. Continue moving up the neck with the slide on the 11th and the index finger stretched back to the 9th fret.

Measure 9-10: this measure can be played by making a half-barre at the 7th fret, then putting the 4th finger in front of the barre at the 8th fret - this only works if you wear the slide on the 3rd finger. If you wear the slide on the 4th finger, then use your 1st and 2nd finger to play the 7-8 together in measure nine and the 5-6 in measure ten.

Chord Tones

Chord tones are notes from the chord. For example, the notes in a C chord are C, E, and G. So, the chord tones for a C chord are C, E, and G. Chord tones can also be called arpeggios. Arpeggios are the notes from a chord but played separately. Here are some examples of chord tones:

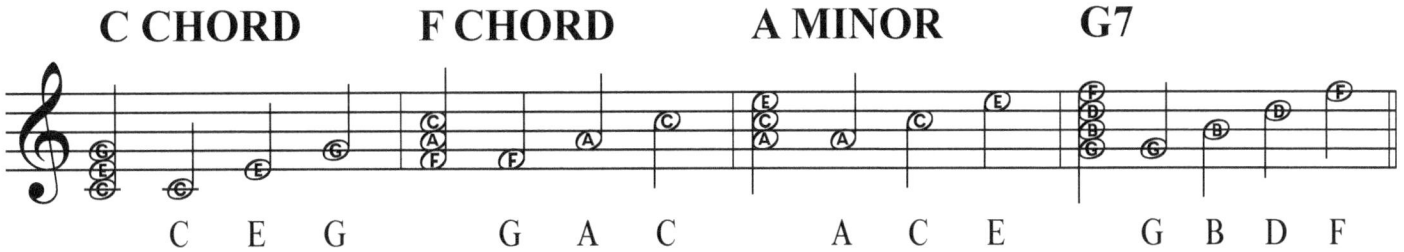

Here are a few examples of chord tones in a popular chord progression:

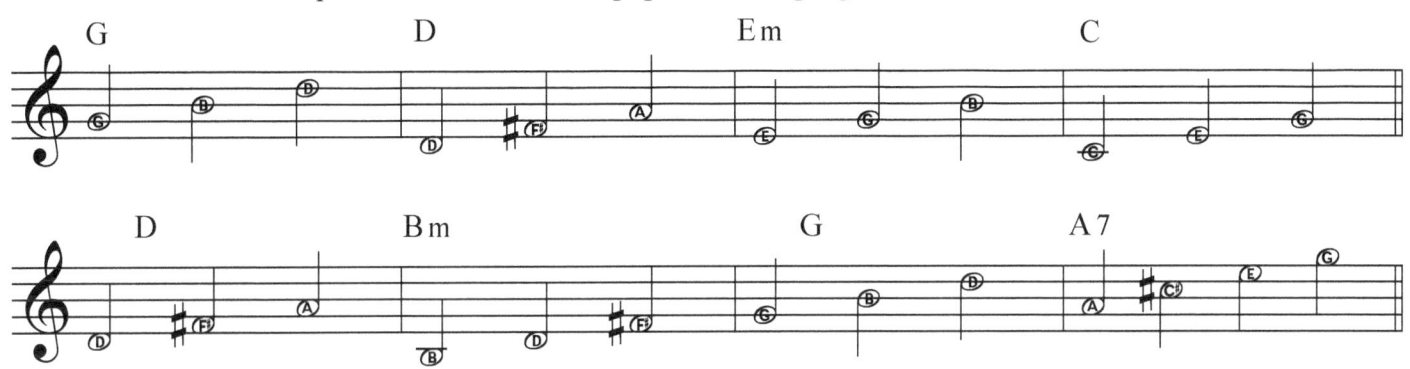

Chord tones in a blues in C:

A • Am • A7
Major, minor, dominant 7th chord tones in all keys.

A — A C♯ E

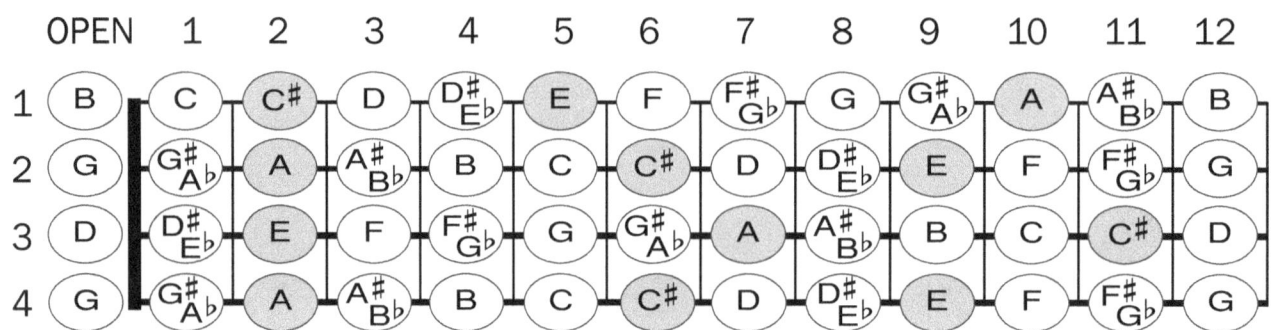

Am — A C E

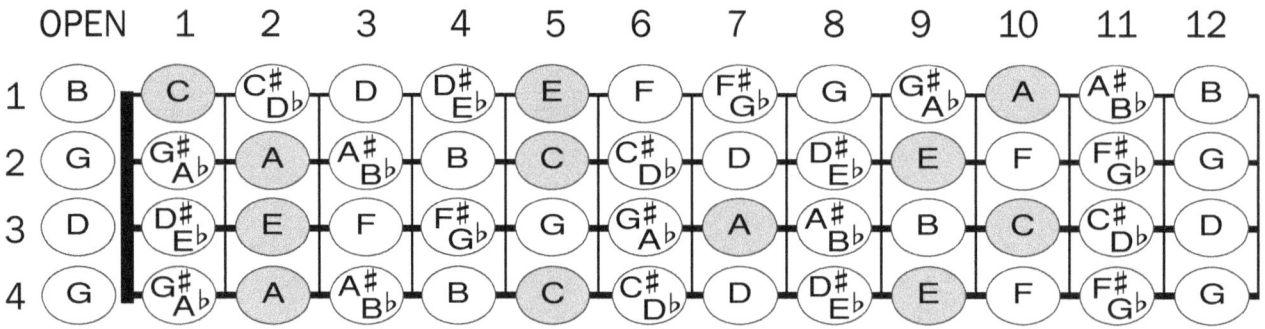

A7 — A C♯ E G

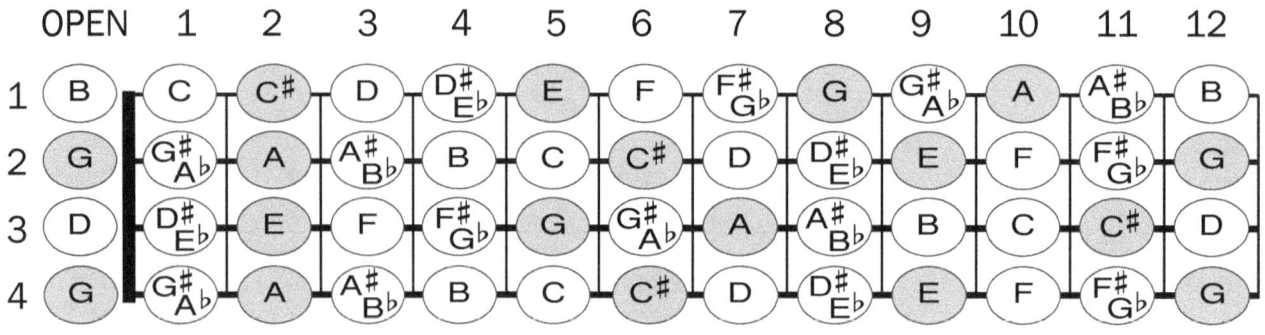

B♭ • B♭m • B♭7

B♭ — B♭ D F

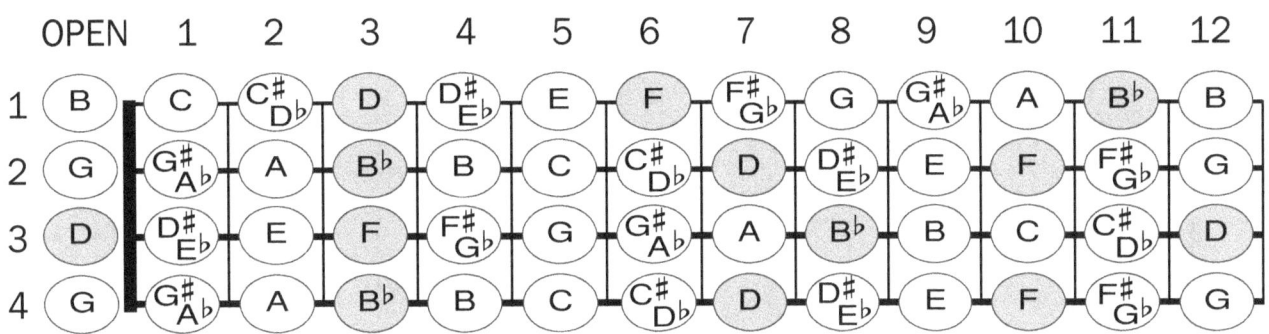

B♭m — B♭ D♭ F

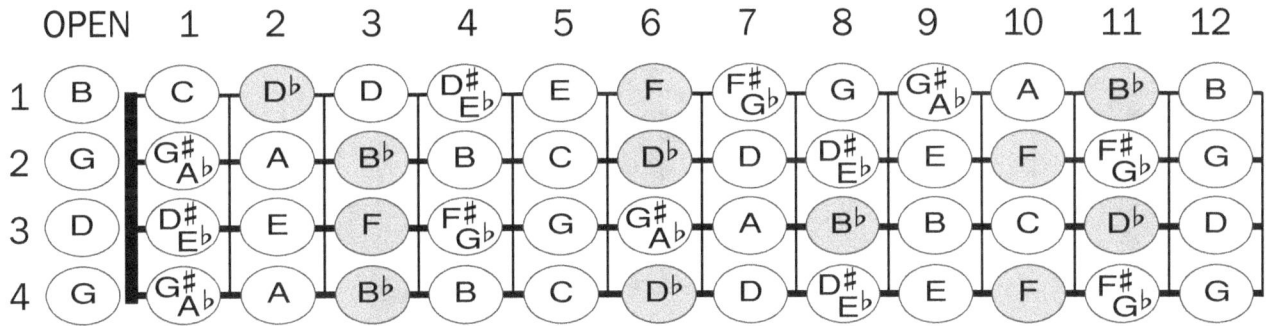

B♭7 — B♭ D F A♭

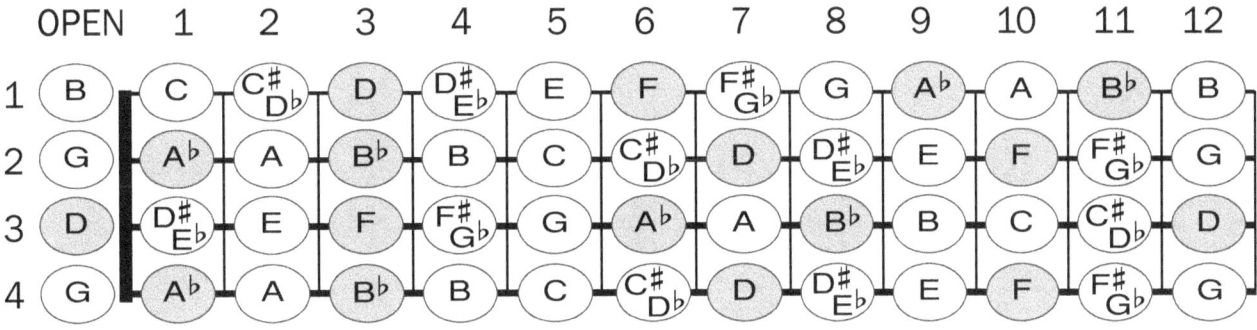

B • Bm • B7

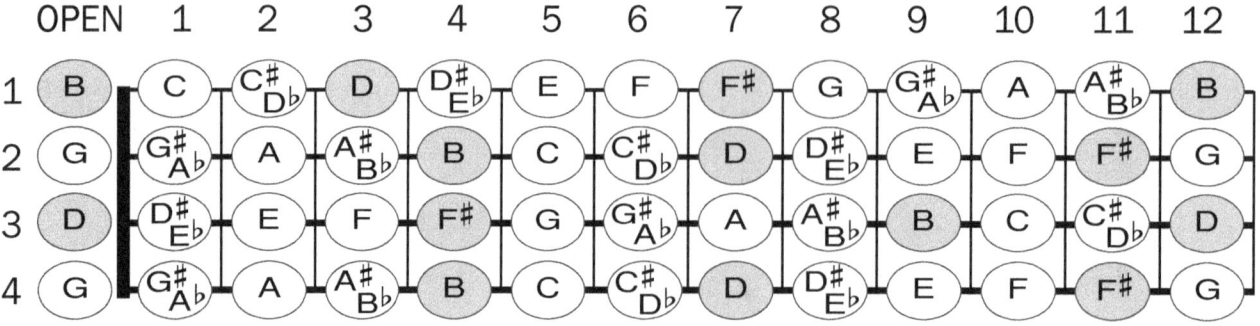

C♭ • C♭m • C♭7

C♭ — C♭ E♭ G♭

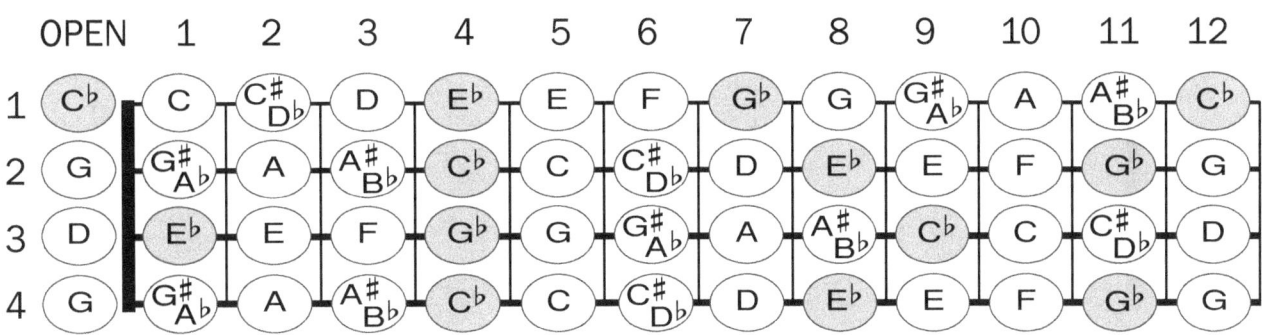

C♭m — C♭ E♭♭ G♭
E♭♭ = D

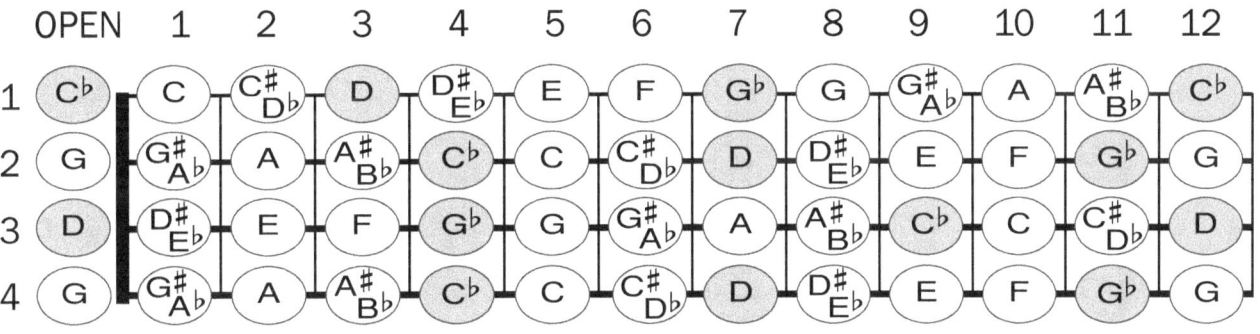

C♭7 — C♭ E♭ G♭ B♭♭
B♭♭ = A

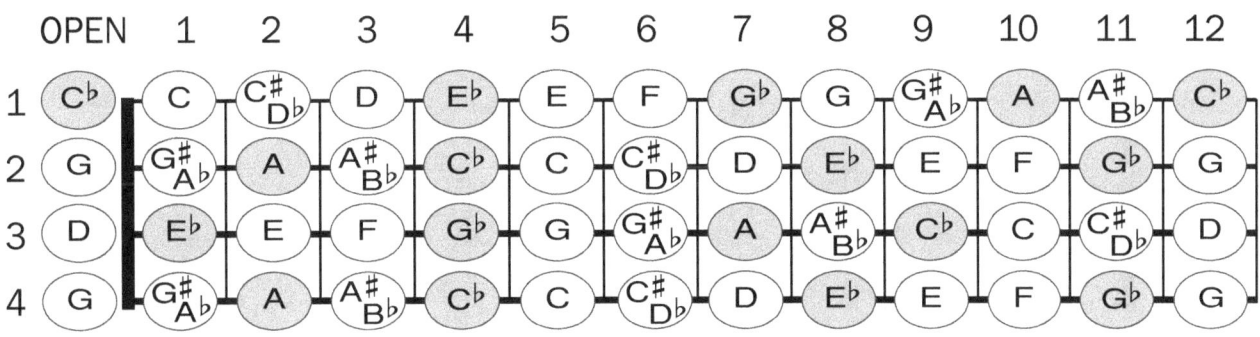

C • Cm • C7

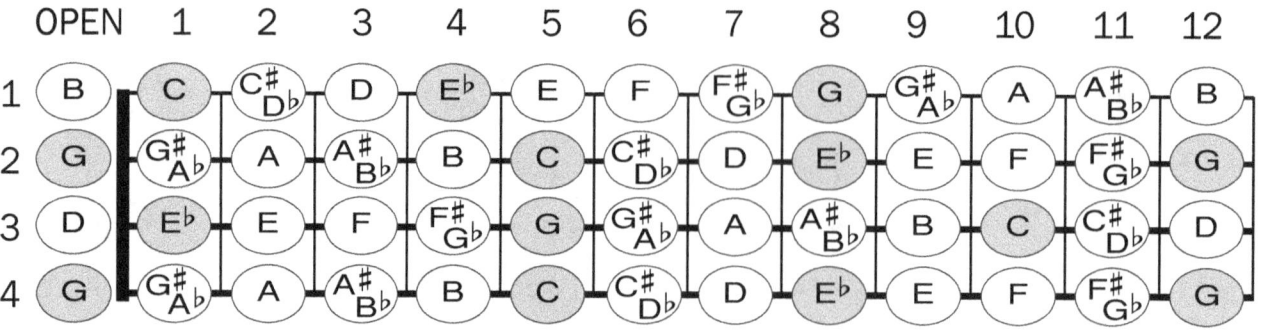

C♯ • C♯m • C♯7

C♯ — C♯ E♯ G♯

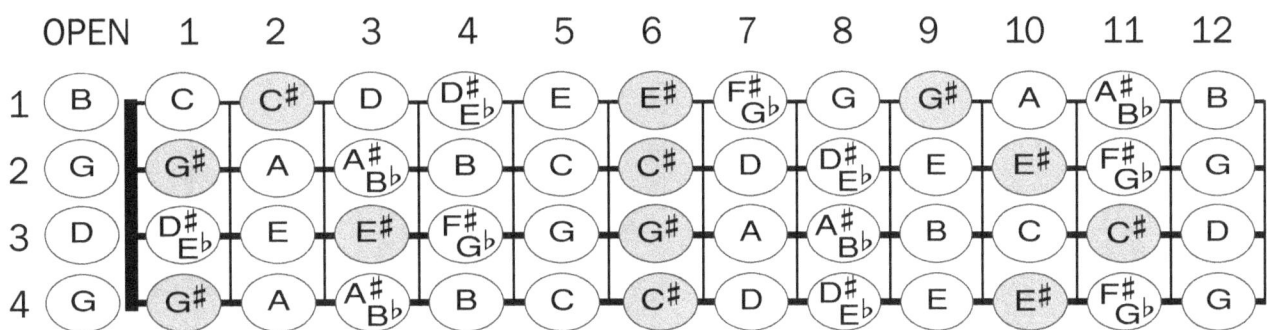

C♯m — C♯ E G♯

B♭♭=A

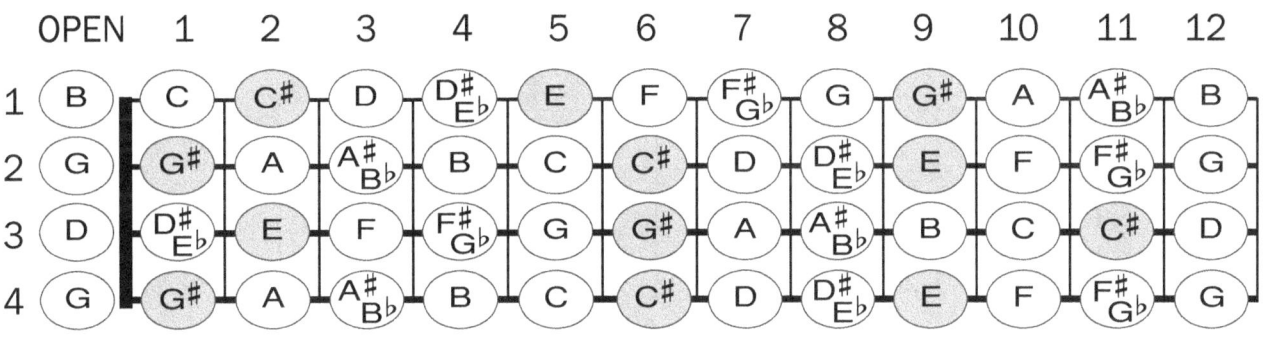

C♯7 — C♯ E♯ G♯ B

D♭ • D♭m • D♭7

D♭ — D♭ F A♭

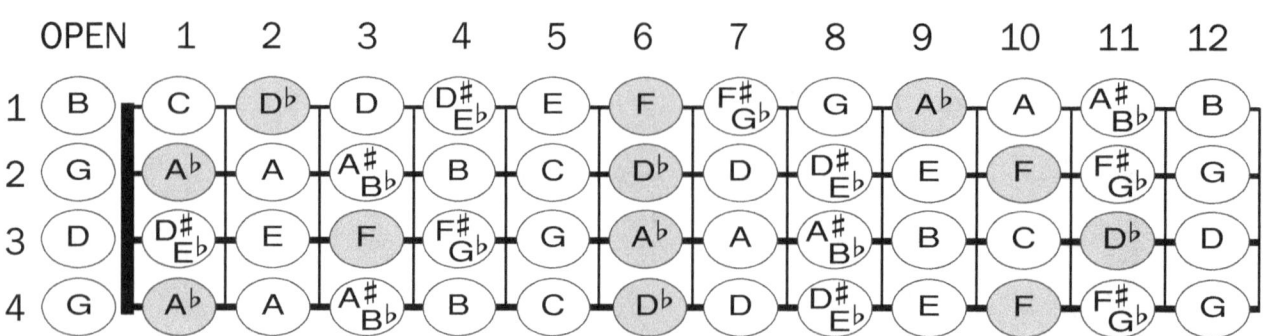

D♭m — D♭ F♭ A♭

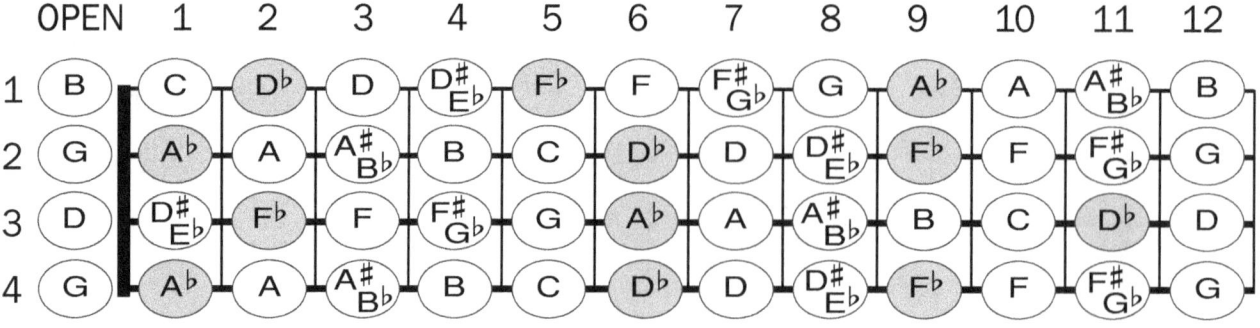

D♭7 — D♭ F A♭ C♭

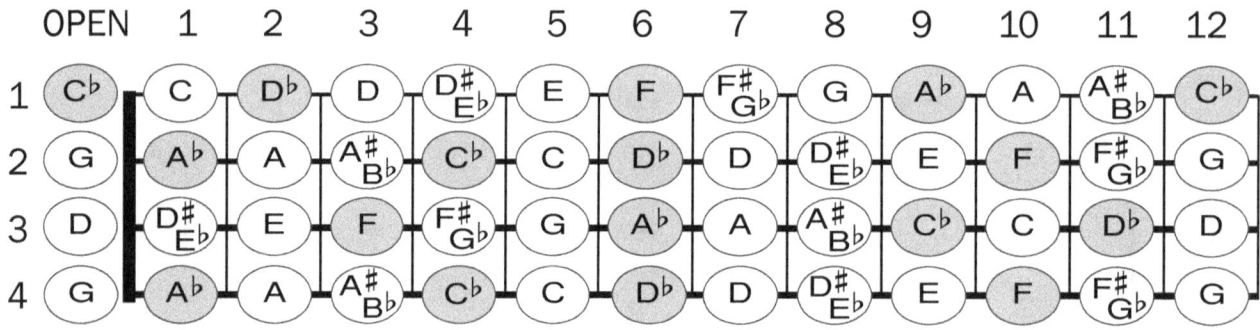

D • Dm • D7

D — DF#A

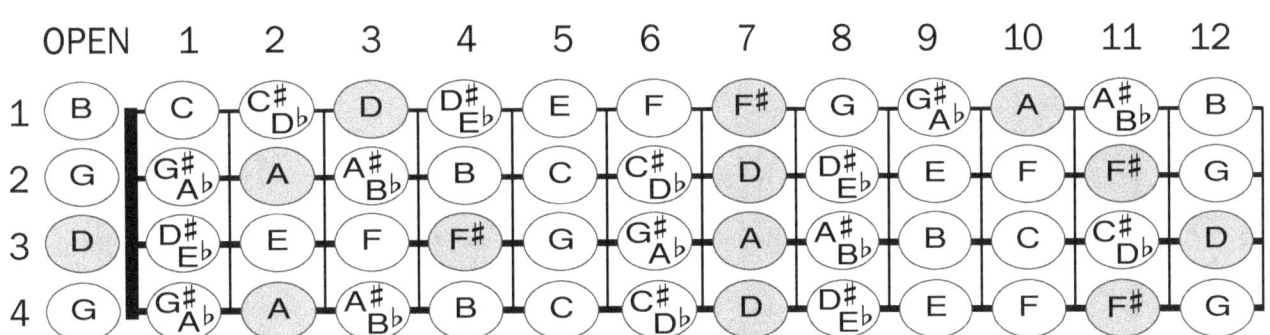

Dm — DFA

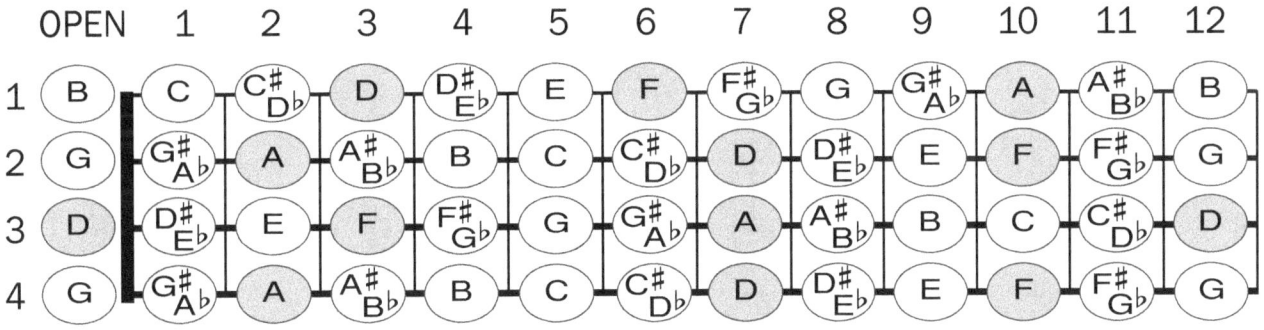

D7 — DF#AC

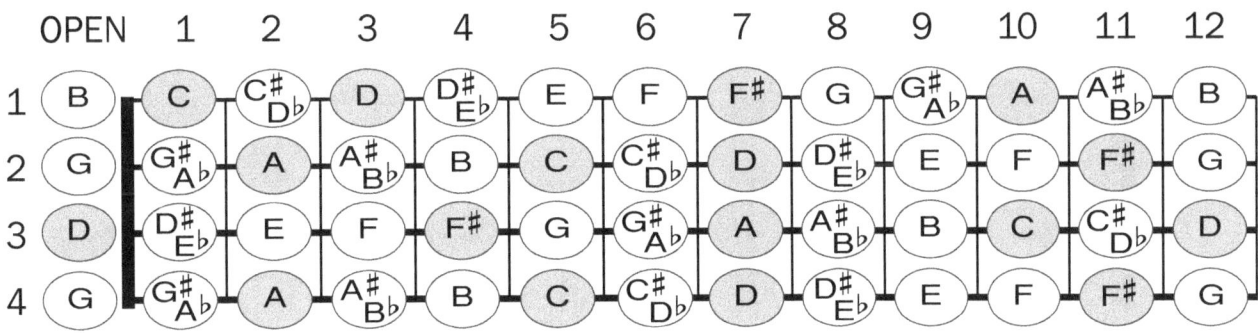

E♭ • E♭m • E♭7

E♭ — E♭ G B♭

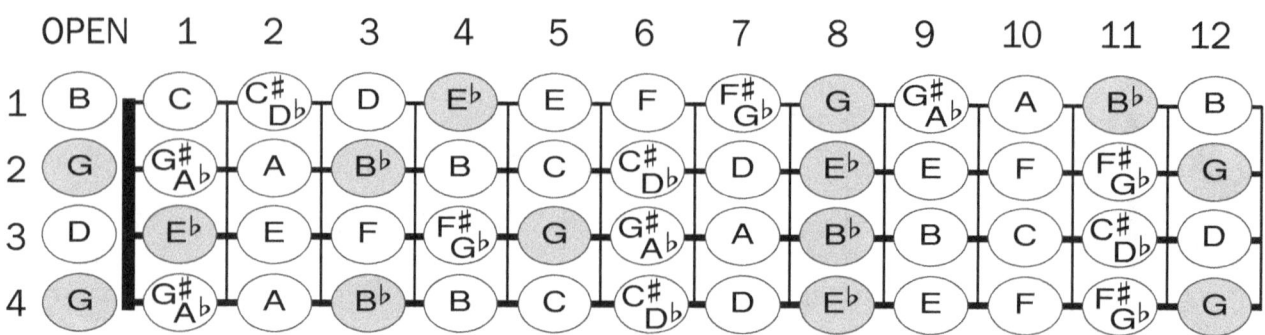

E♭m — E♭ G♭ B♭

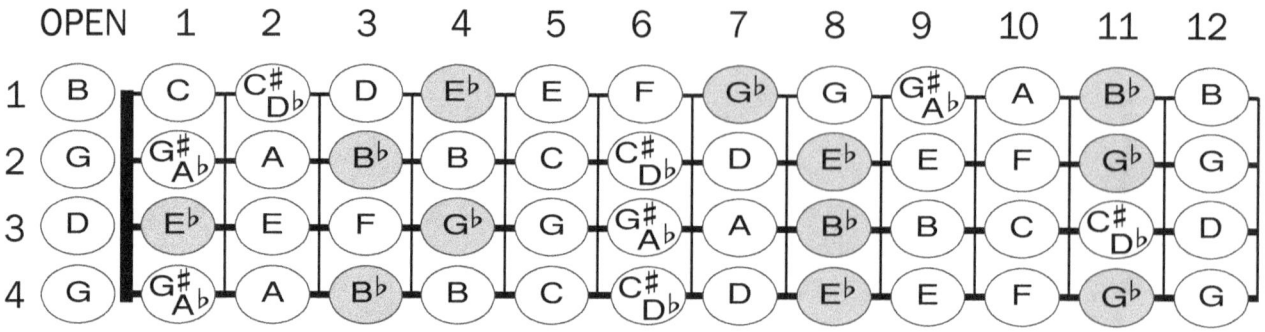

E♭7 — E♭ G B♭ D♭

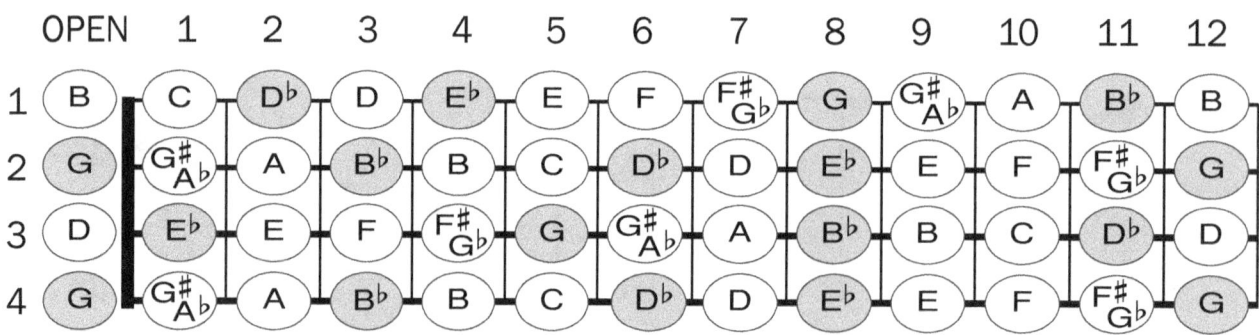

E • Em • E7

E — EG#B

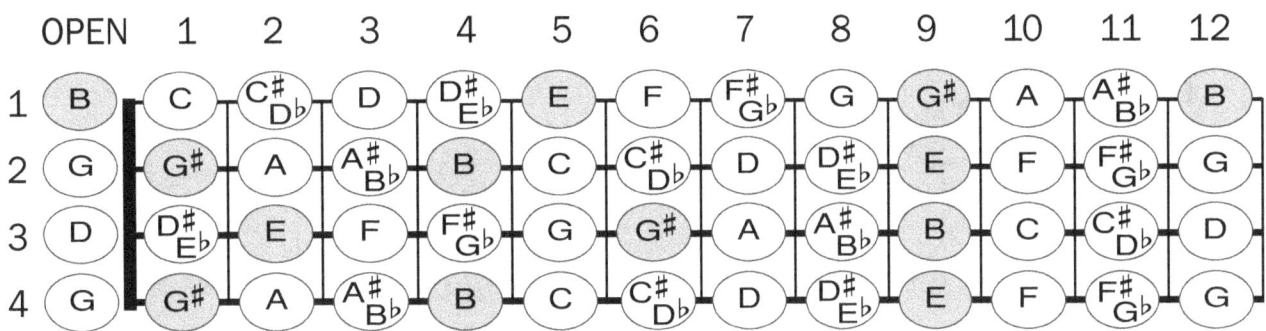

Em — EGB

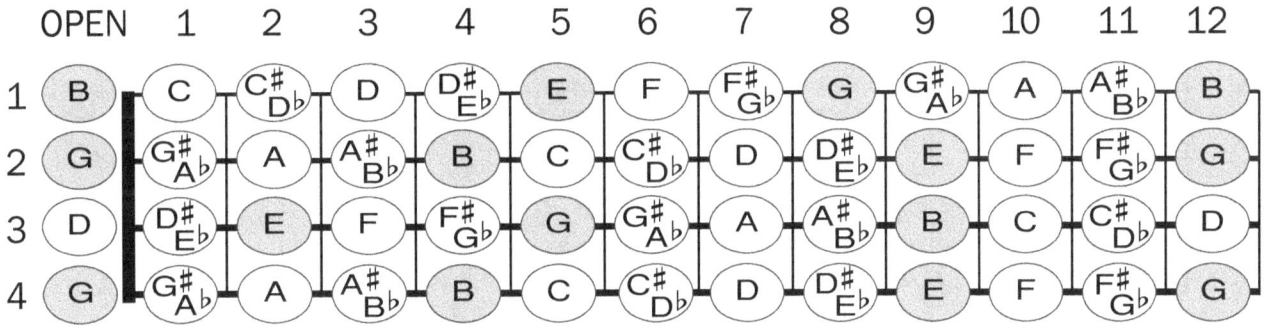

E7 — EG#BD

F • Fm • F7

F — FAC

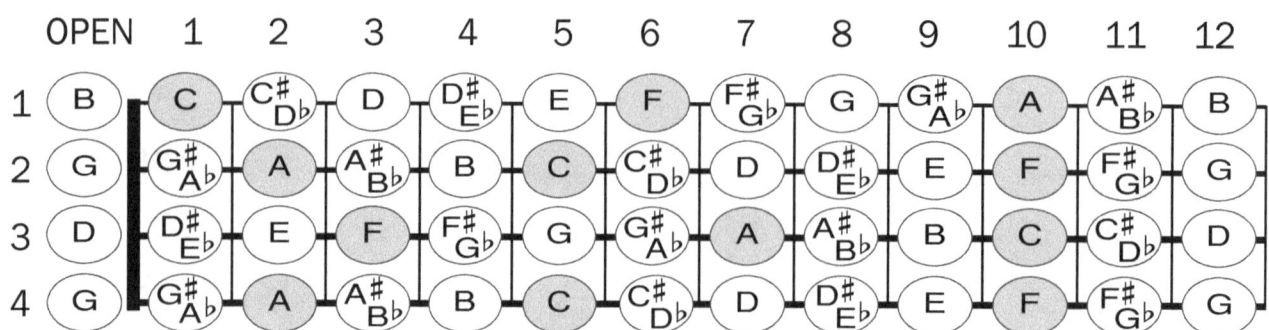

Fm — FA♭C

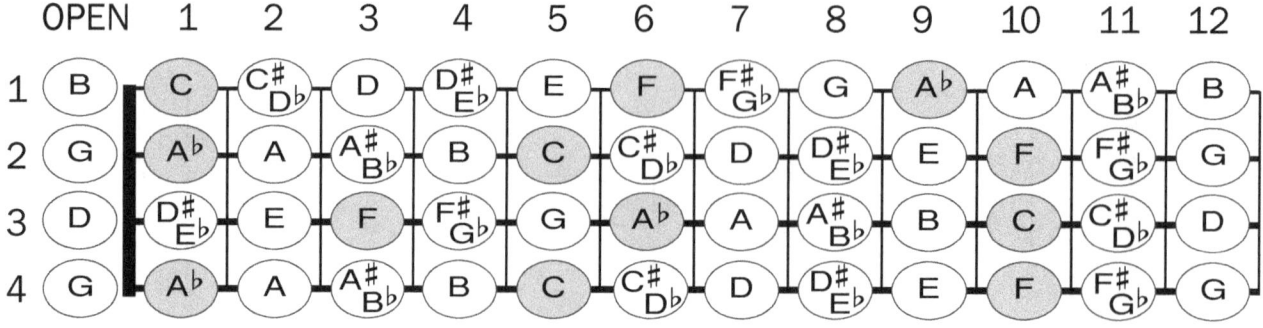

F7 — FACE♭

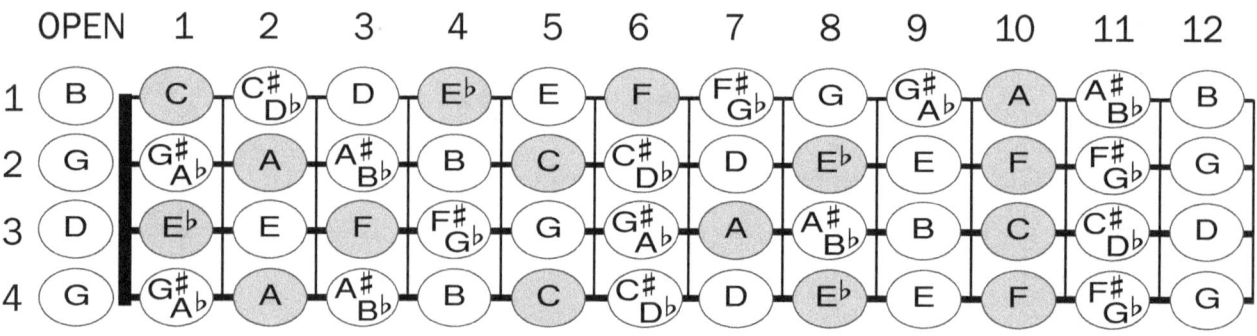

F♯ • F♯m • F♯7

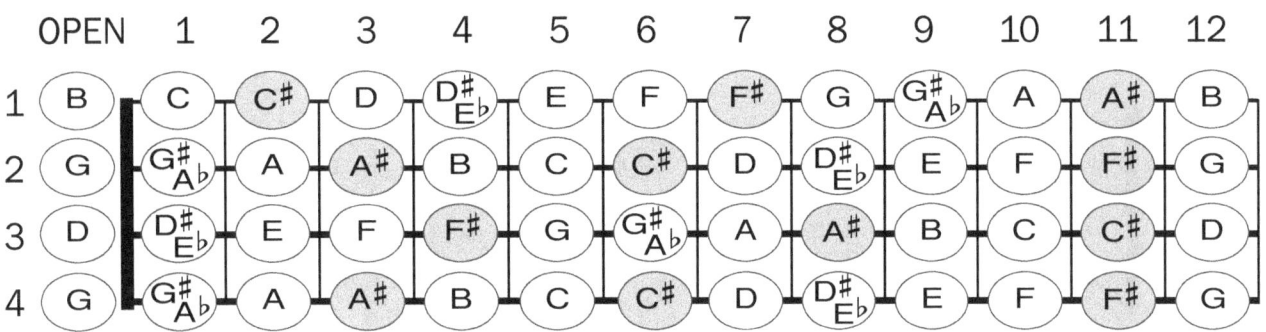

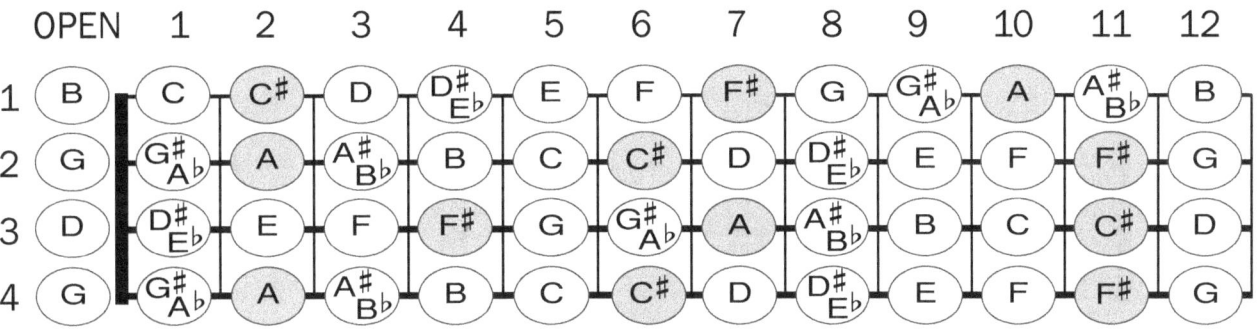

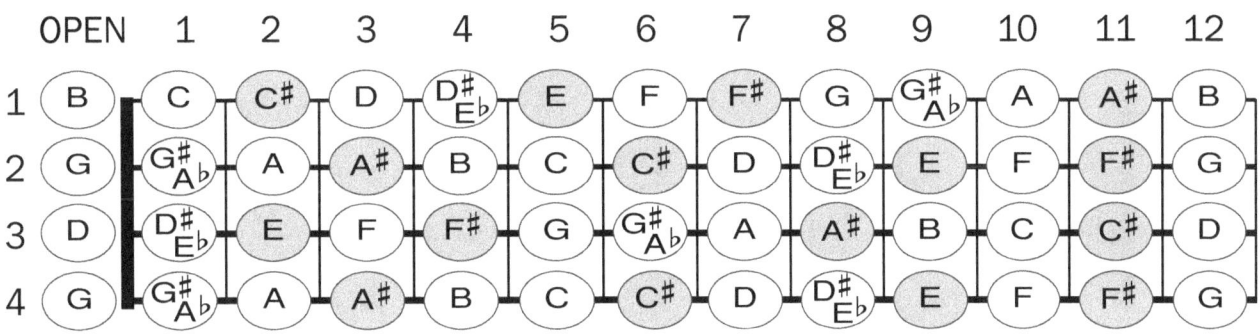

Gb • Gbm • Gb7

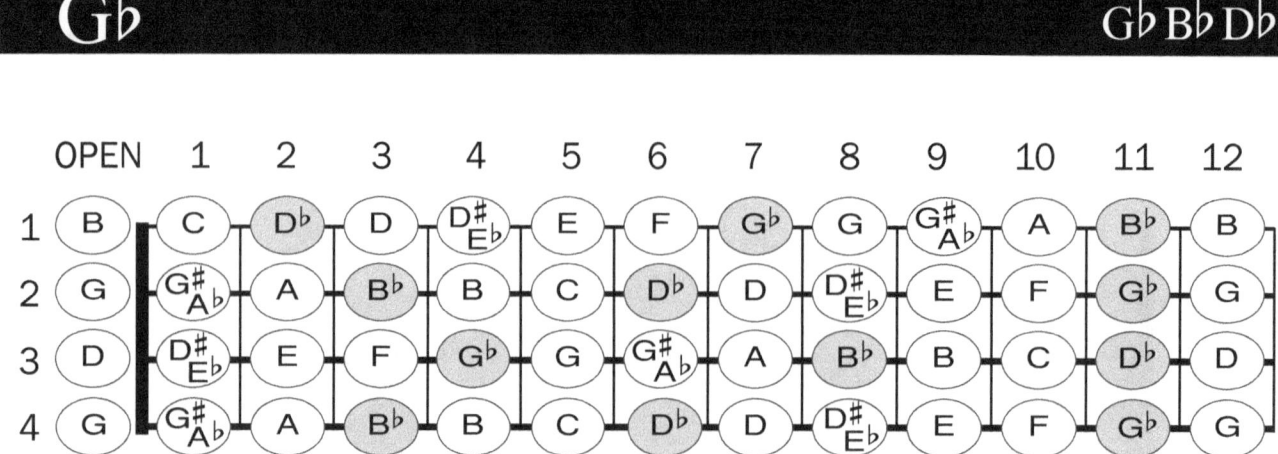

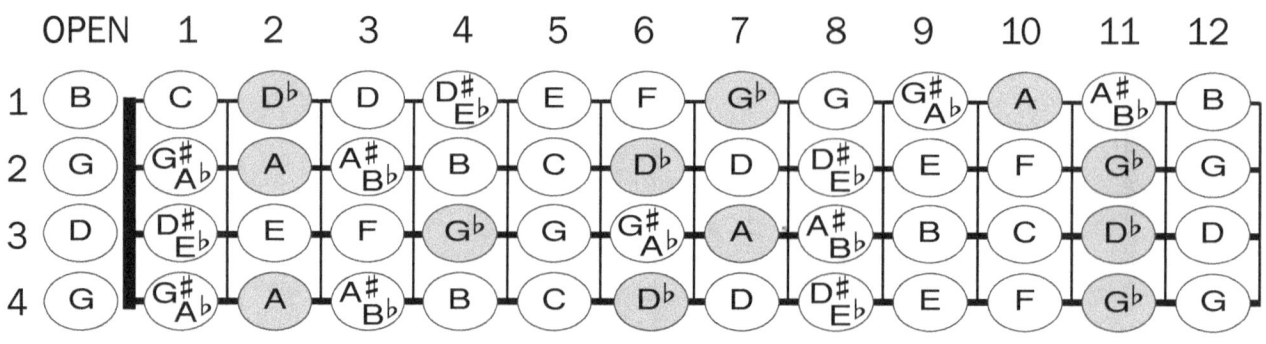

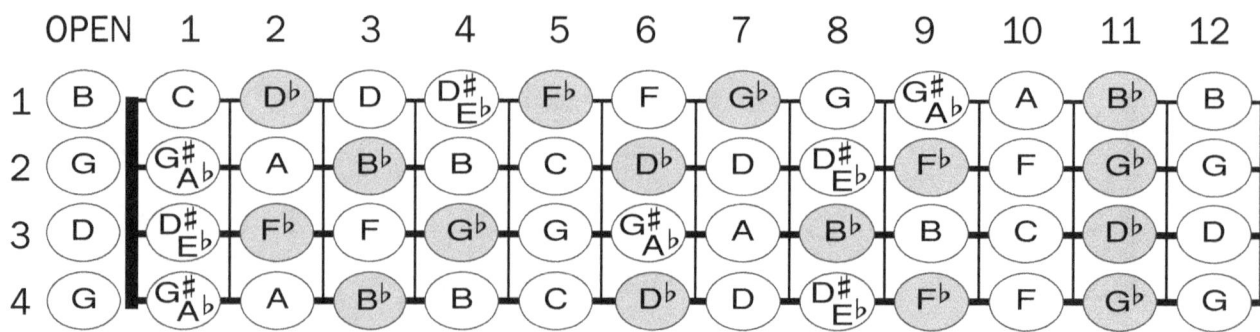

G • Gm • G7

G — GBD

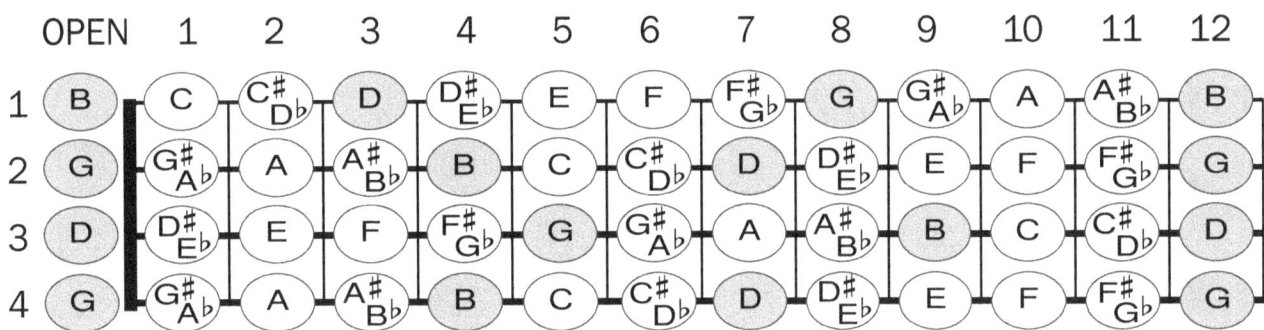

Gm — GB♭D

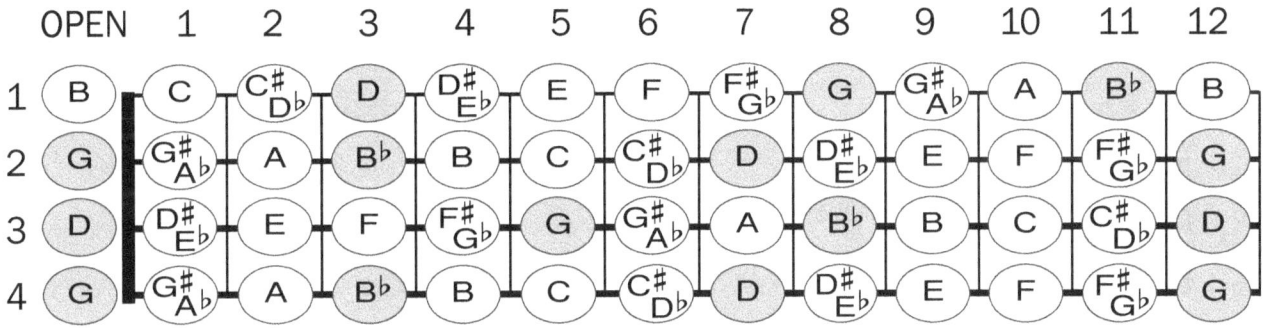

G7 — GBDF

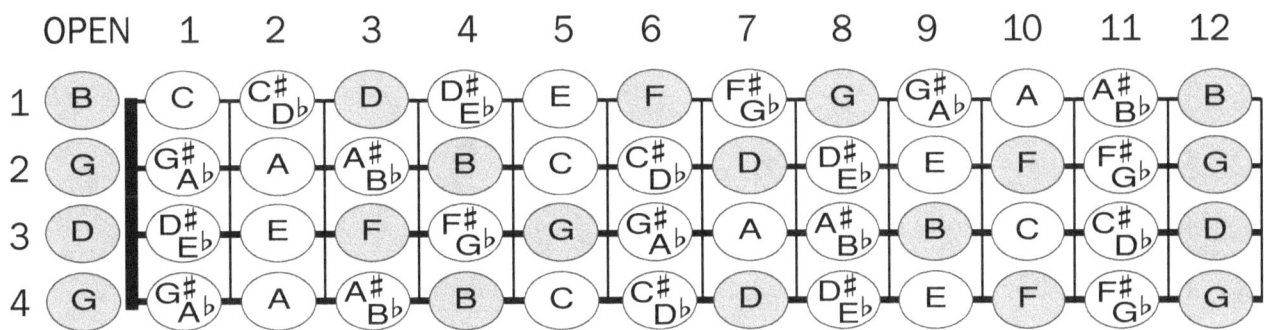

A♭ • A♭m • A♭7

A♭ — A♭ C E♭

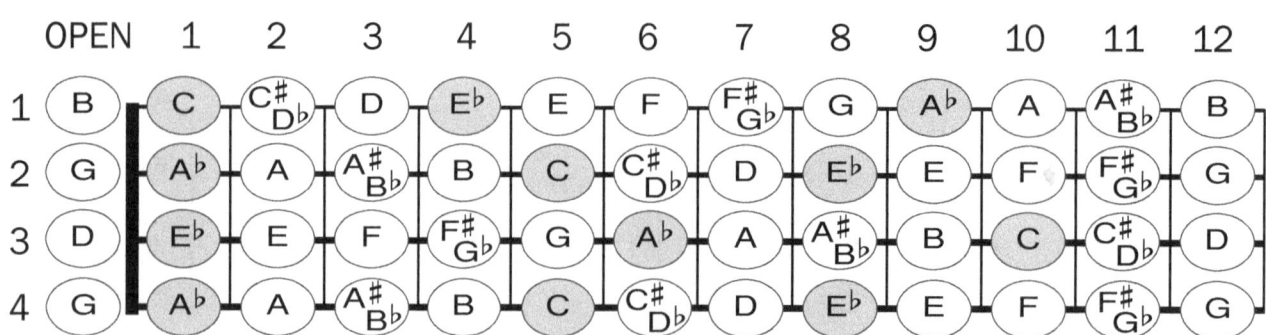

A♭m — A♭ C♭ E♭

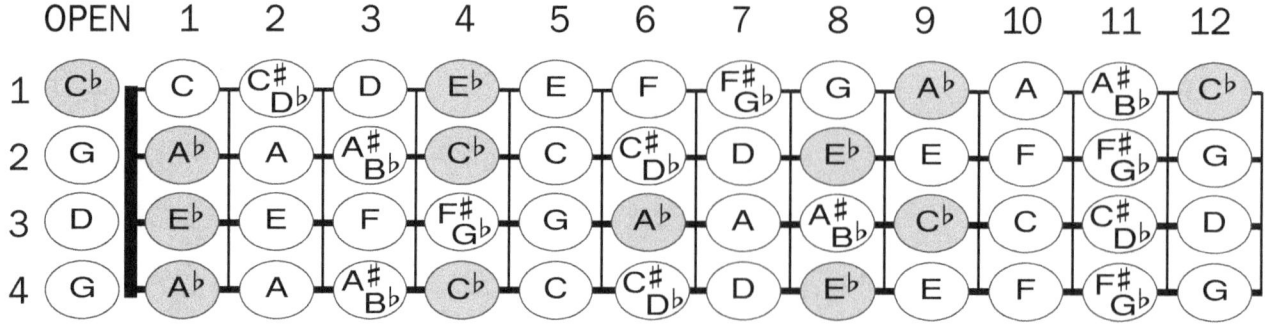

A♭7 — A♭ C E♭ G♭

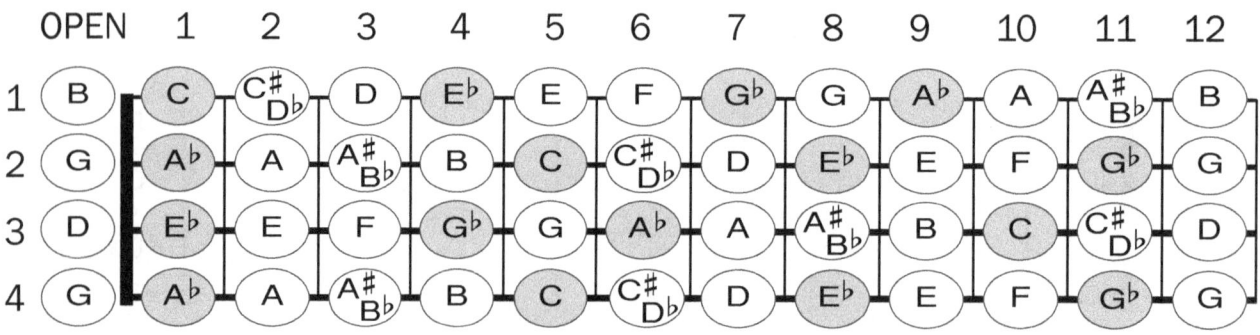

A SCALES
MAJOR - MINOR - BLUES

Here are the major, minor and blues scales shown in three positions. Look to the opposite page for the scale diagrams.

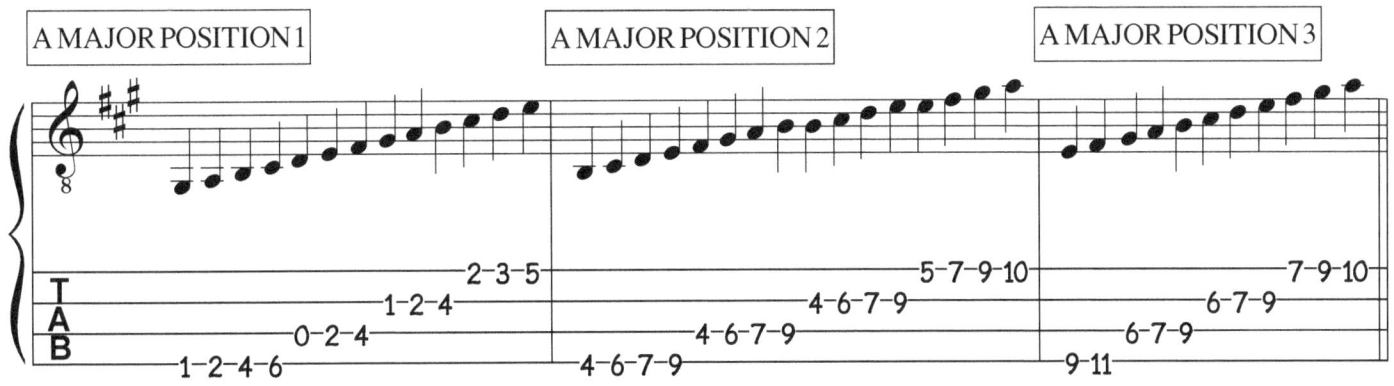

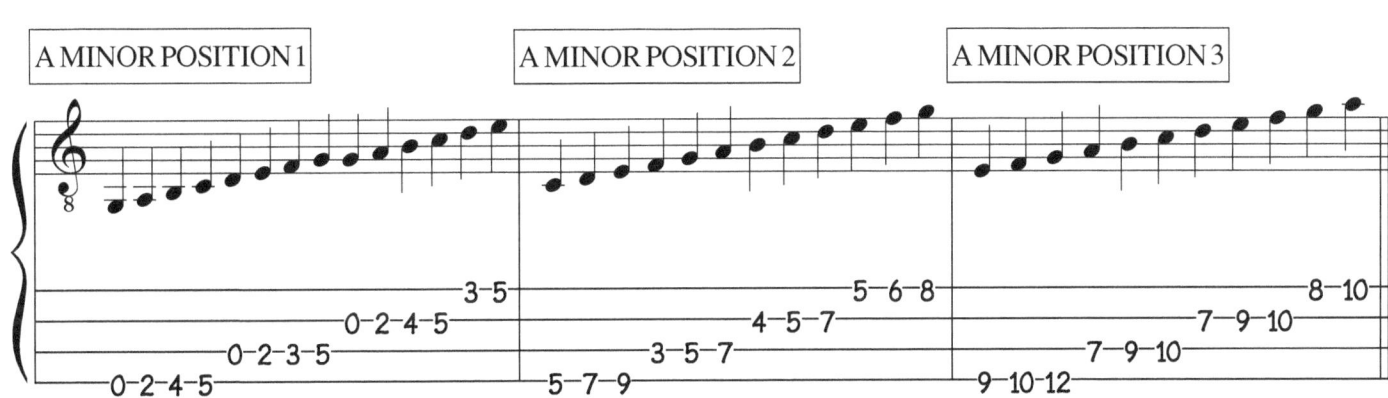

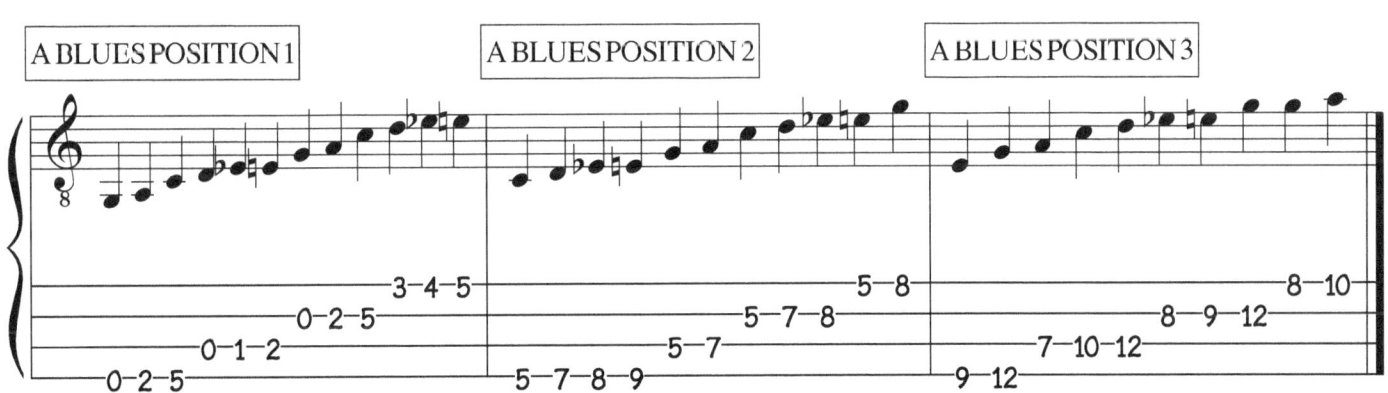

A MAJOR - MINOR - BLUES

A MAJOR — A B C# D E F# G#

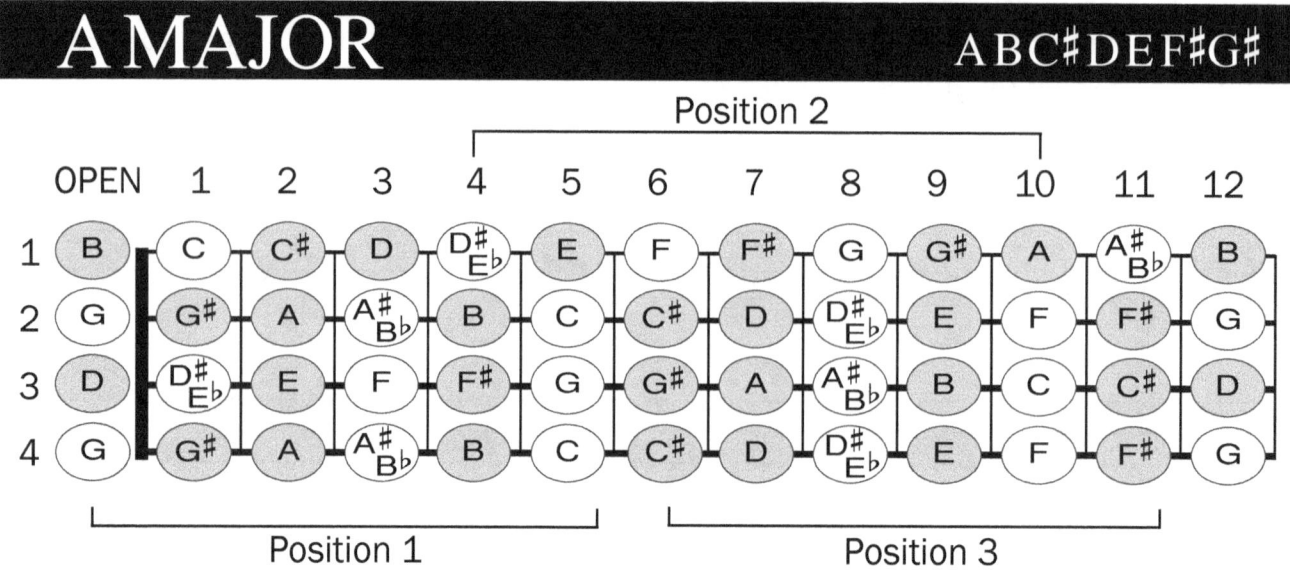

A MINOR — A B C D E F G

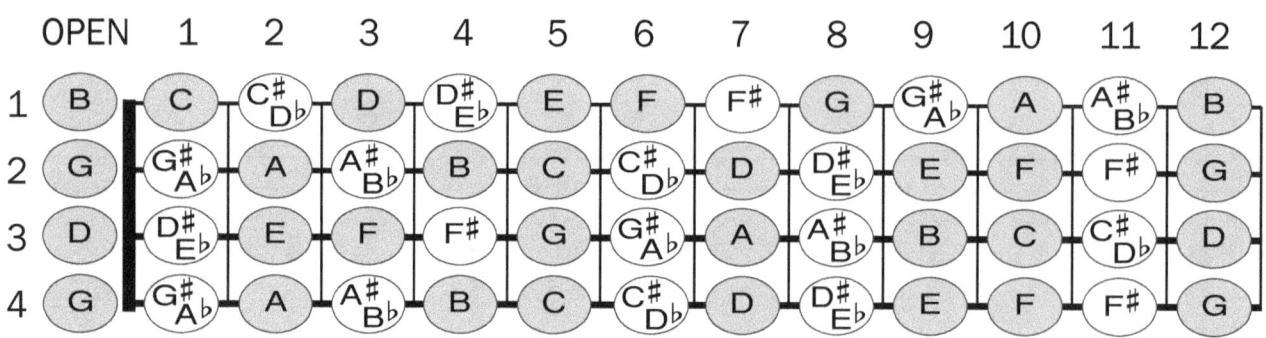

A BLUES — A C D E♭ E G

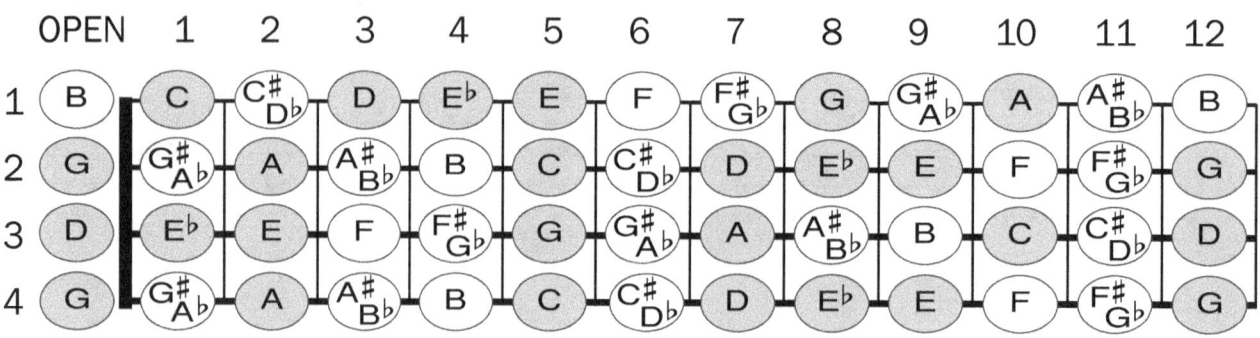

B♭ SCALES
MAJOR - MINOR - BLUES

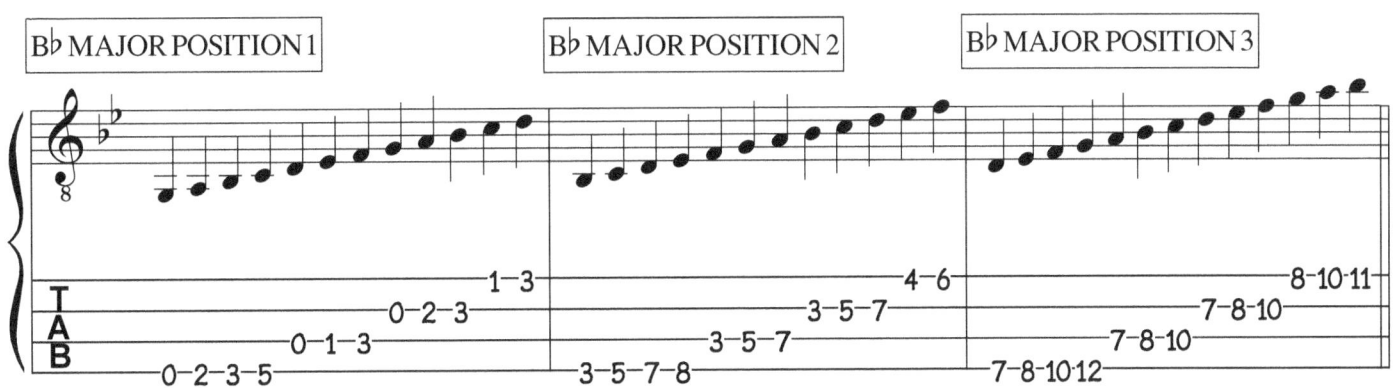
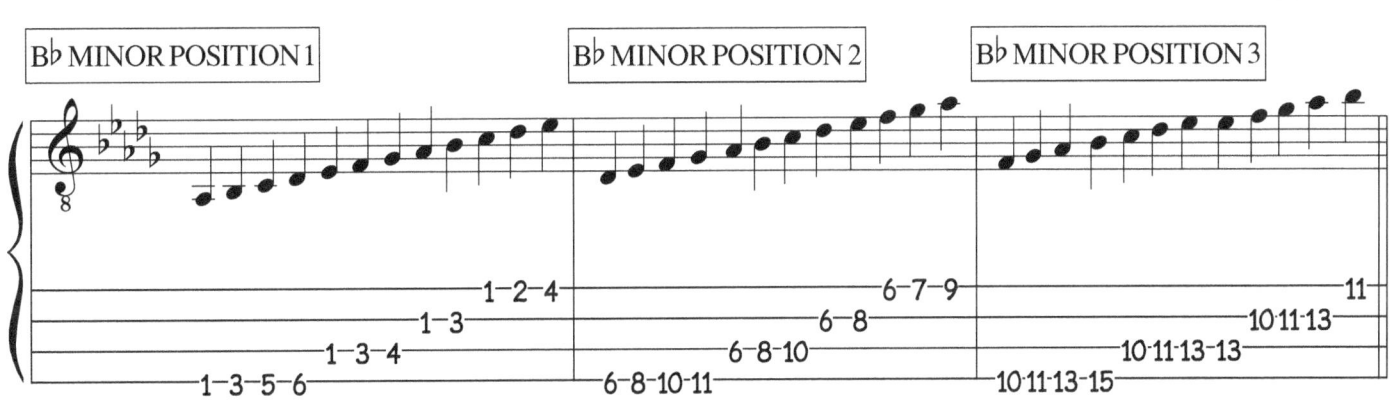
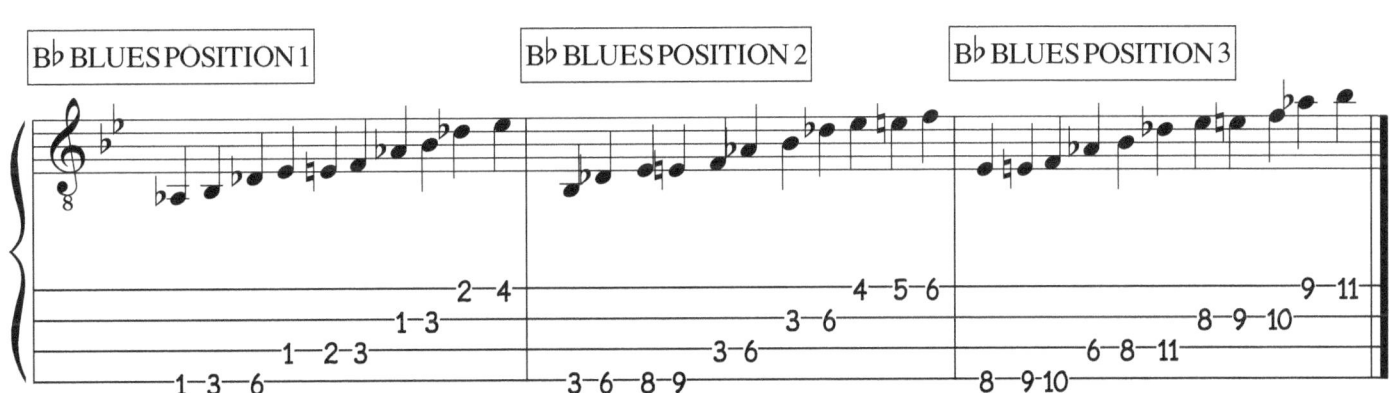

B♭ MAJOR - MINOR - BLUES

B♭ MAJOR — B♭ C D E♭ F G A

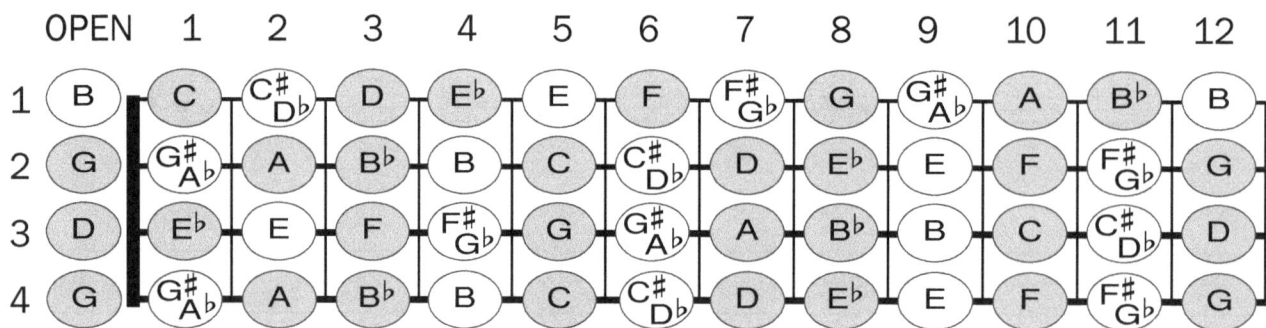

B♭ MINOR — B♭ C D♭ E♭ F G♭ A♭

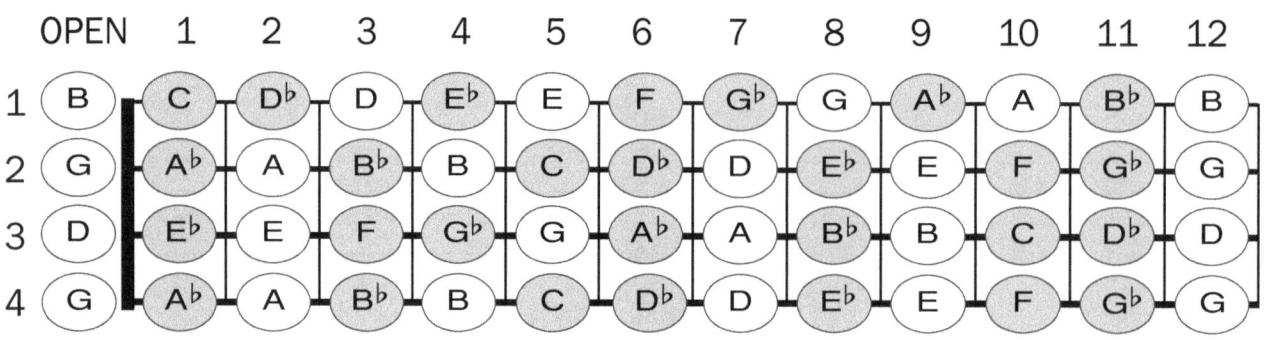

B♭ BLUES — B♭ D♭ E♭ F♭ F A♭

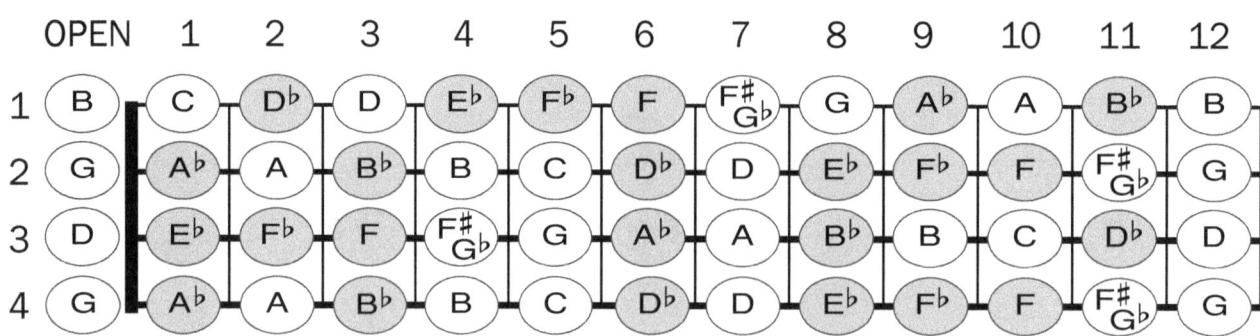

B SCALES
MAJOR - MINOR - BLUES

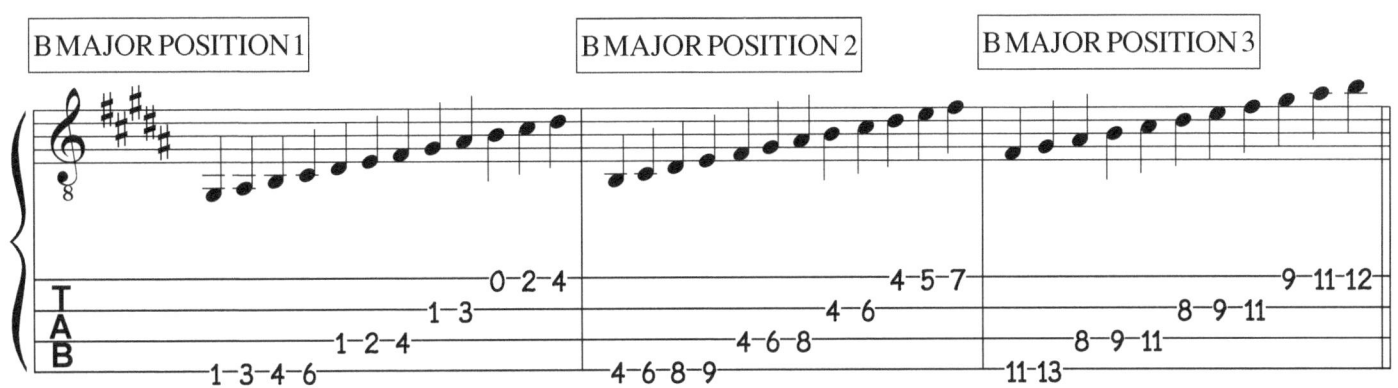

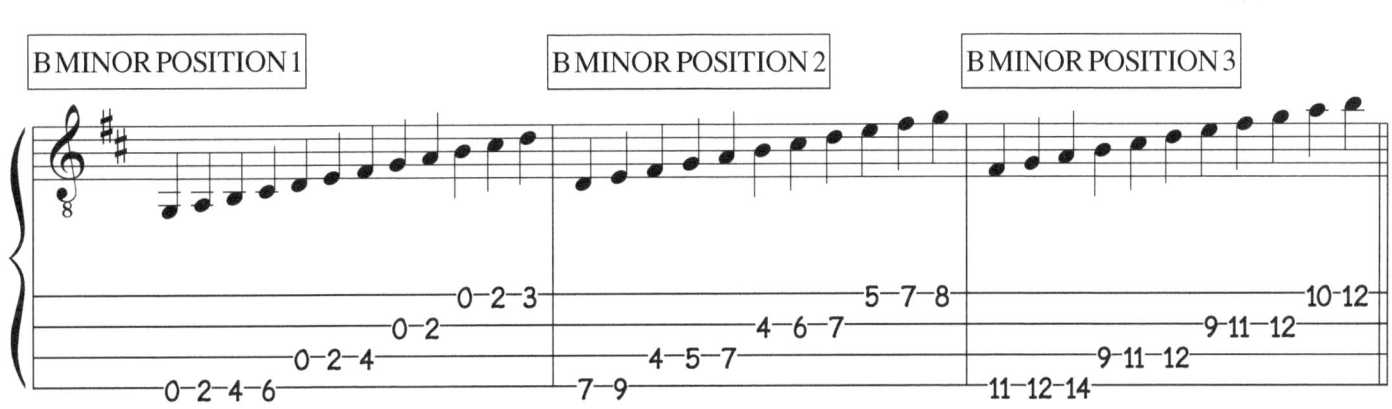

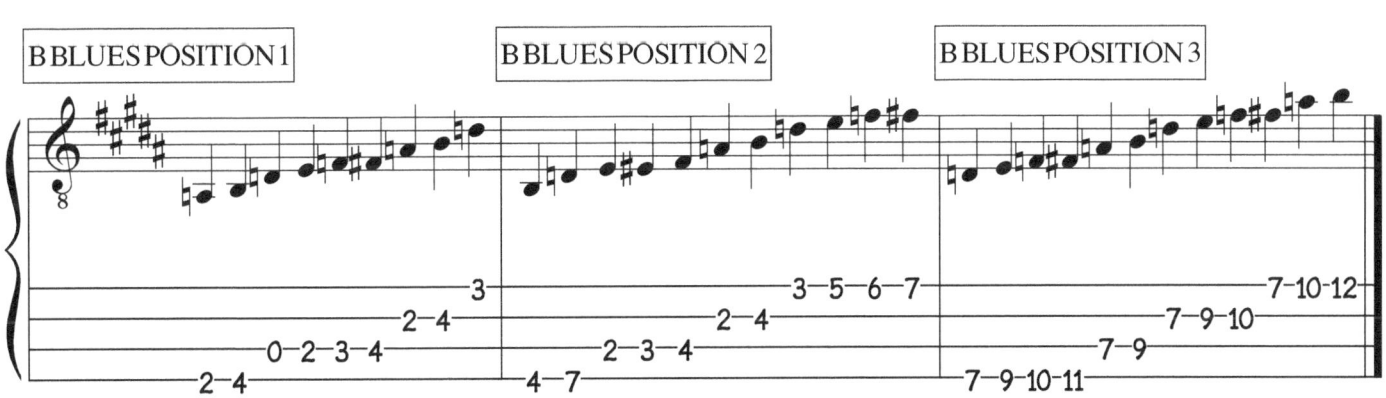

B MAJOR - MINOR - BLUES

B MAJOR — B C# D# E F# G# A#

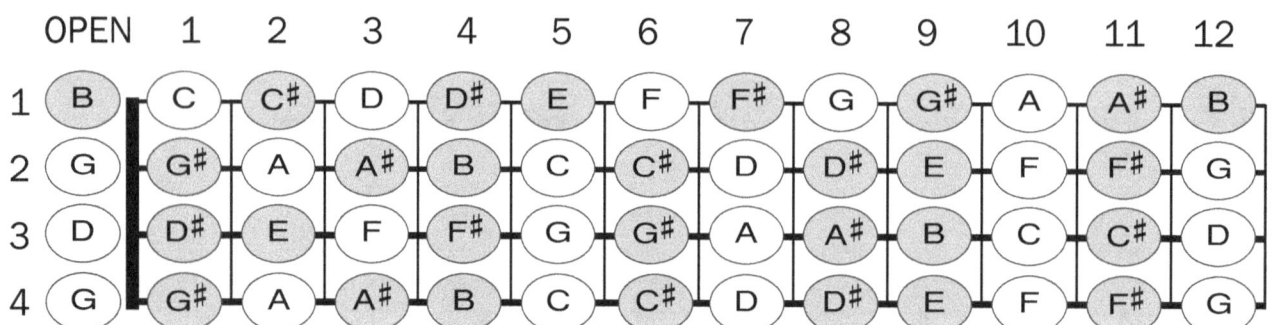

B MINOR — B C# D E F# G A

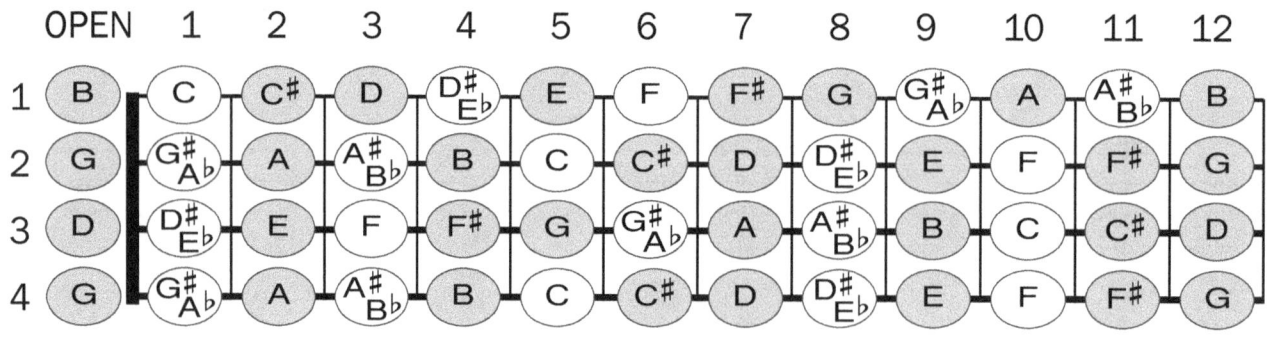

B BLUES — B D E F F# A

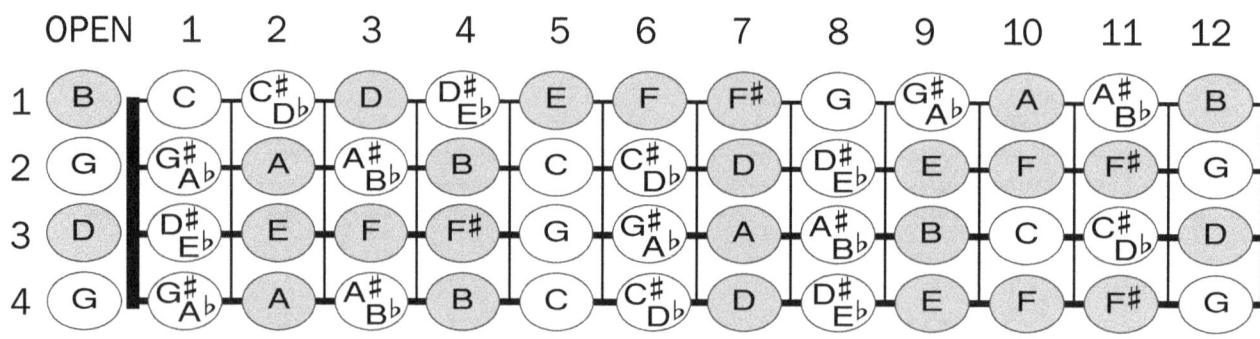

C SCALES
MAJOR - MINOR - BLUES

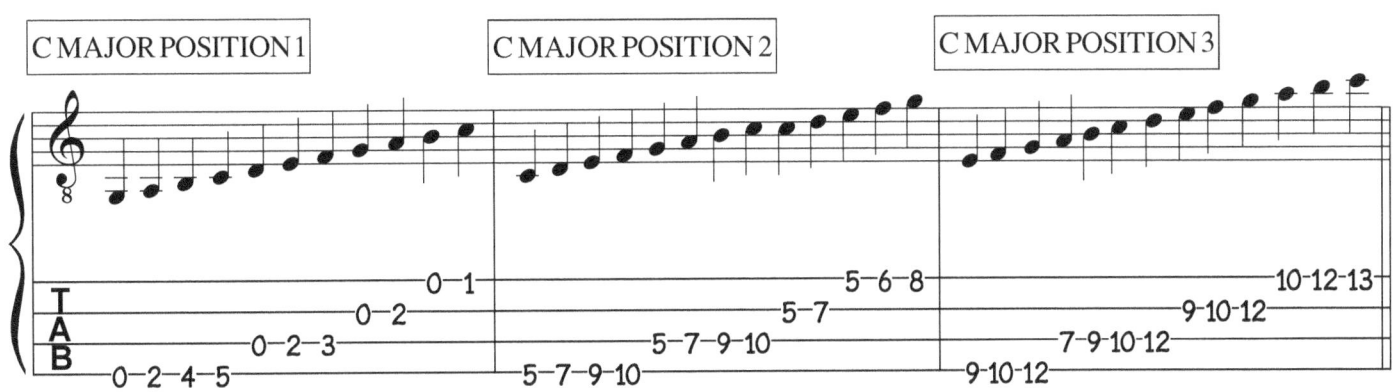
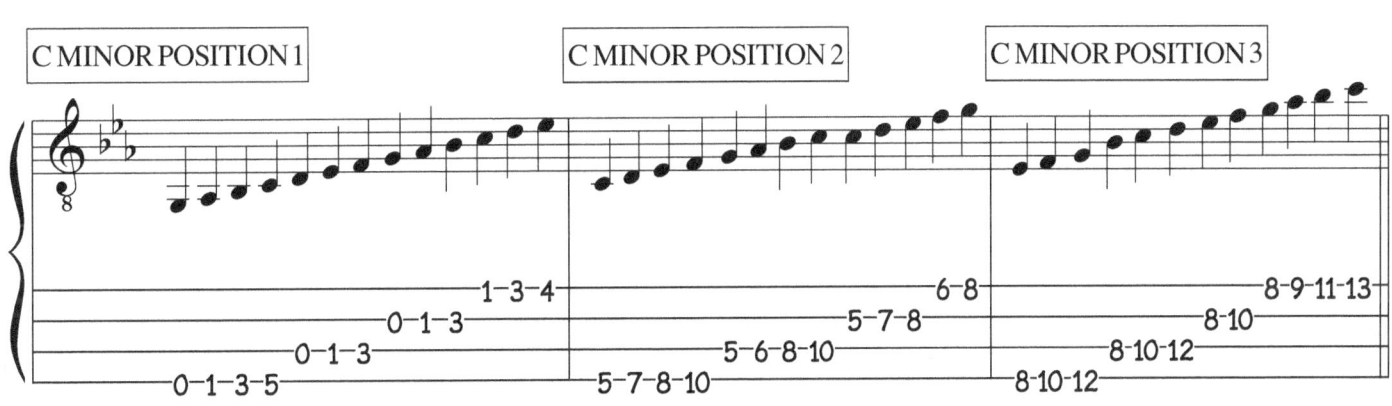
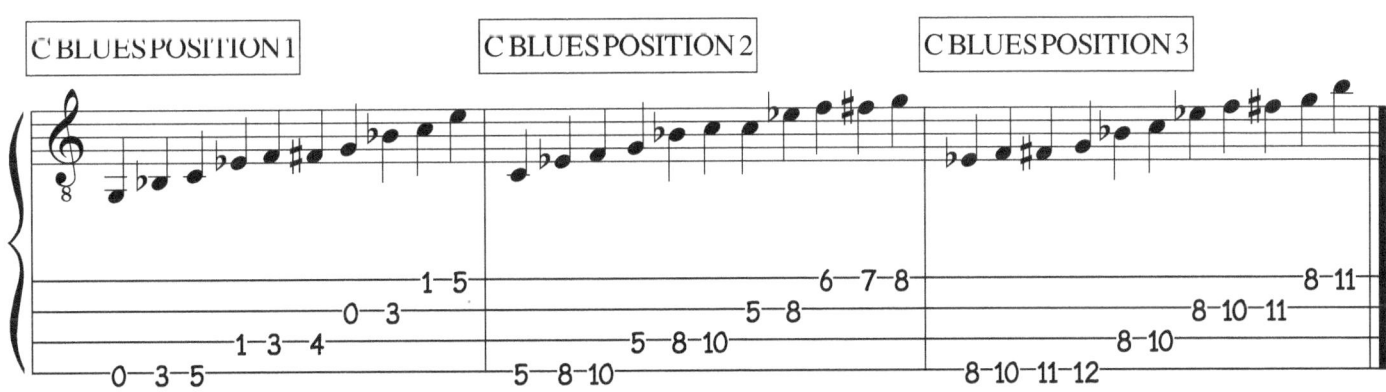

C MAJOR - MINOR - BLUES

C MAJOR — CDEFGAB

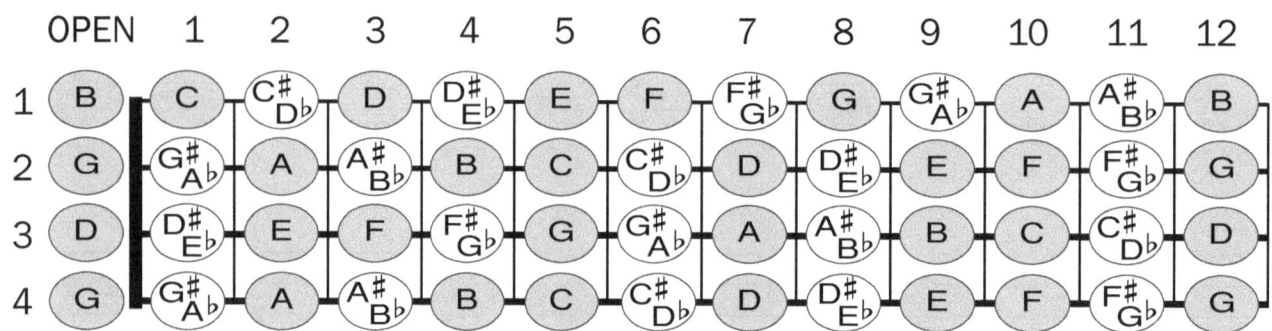

C MINOR — CDE♭FGA♭B♭

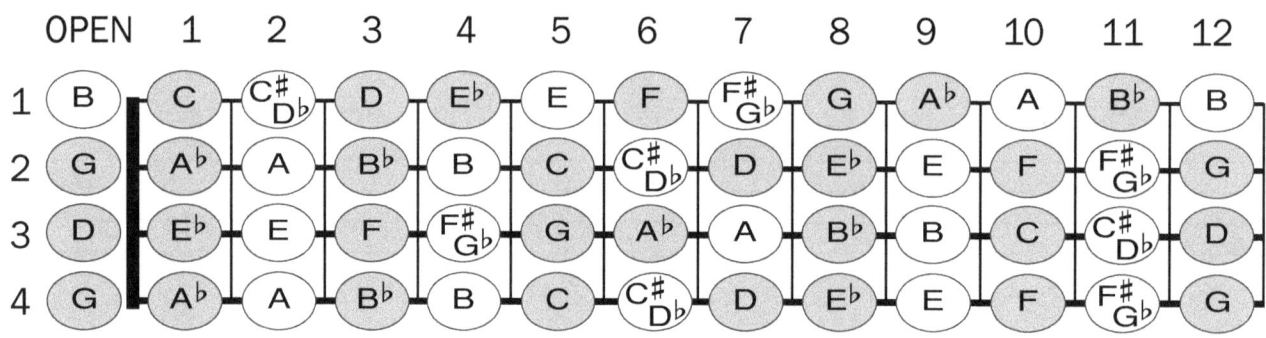

C BLUES — CE♭FG♭GB♭

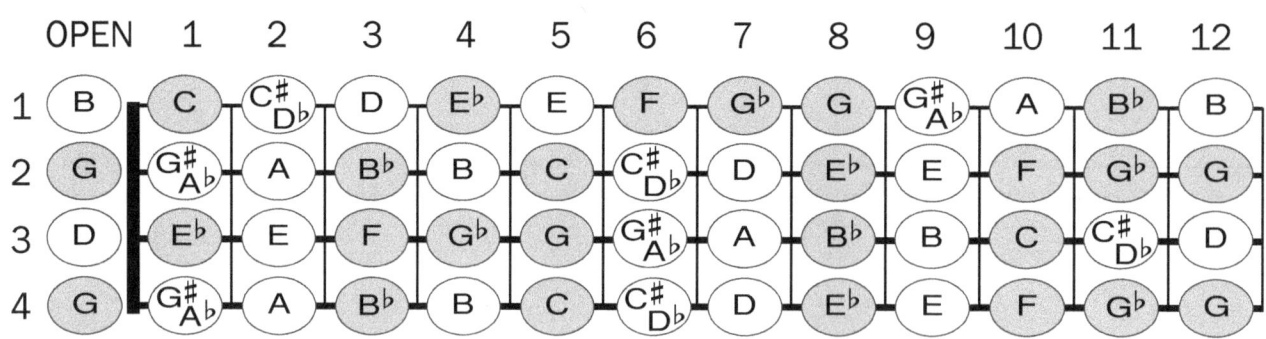

C♯ D♭ SCALES
MAJOR - MINOR - BLUES

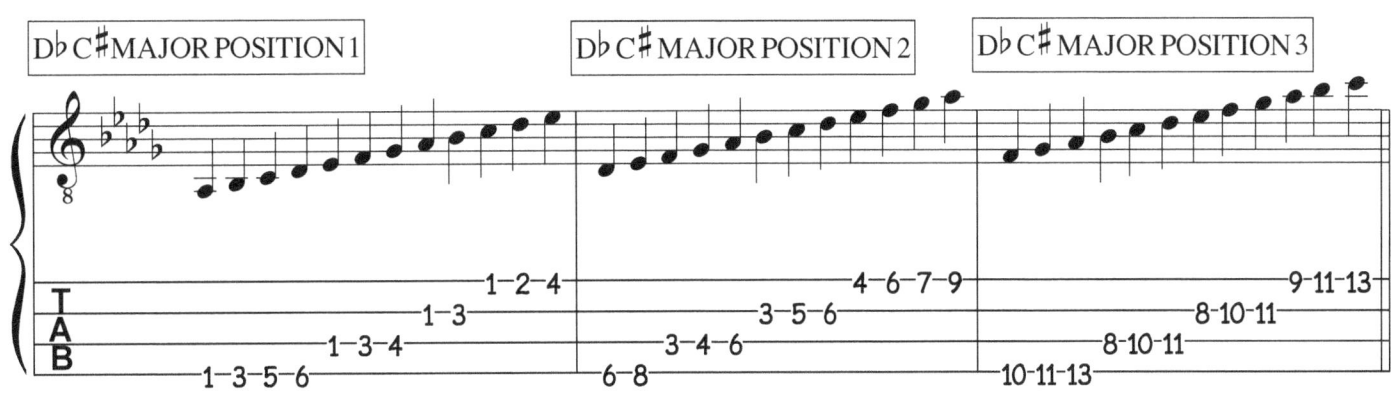

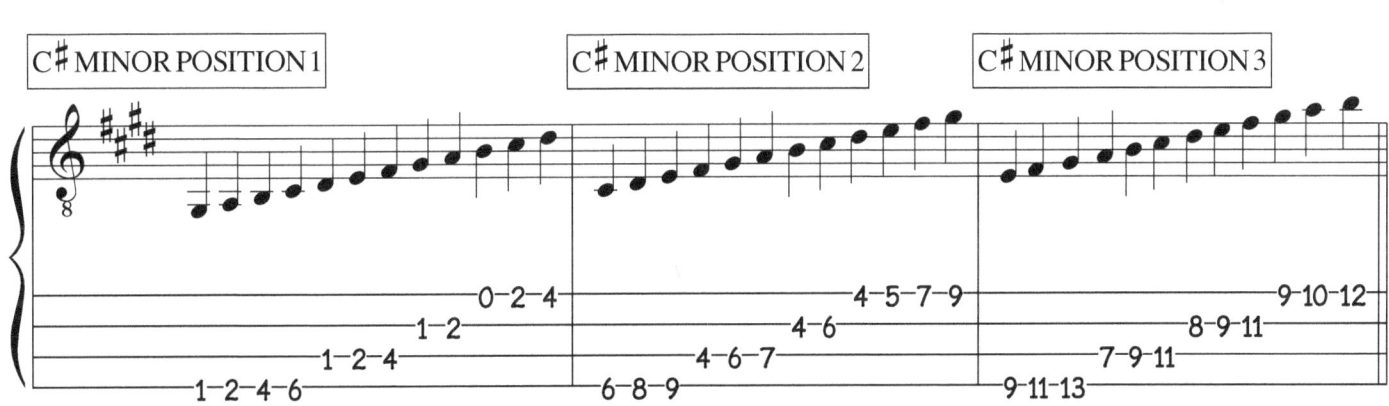

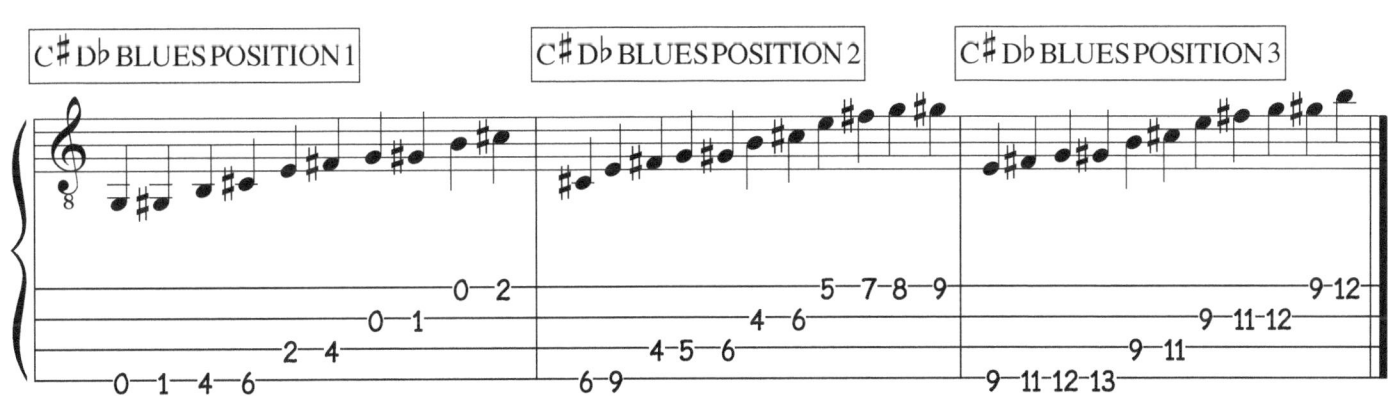

C♯ - D♭ MAJOR - MINOR - BLUES

C♯ - D♭ MAJOR

C♯ D♯ E♯ F♯ G♯ A♯ B♯
D♭ E♭ F G♭ A♭ B♭ C
E♯ = F

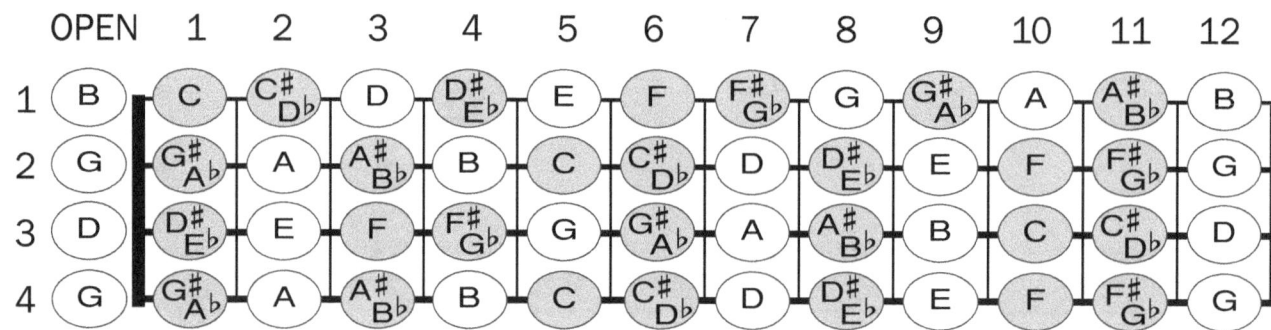

C♯ MINOR

C♯ D♯ E F♯ G♯ A B

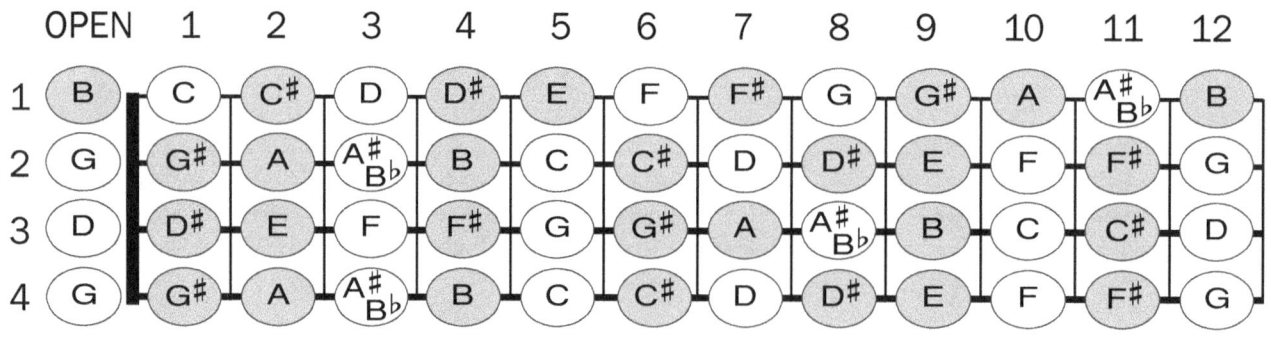

C♯ - D♭ BLUES

C♯ E F♯ G G♯ B

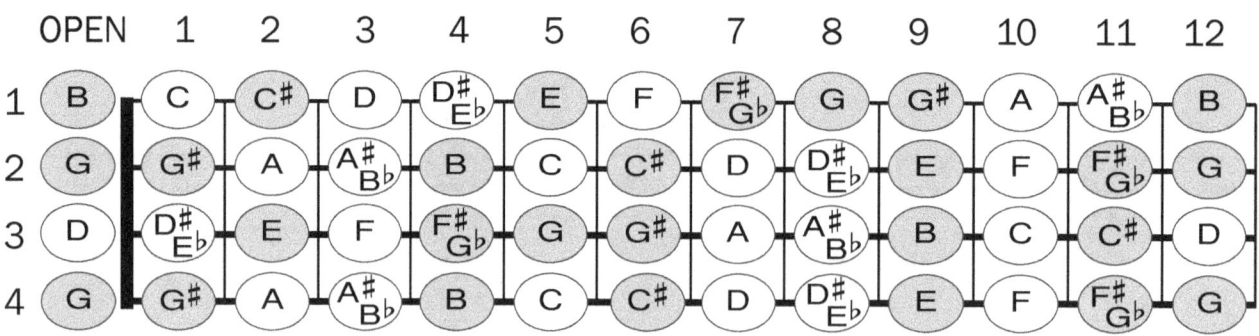

D SCALES
MAJOR - MINOR - BLUES

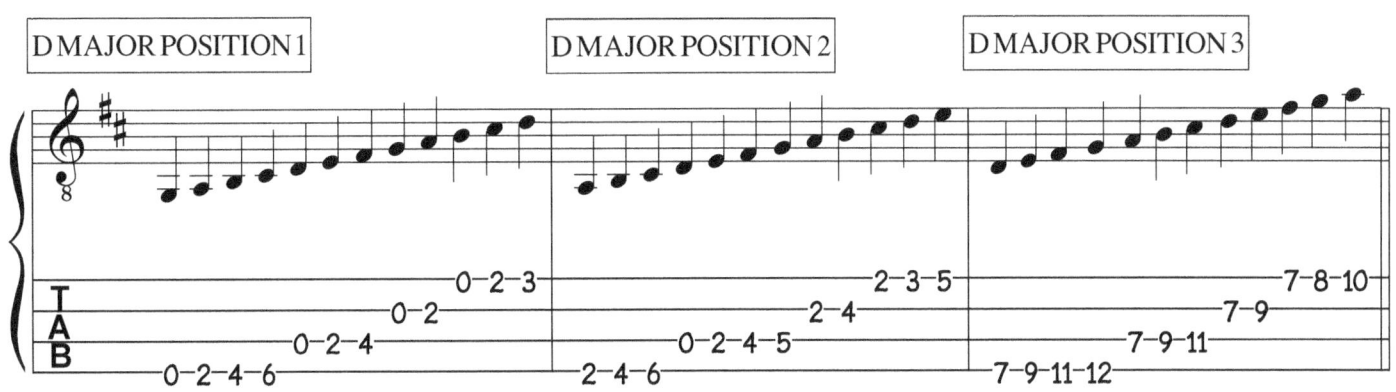

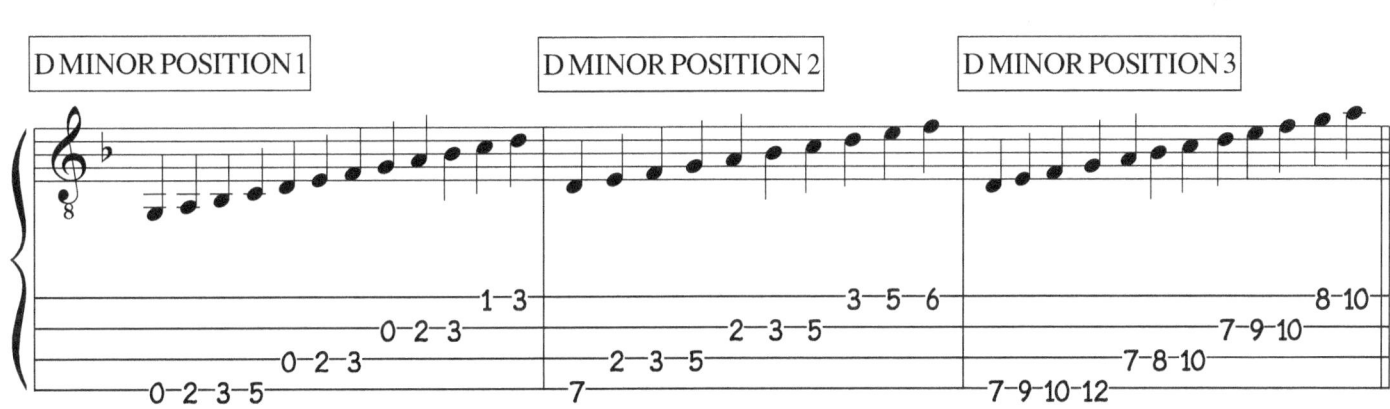

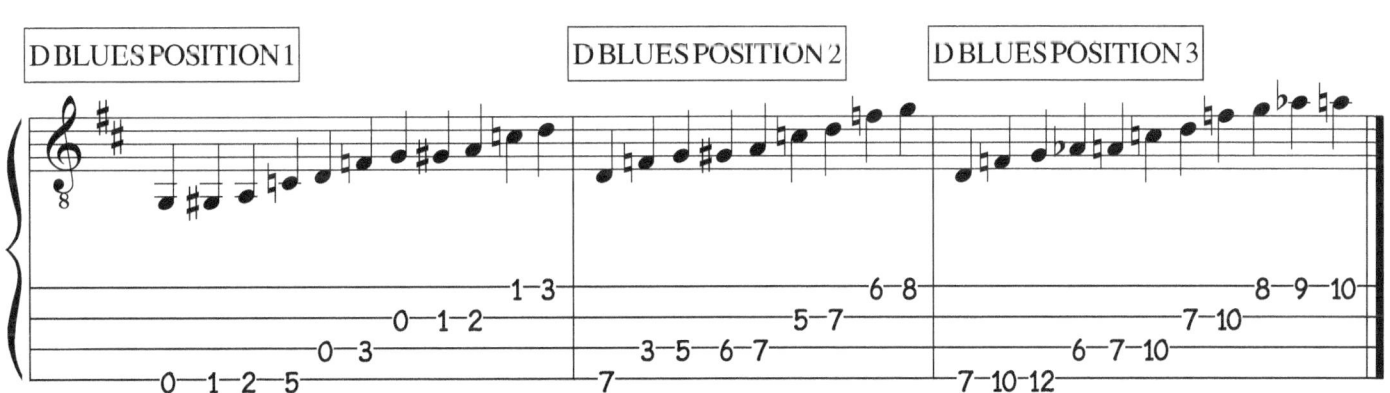

D MAJOR - MINOR - BLUES

D MAJOR — DEF#GABC#

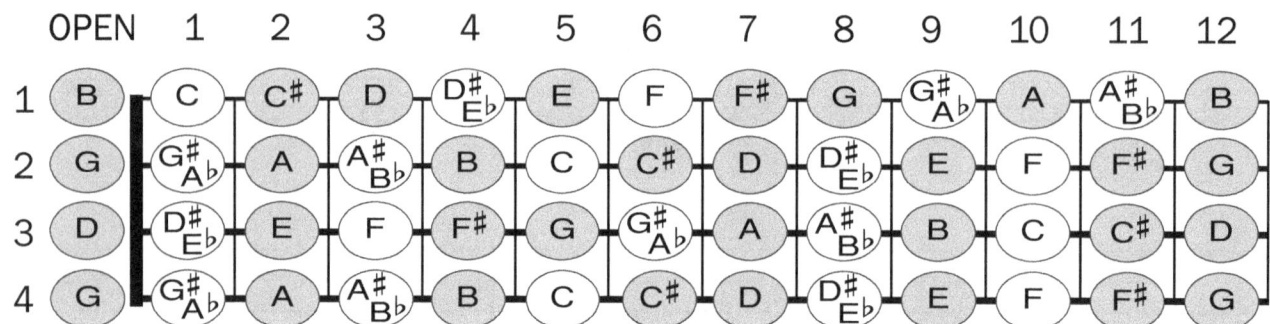

D MINOR — DEFGAB♭C

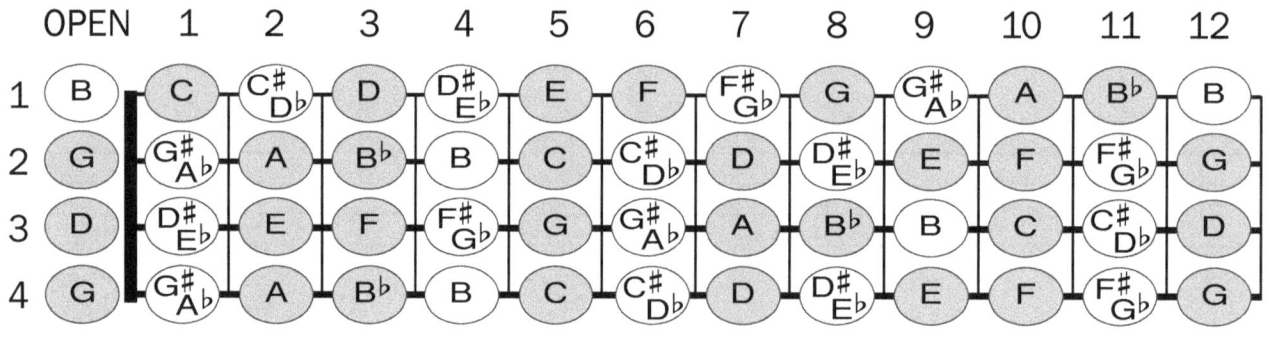

D BLUES — DFGA♭AC

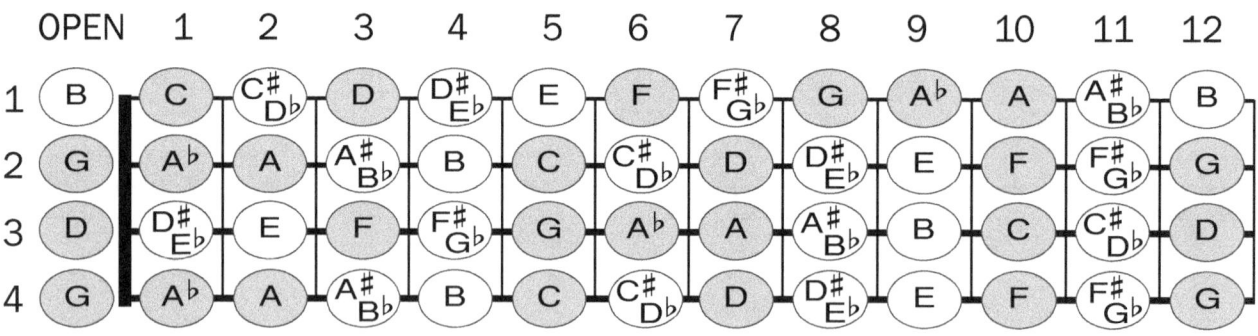

E♭ SCALES
MAJOR - MINOR - BLUES

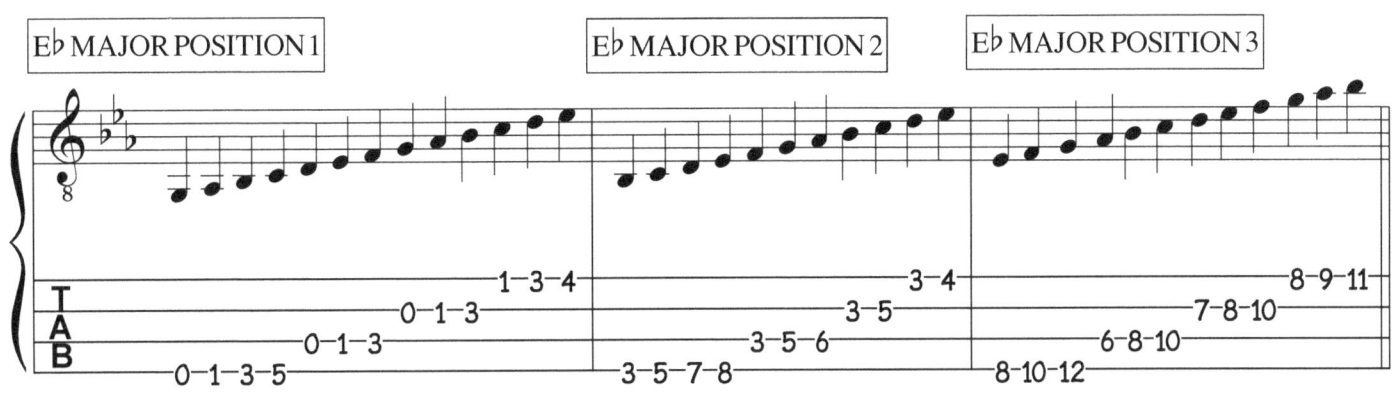
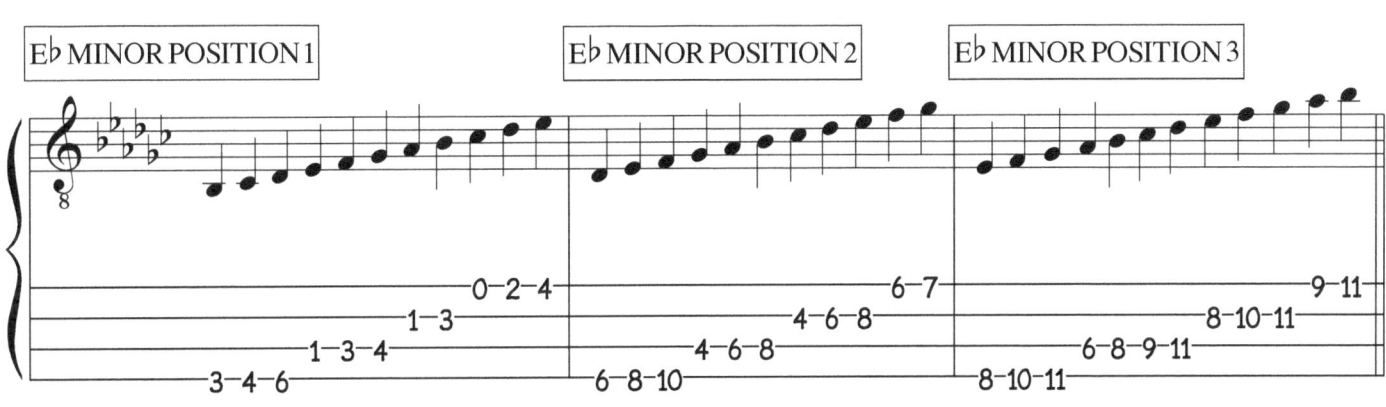
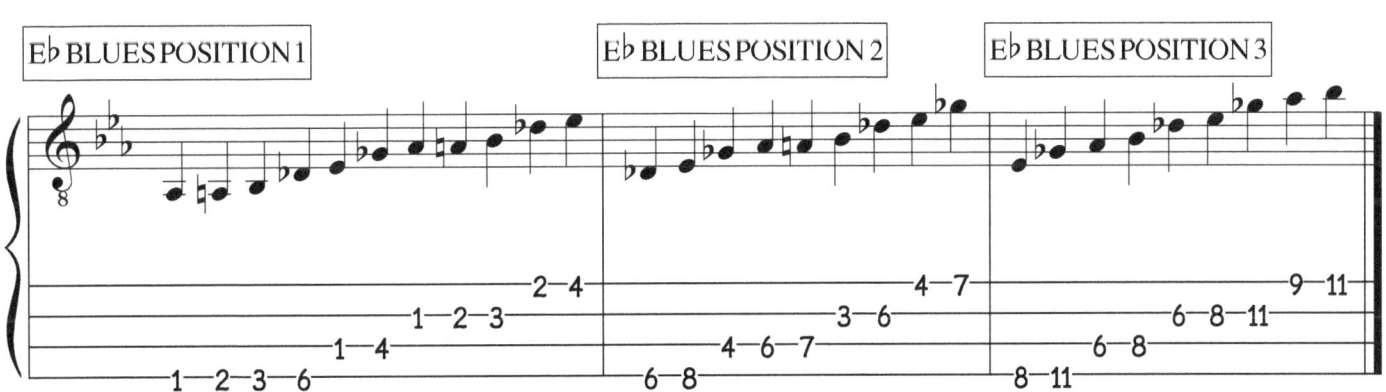

E♭ MAJOR - MINOR - BLUES

E♭ MAJOR — E♭ F G A♭ B♭ C D

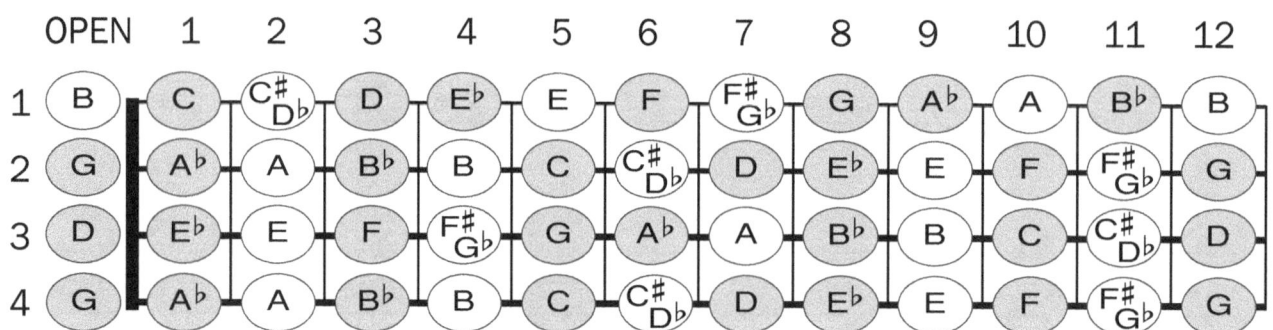

E♭ MINOR — E♭ F G♭ A♭ B♭ C♭ D♭

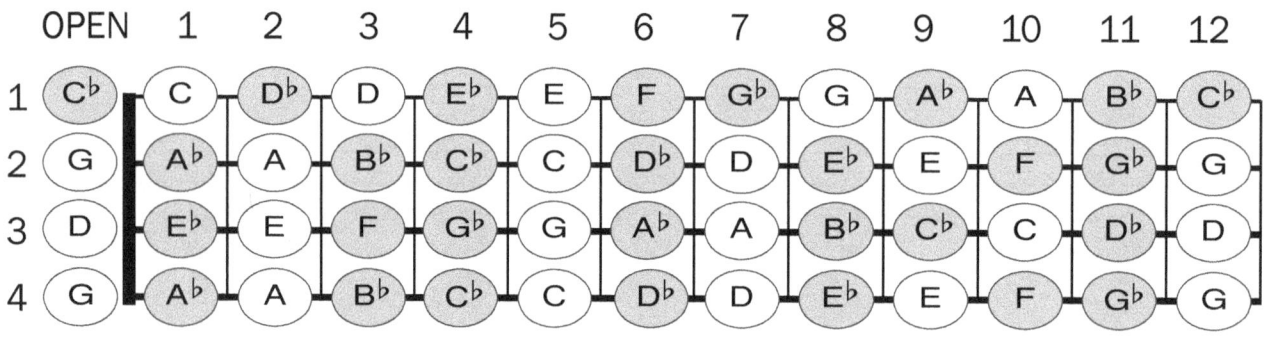

E♭ BLUES — E♭ G♭ A♭ A B♭ D♭

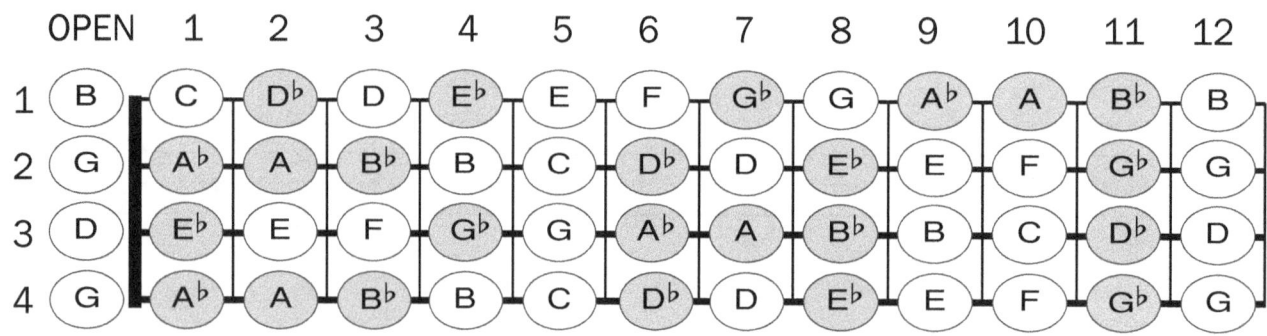

E SCALES
MAJOR - MINOR - BLUES

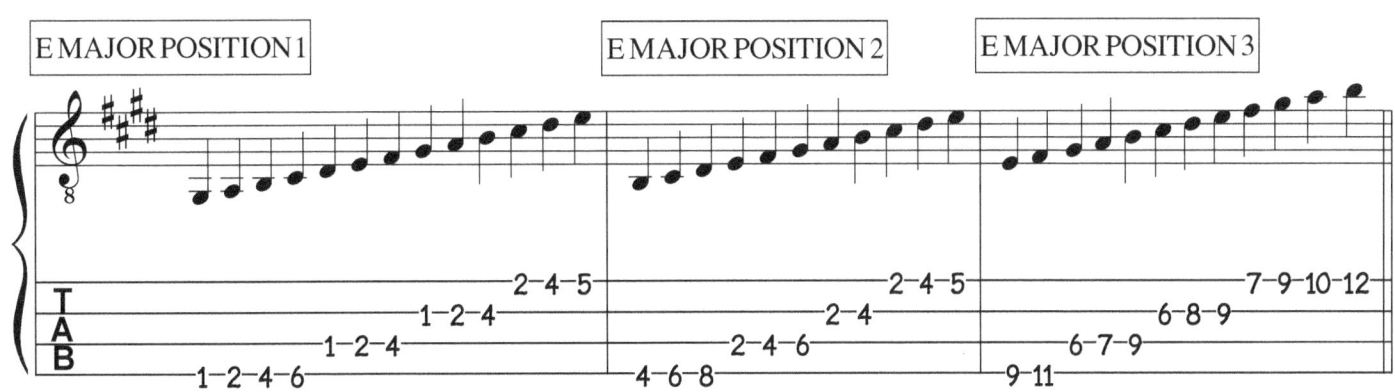

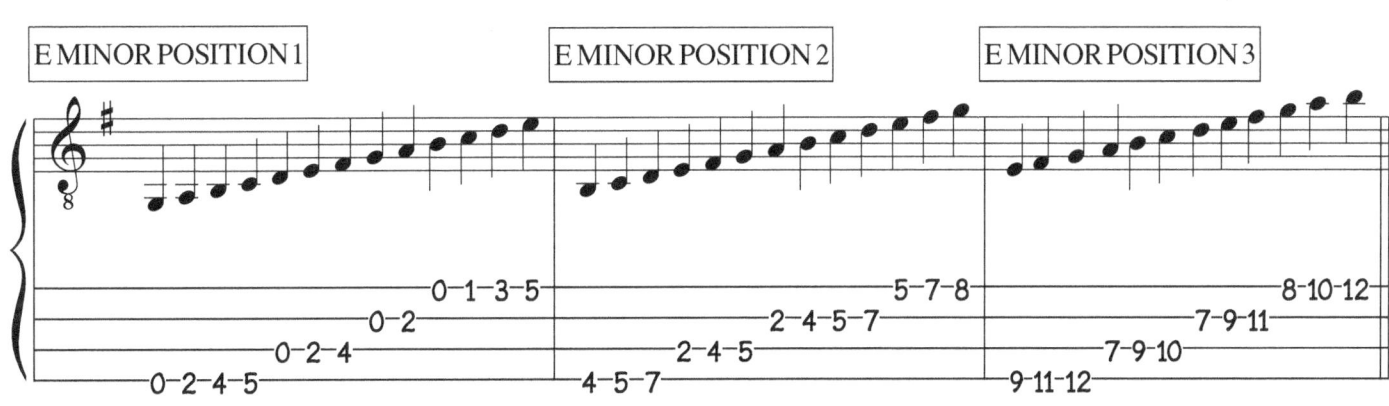

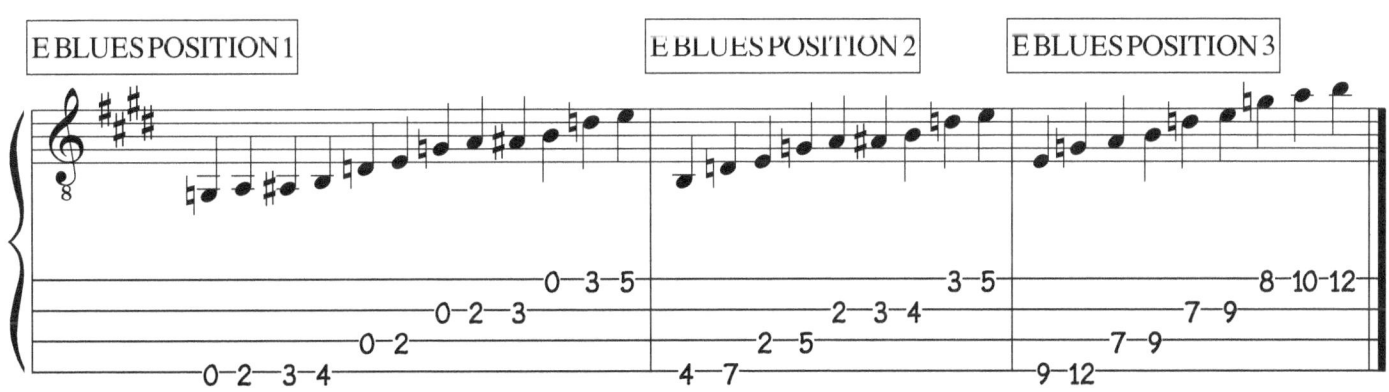

E MAJOR - MINOR - BLUES

E MAJOR — E F# G# A B C# D#

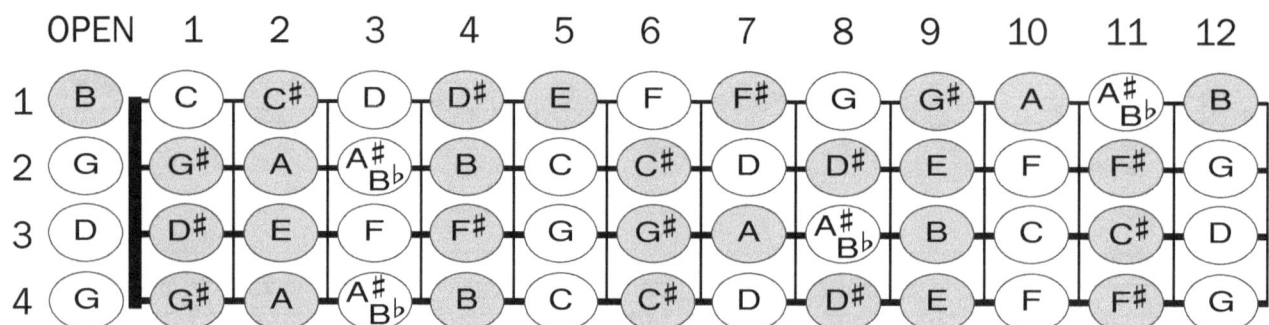

E MINOR — E F# G A B C D

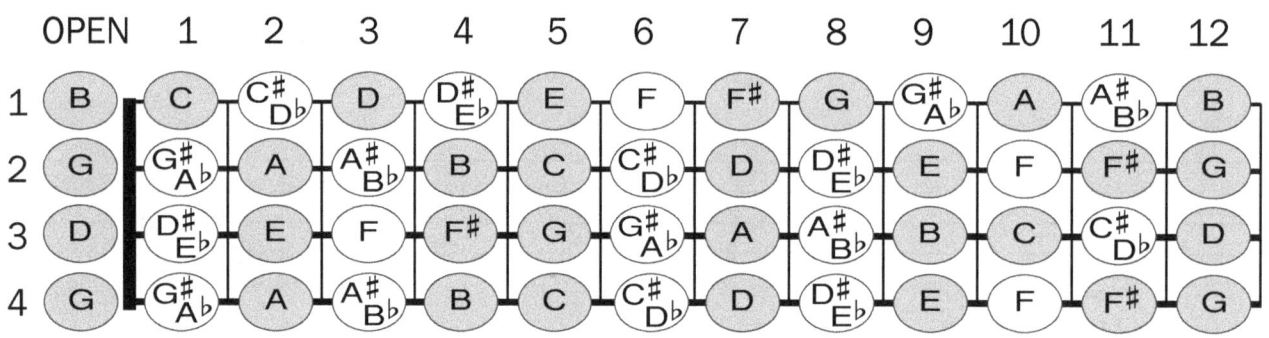

E BLUES — E G A Bb B D

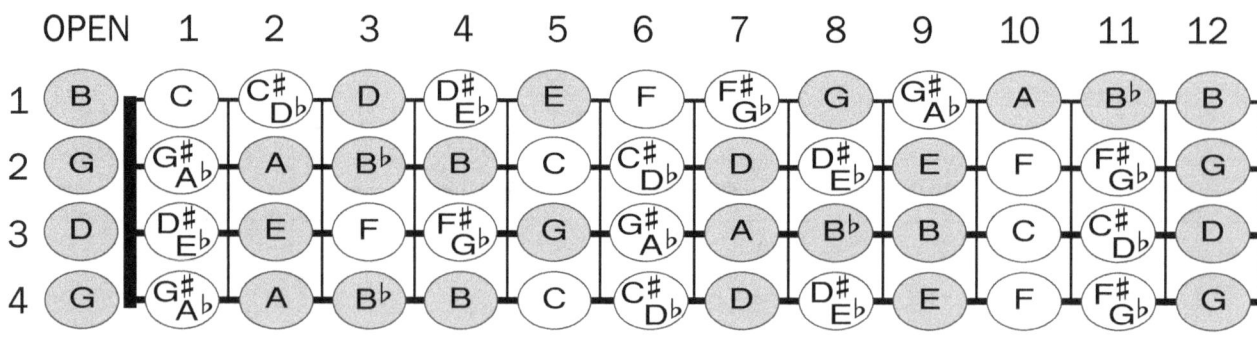

F SCALES
MAJOR - MINOR - BLUES

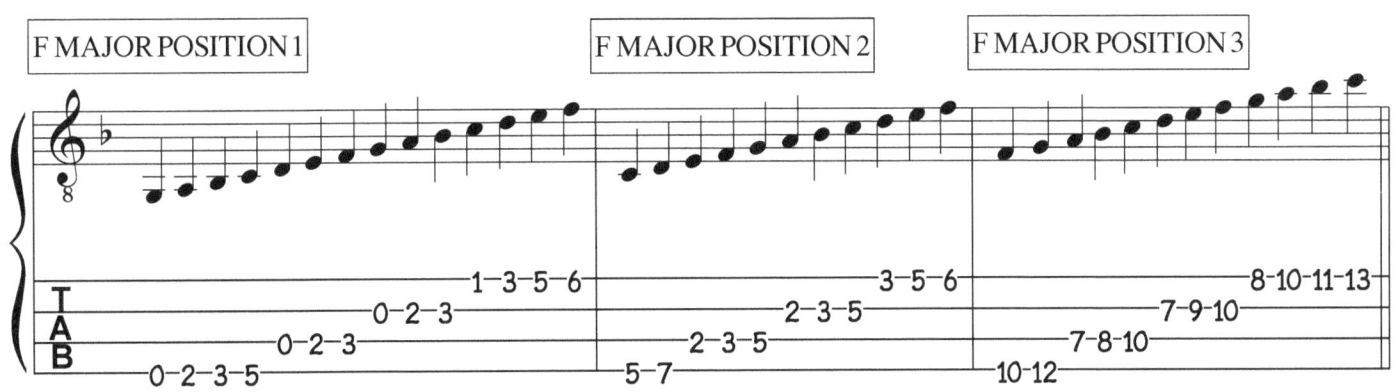

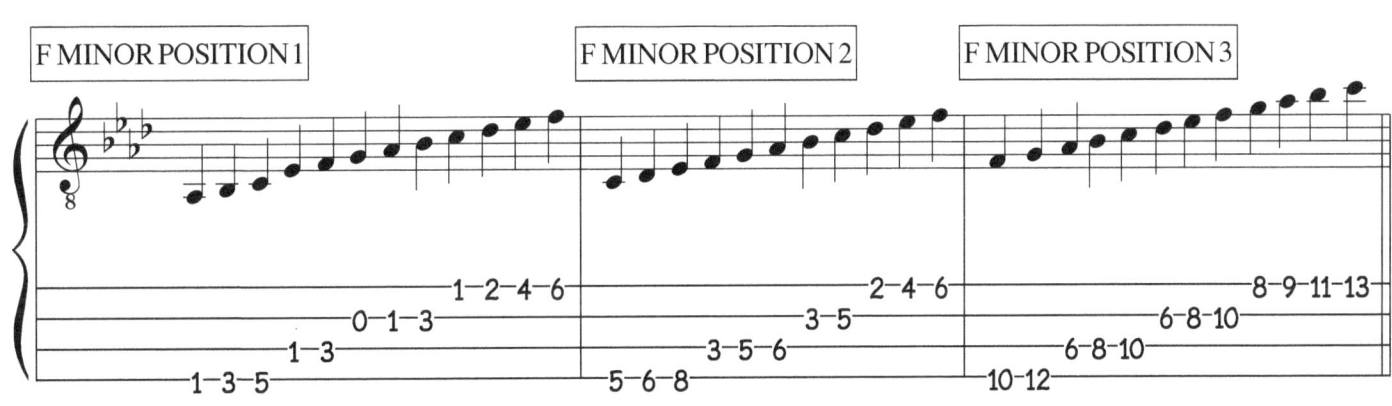

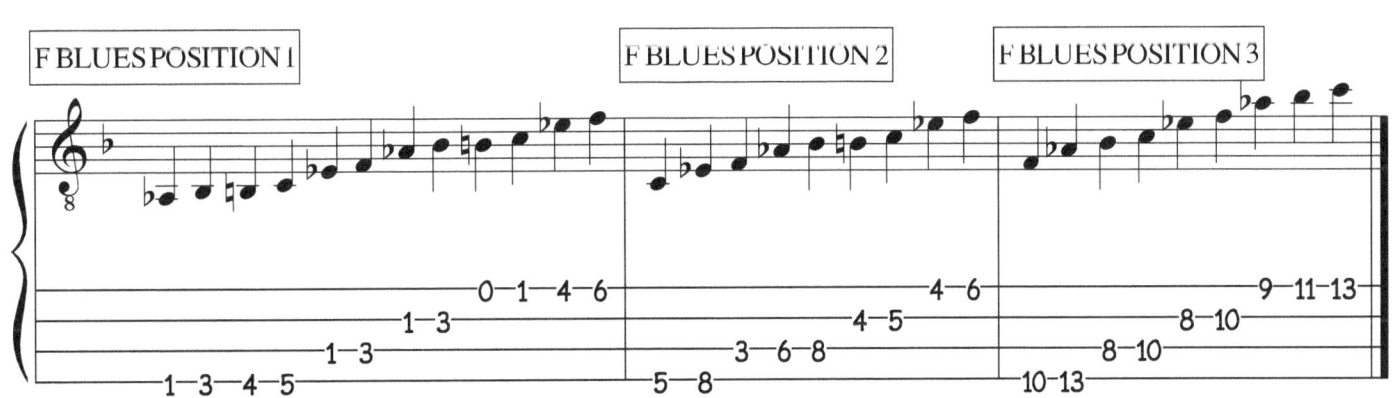

F MAJOR - MINOR - BLUES

F MAJOR — F G A B♭ C D E

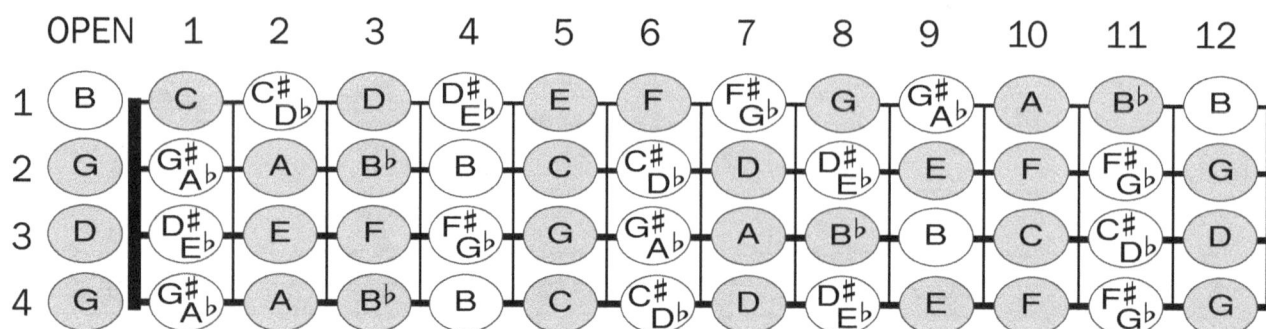

F MINOR — F G A♭ B♭ C D♭ E♭

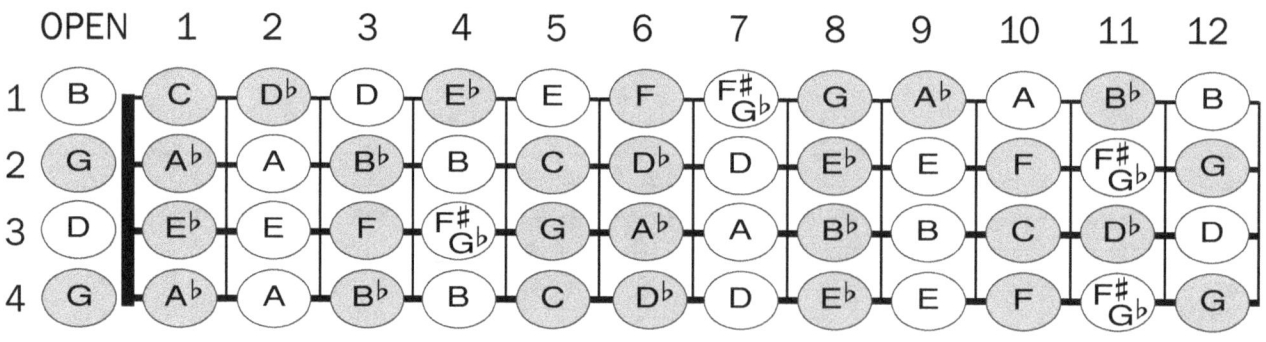

F BLUES — F A♭ B♭ C♭ C E♭

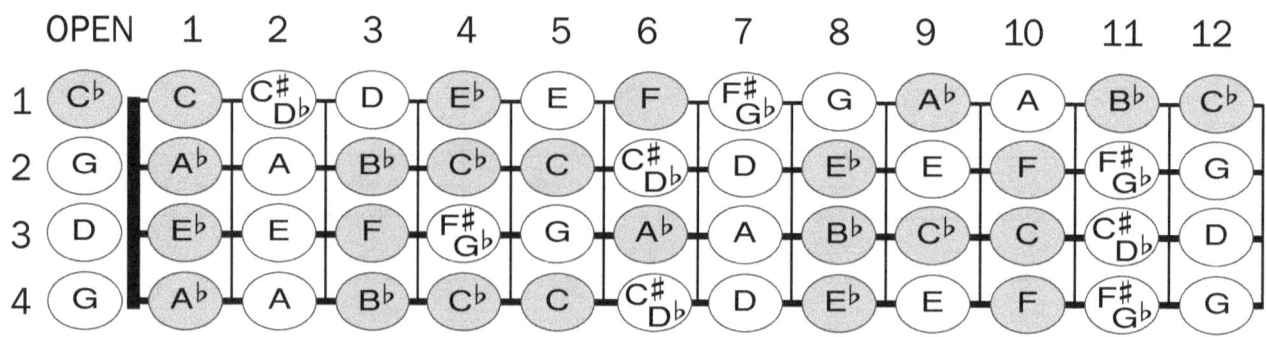

F#(G♭) SCALES
MAJOR - MINOR - BLUES

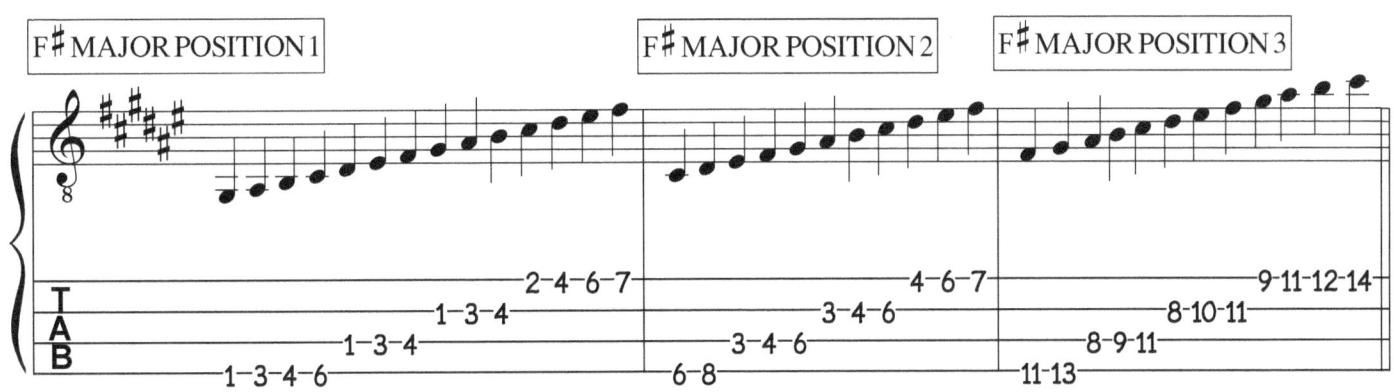

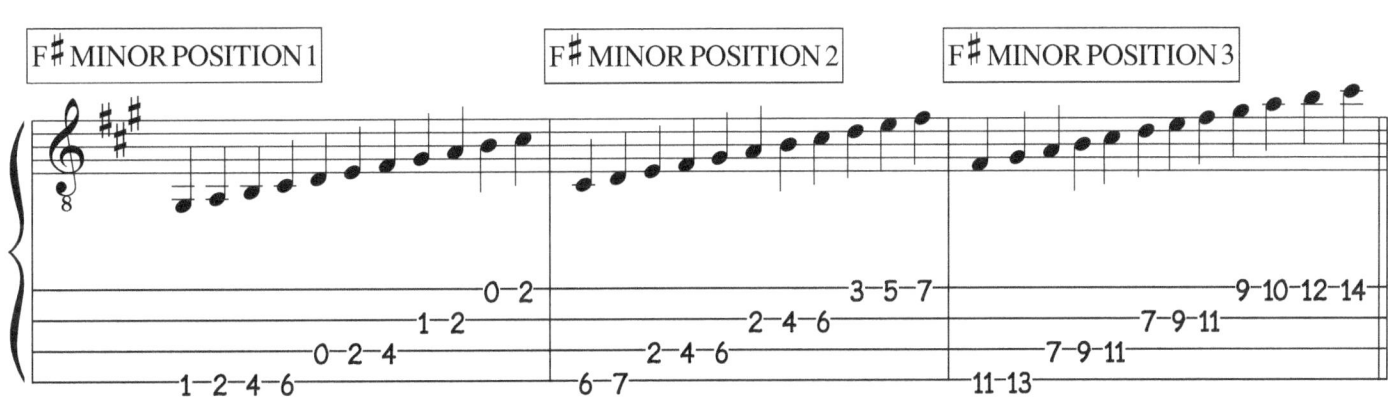

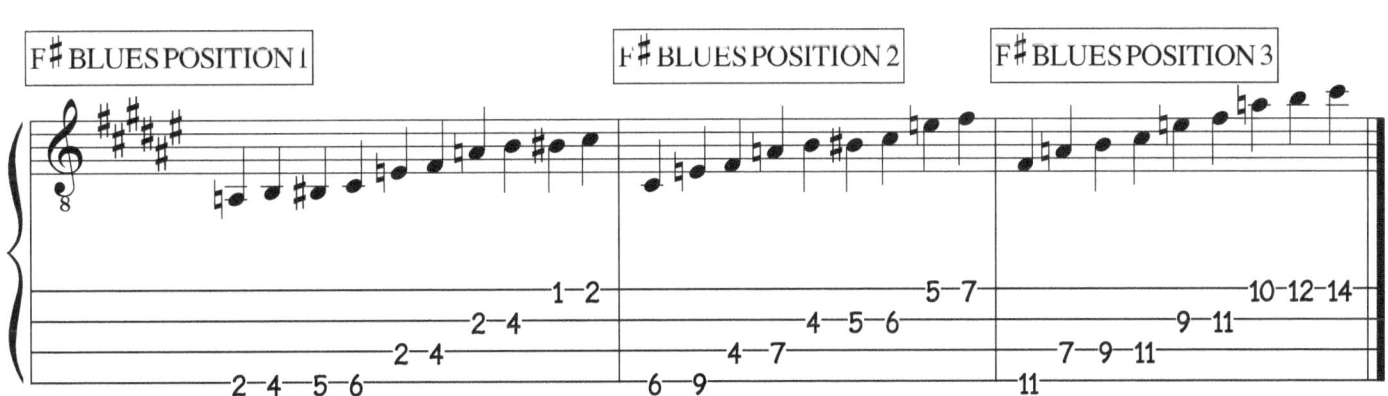

F# - G♭ MAJOR - MINOR - BLUES

F# - G♭ MAJOR

G♭ A♭ B♭ C♭ D♭ E♭ F
F# G# A# B C# D# E#
E# = F

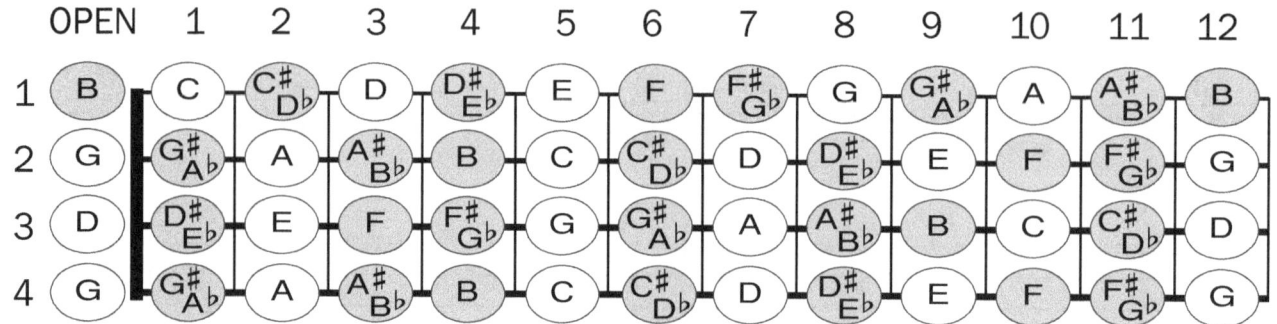

F# MINOR

F# G# A B C# D E F#

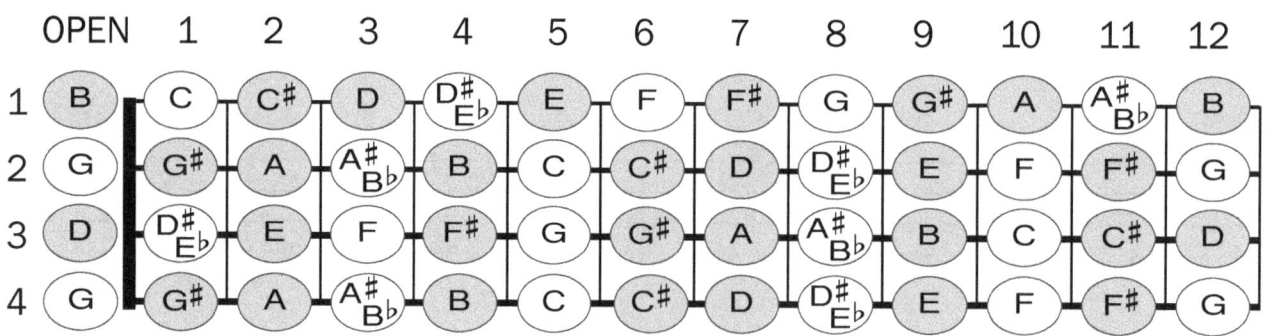

F# - G♭ BLUES

F# A B C C# E

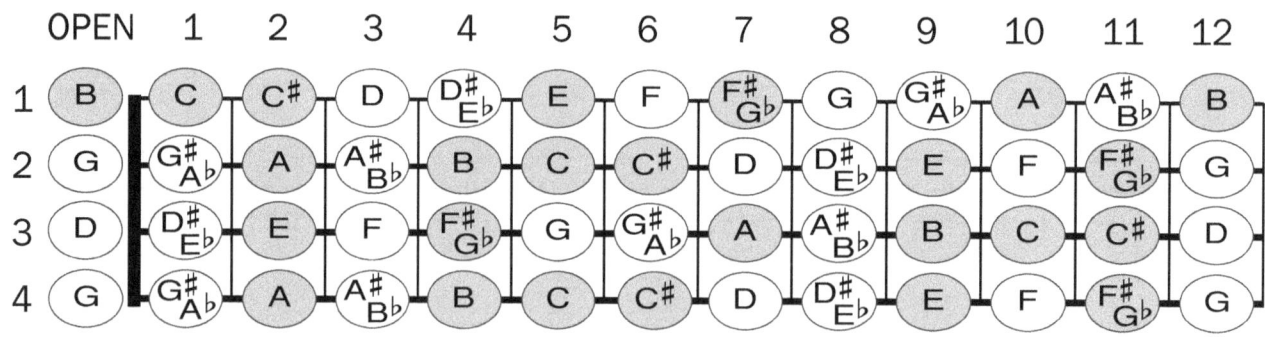

G SCALES
MAJOR - MINOR - BLUES

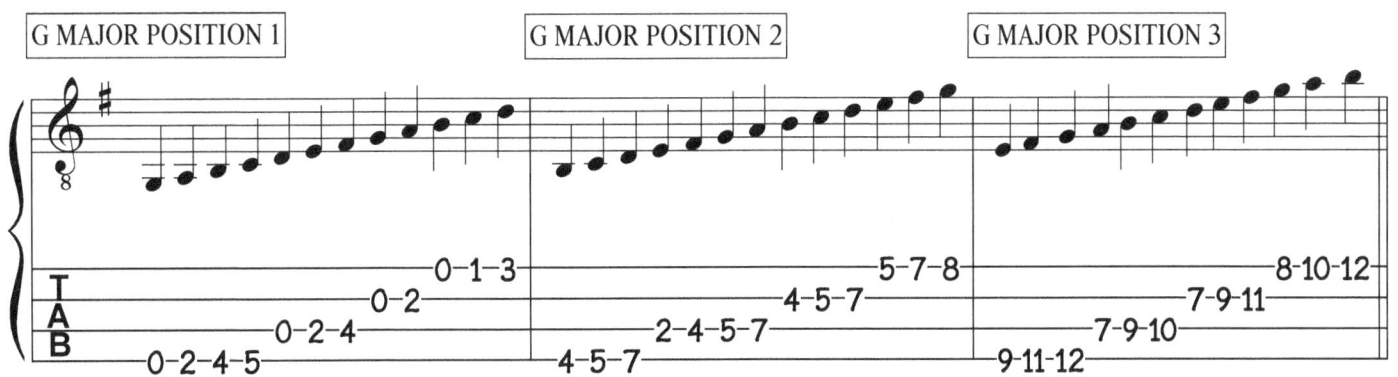

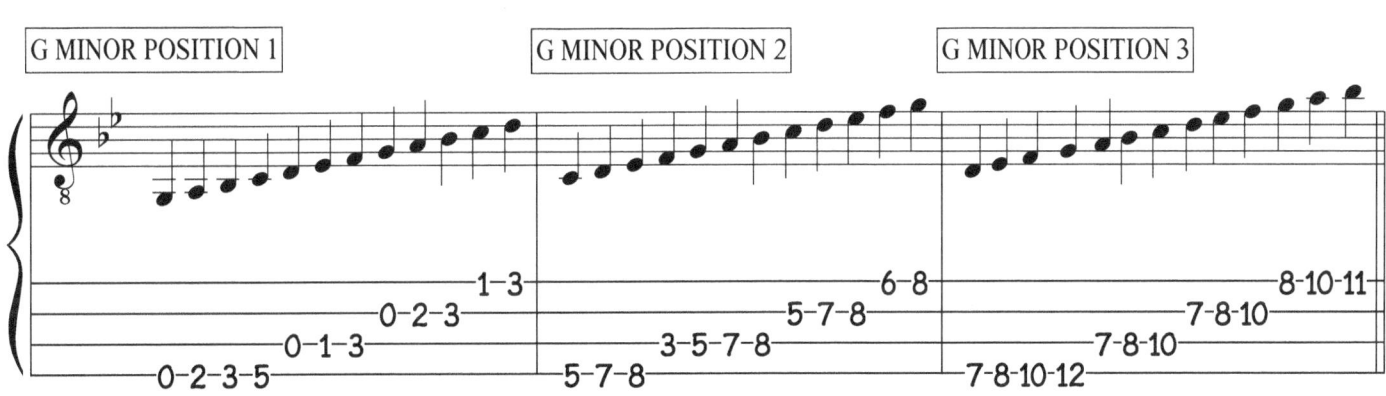

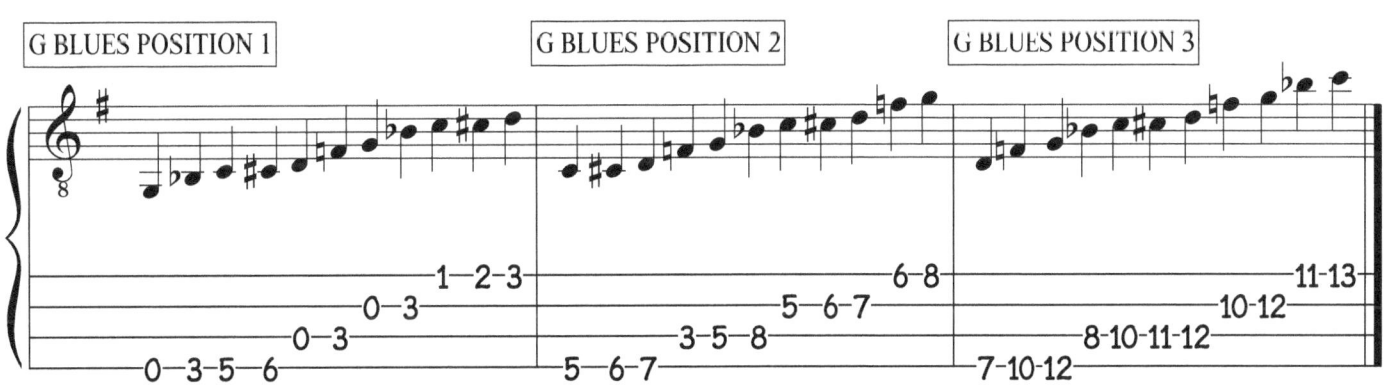

G MAJOR - MINOR - BLUES

G MAJOR — G A B C D E F♯

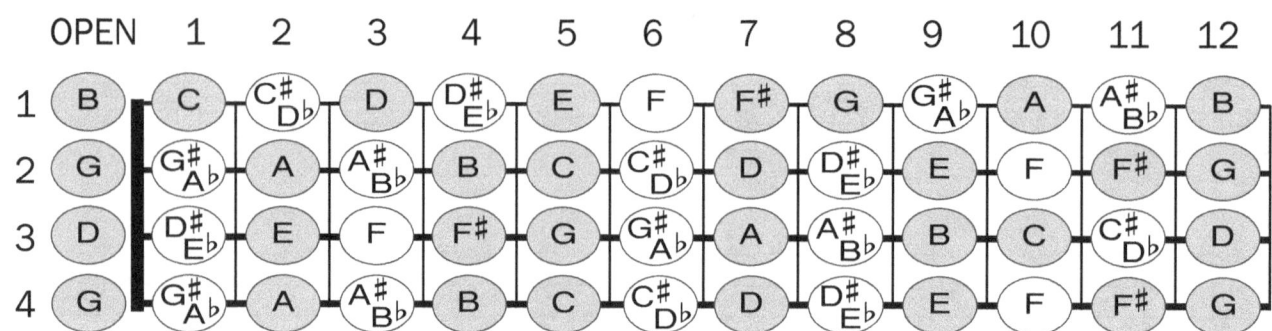

G MINOR — G A B♭ C D E♭ F

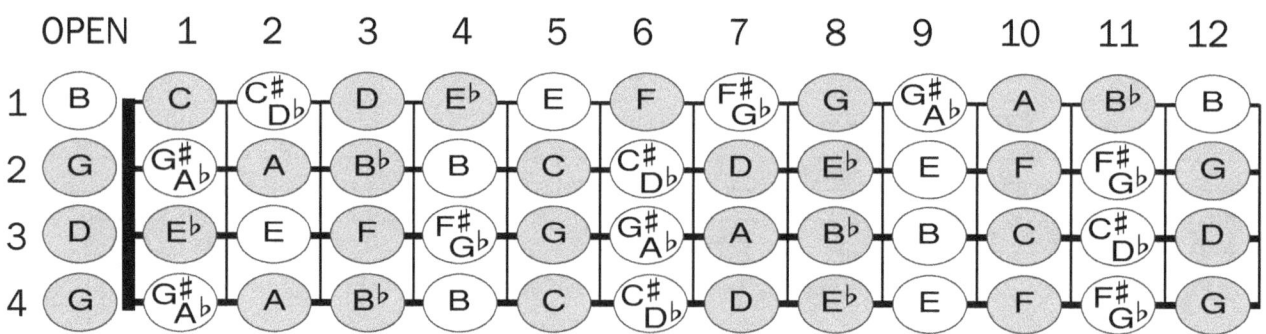

G BLUES — G B♭ C D♭ D F

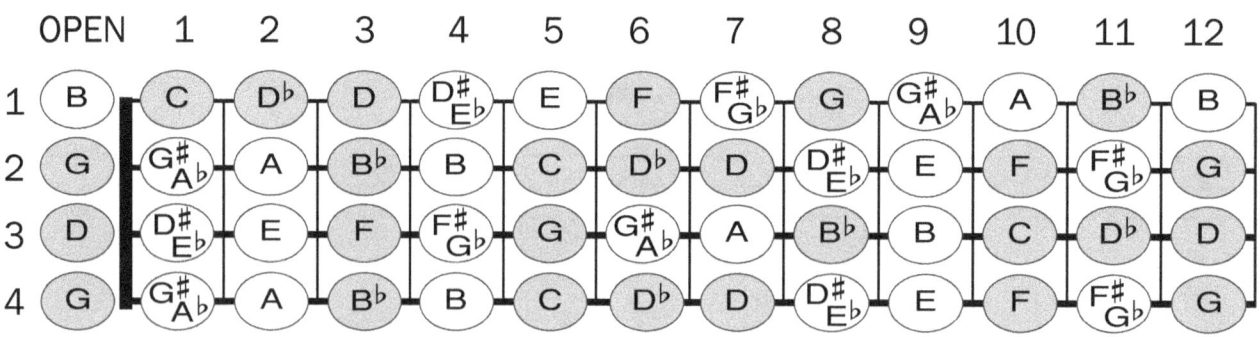

A♭ - G♯ SCALES
MAJOR - MINOR - BLUES

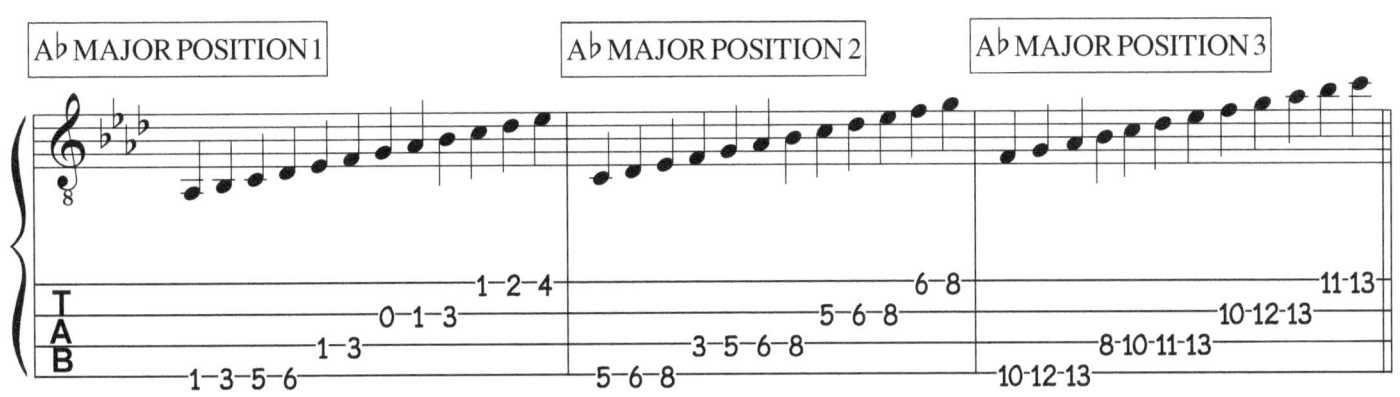

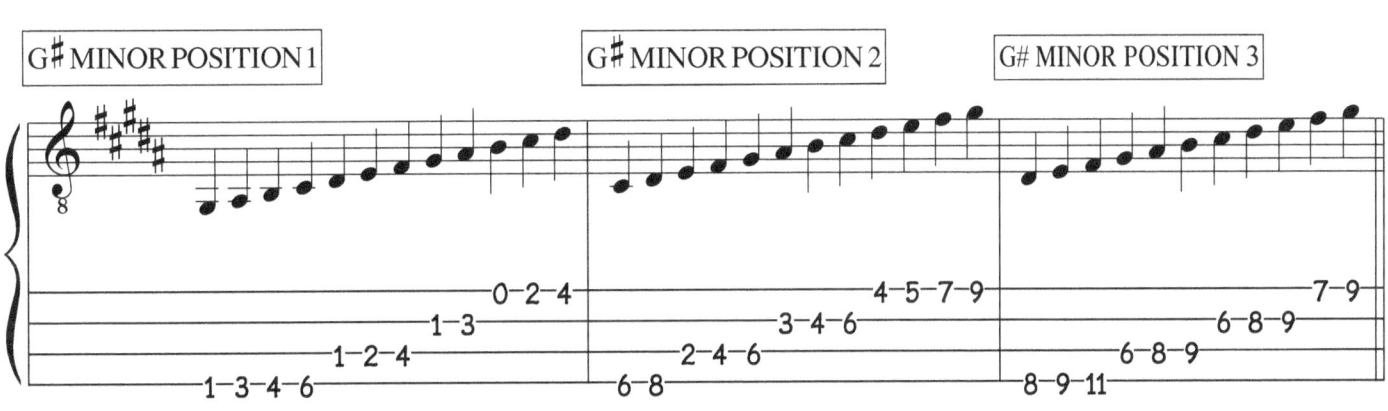

A♭ - G♯ MAJOR - MINOR - BLUES

A♭ MAJOR — A♭ B♭ C D♭ E♭ F G

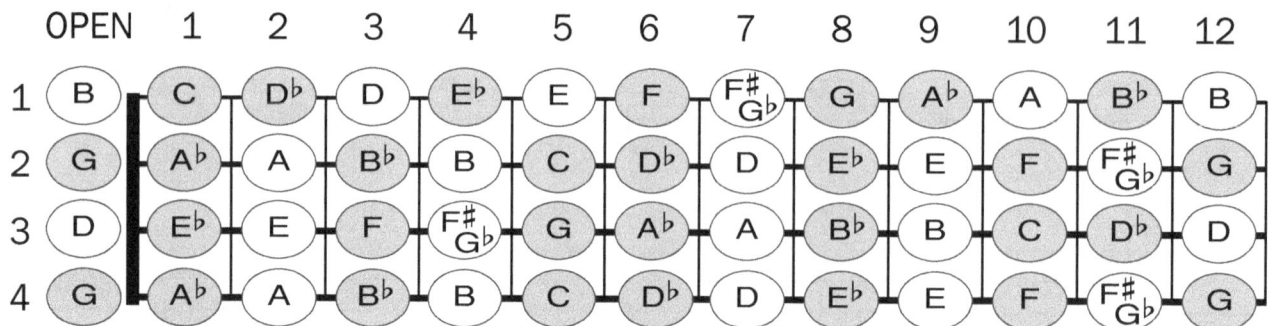

A♭ - G♯ MINOR — A♭ B♭ C♭ D♭ E♭ F♭ G♭ / G♯ A♯ B C♯ D♯ E F♯
B=C♭

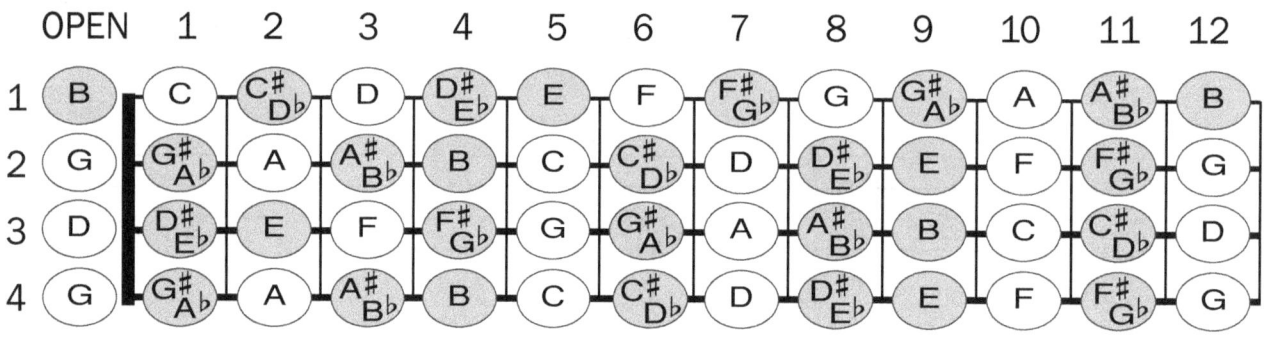

A♭ - G♯ BLUES — A♭ C♭ D♭ D E♭ G♭
B=C♭

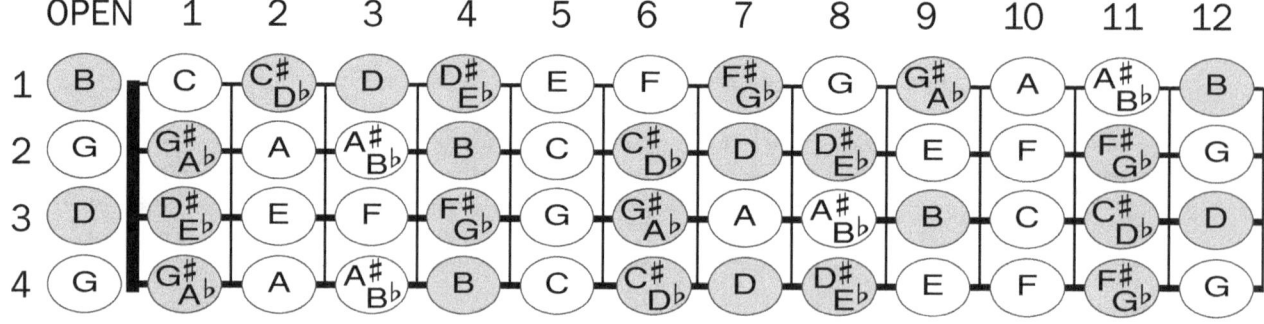

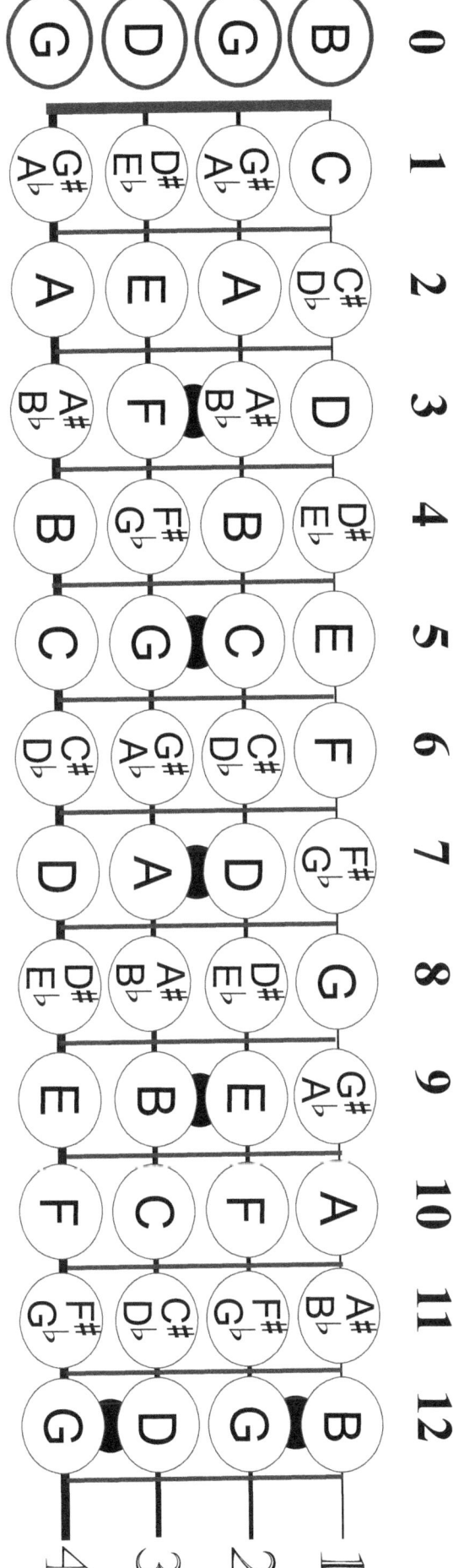

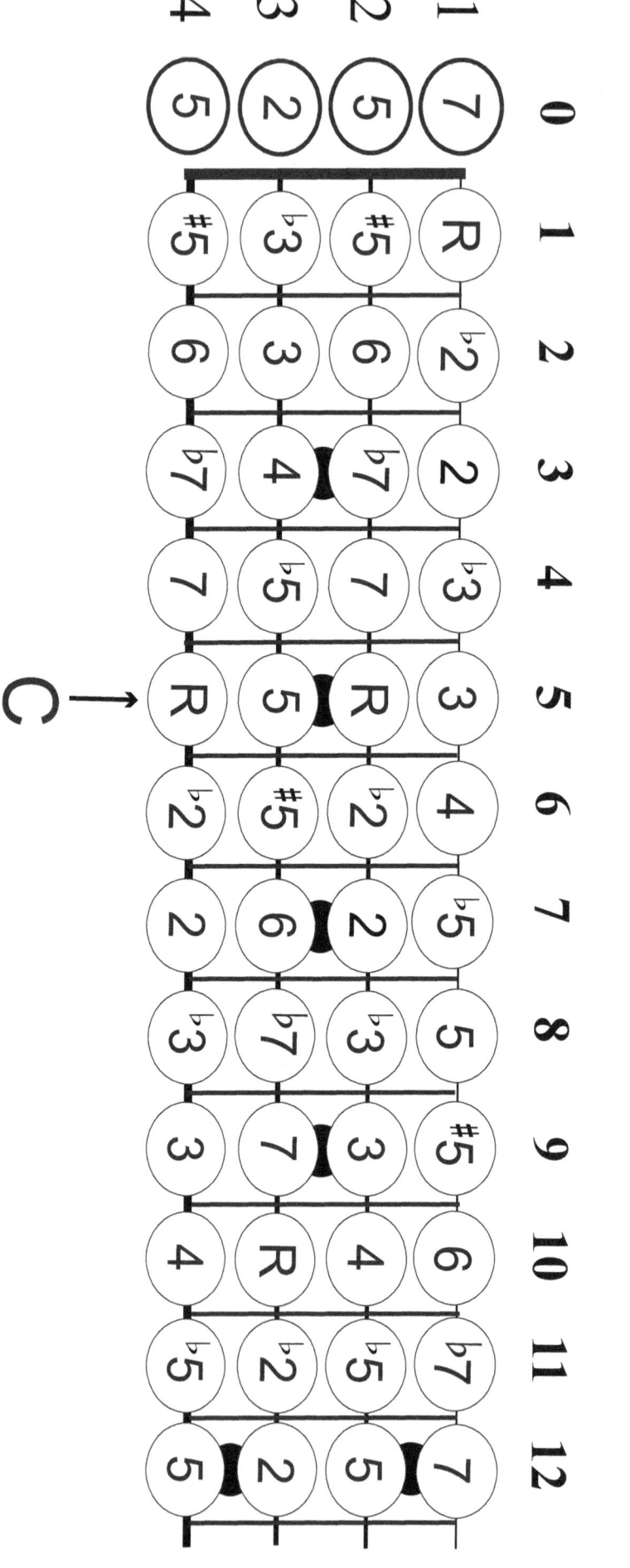

CIGAR BOX GUITAR NOTE CHART
TUNING - G D G B

1st String - B

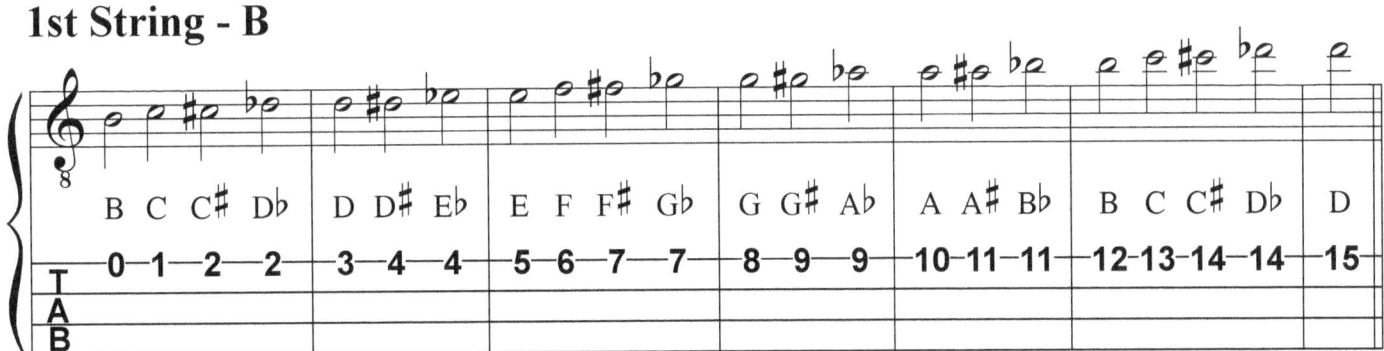

2nd String - G

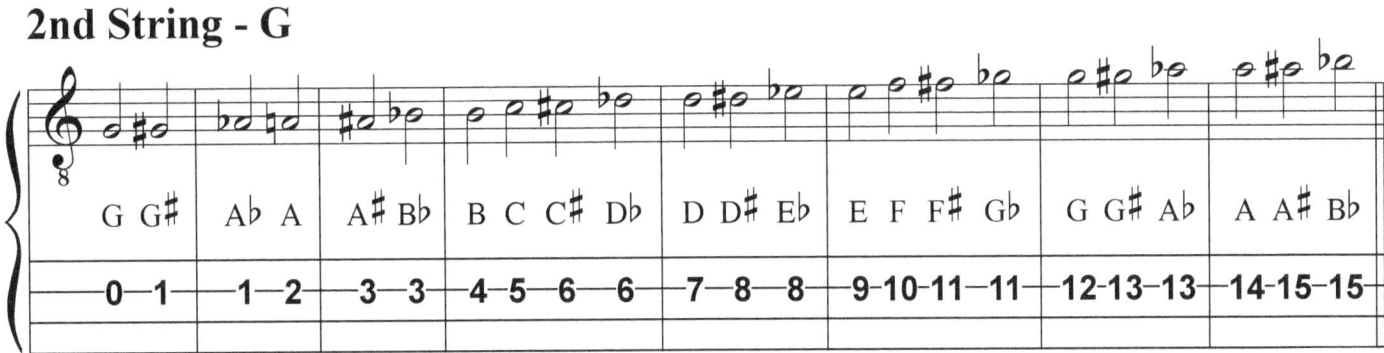

3rd String - D

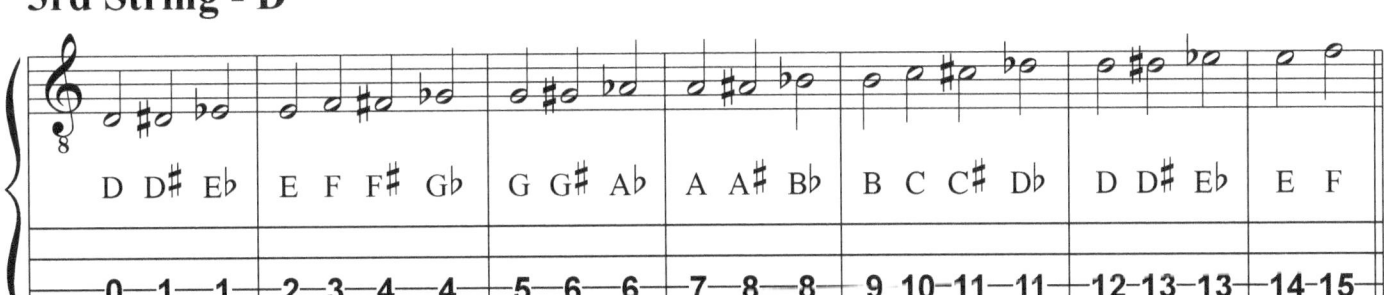

4th String - G

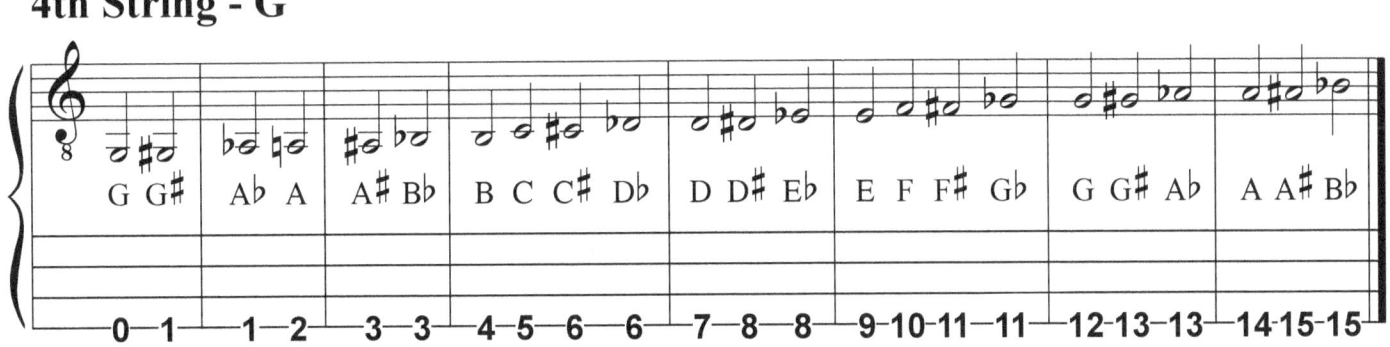

CIGAR BOX GUITAR NOTATION GUIDE

Downstroke
Pick down towards ground.

Upstroke
Pick up towards sky.

Accent
Strike the string harder to produce a louder sound.

Strong Accent (Martelato)
Pluck the string forcibly to produce a strong accent.

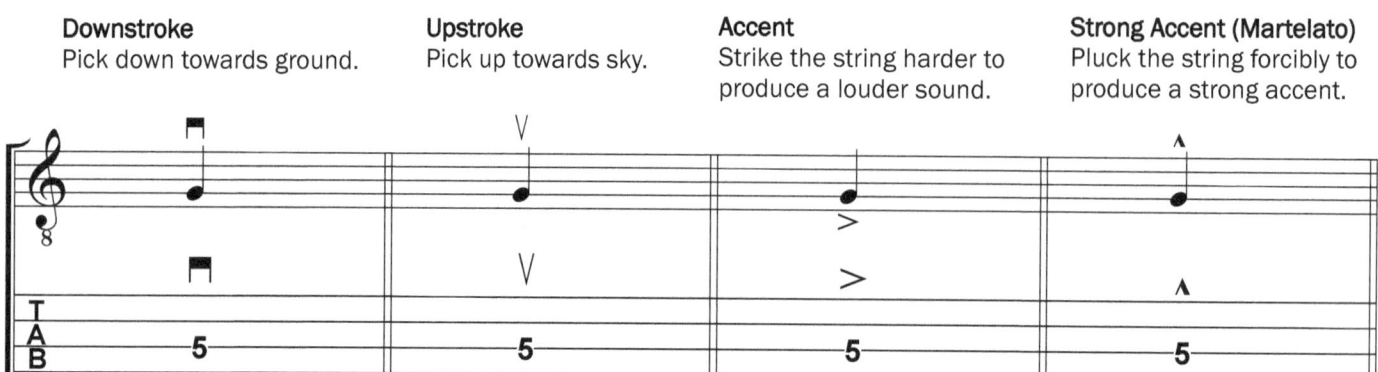

Staccato
Shorten note lenght.

Accent with Staccato
Strike the string harder and let ring shorter. (Marcatto)

Tenuto
Slight accent. Hold note for full value.

Accent with Tenuto
Strike string harder and let ring for full value of note.

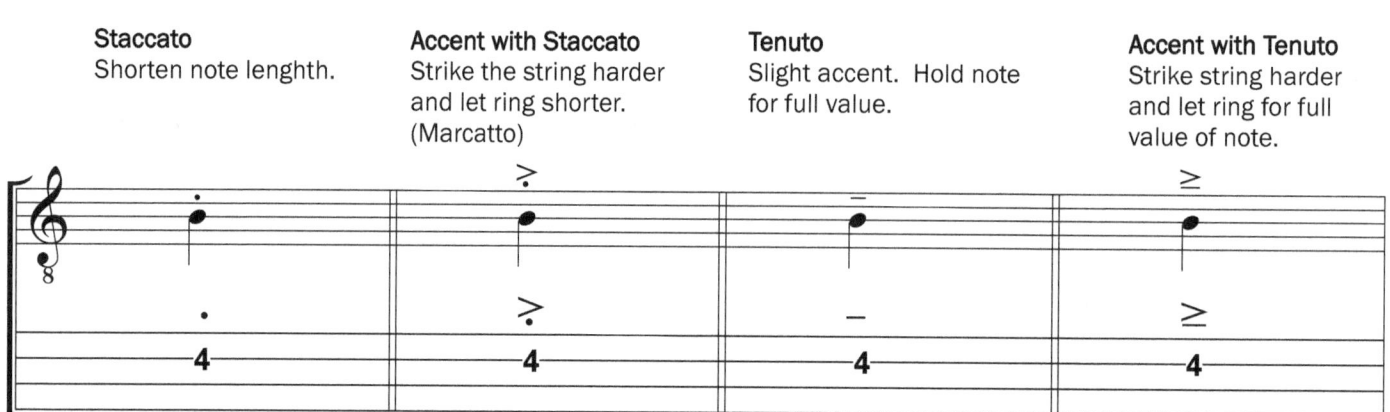

Hammer On
Play first note then hammer down finger without playing higher second note.

Pull Off
Play first note then grip on string and pull off to second lower note without playing.

Shift Slide
Slide finger/slide up or down to the next note on the same string. Pluck both notes.

Legato Slide
Slide finger/slide up or down to the next note on the same string.
Play only the first note.

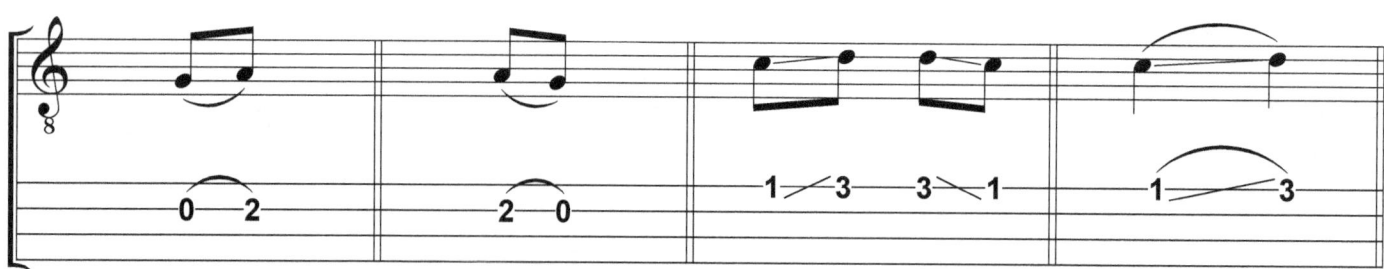

Palm Muting (P.M.)
Place palm on strings near bridge to muffle the sound.

Left Hand Mute
Place left hand finger(s) on strings to mute sound. A percussive sound.

Grace Note
The smaller grace note is rhythmically combined with large note. Play quickly before larger note.

Ghost Note (Parenthesis)
An optional note or bracketed note played quickly before main note.

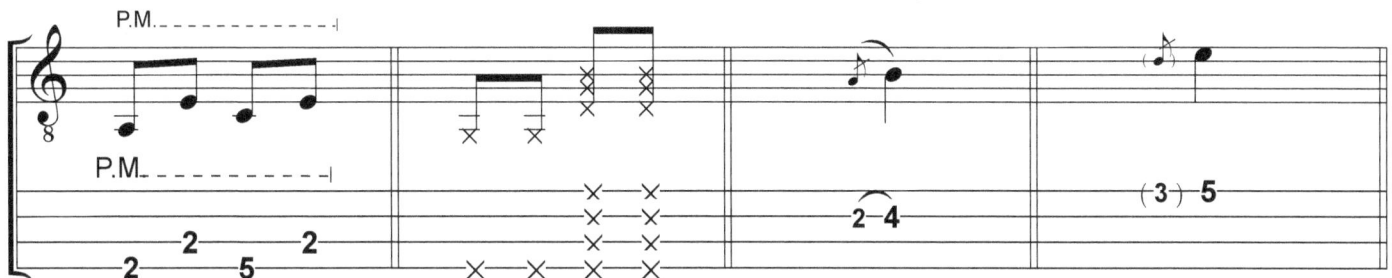

Vibrato
Bend string up and down. Can be slow or fast.

Wide Vibrato
Bend string up and down but with wider arc. Can be slow or fast.

Slight Bend
Slightly Bend the note up a 1/4 tone.

1/2 Tone Bend
Bend the note up a half tone or to sound 1 fret higher.

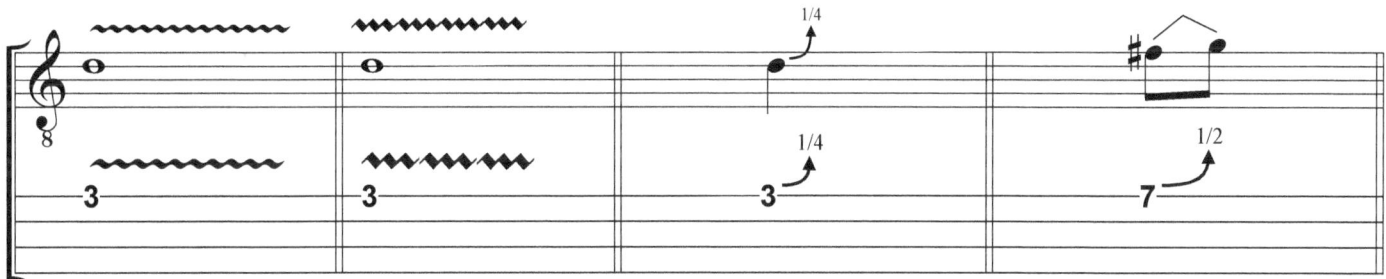

Whole Step Bend
Bend the note up a full whole tone or to sound 2 frets higher.

Bend and Release
Bend the note up and release back down to the original note.

Pre-Bend
Bend the note up then play note.

Pre-Bend
Bend the note up then play note.

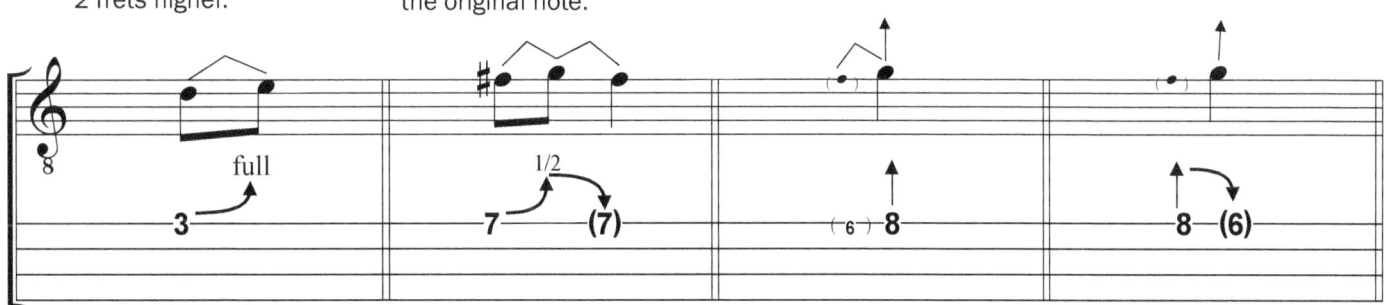

Hold Bend
Hold bend up until the end of the dashed line.

Multiple Bends
Several bends combined together.

Bend Neck
Grab headstock while holding body firm and bend neck.

Behind Nut Bend
Bend the string behind the nut at the headstock.

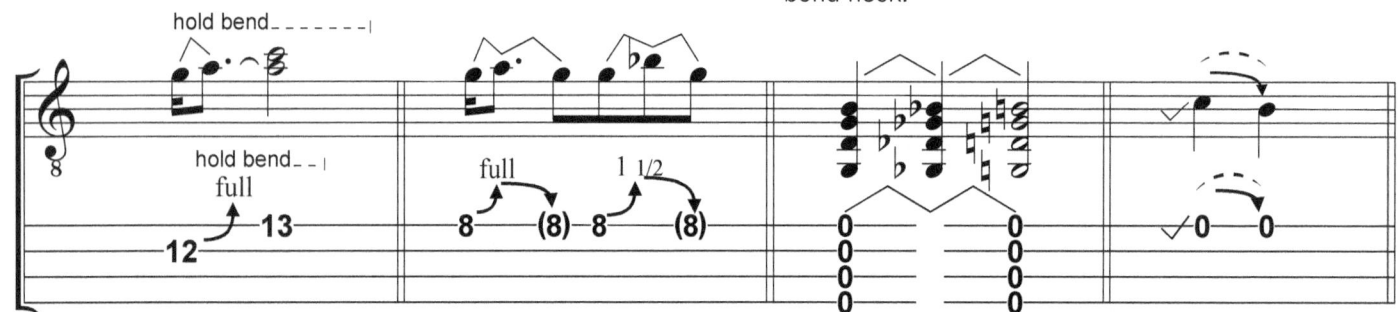

Rake
A percussive clicking sound before playing a note. Mute the strings (x) with the left hand. Often a muted arpeggio.

Arpeggiate
Strum the chord in the direction of the arrow.

Trill
Quickly alternate between two notes using hammer ons and pull offs.

Tapping (+)
Tap fret with finger or pick.

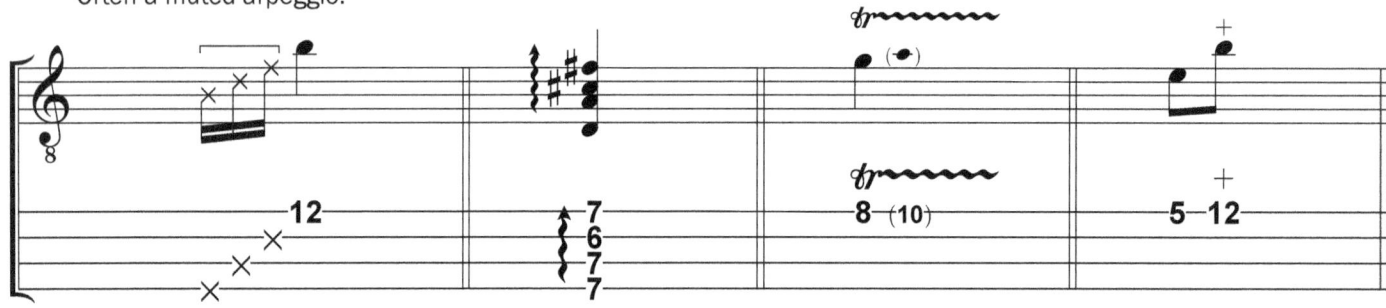

Natural Harmonic
Lightly place finger over fret indicated and pluck.

Artificial Harmonic
Hold done note indicated and lightly pluck pick finger higher up string with thumb.

Pick Slide (P.S.)
Place pick edge on string and scrape down or up string.

Tremelo Picking
Rapidly pick down and up on string.

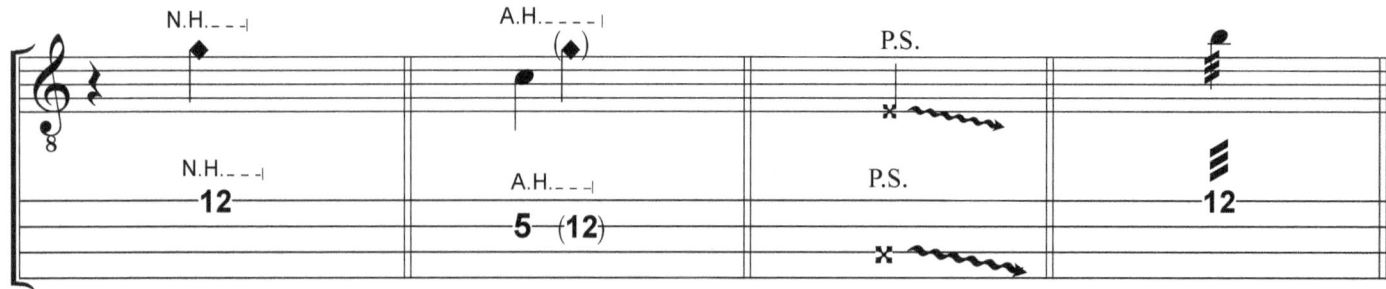

CIGAR BOX GUITAR BOOK COLLECTION

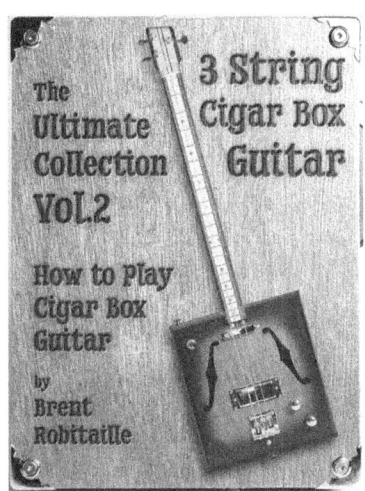

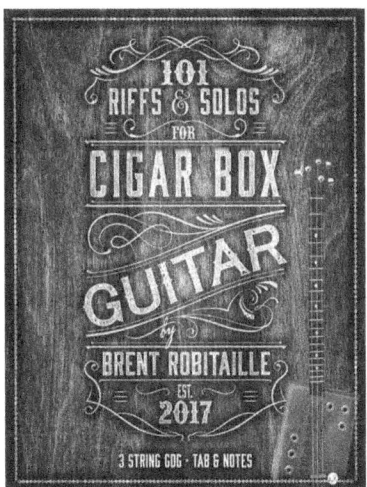

WWW.BRENTROBITAILLE.COM

More Great Music From Kalymi Publishing

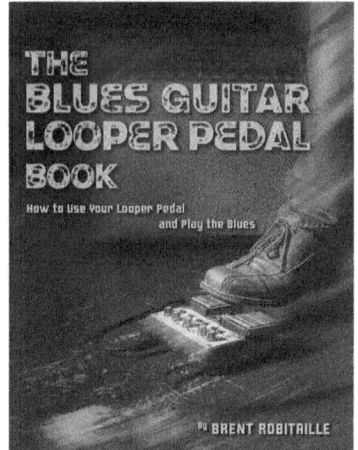

THE BLUES GUITAR LOOPER PEDAL BOOK

- 2, 4, 8, 12, & 16 Bar Blues Loops
- Riffs, Bass, Chords, and Rhythm for Each Loop
- 10 Tips for Making Great Loops
- 10 Tips for Better Guitar Solos
- Blues Scales & Fingerboard Charts - Slide Guitar Exercises
- Blues Progressions & Strumming Patterns
- Free Audio Tracks Online

Improve Your Guitar Chord Playing

- 12 Tips, tricks, and exercises to improve your chord switching
- Step by step chord switching exercises excellent for beginners
- 45 common chord progressions in pop, rock, folk, and blues.
- Barre chord tips with strengthening exercises
- Master the fingerboard with triangle patterns and diagrams
- Key and capo charts to transpose from key to key

Guitar - Mandolin - Fiddle - Ukulele

WWW.BRENTROBITAILLE.COM

www.ingramcontent.com/pod-product-compliance
Lightning Source LLC
Chambersburg PA
CBHW081417080526
44589CB00016B/2574